CHRIS TARRANT

It's Not a Proper Job

GREAT NORTHERN

Great Northern Books
PO Box 1380, Bradford,
West Yorkshire, BD5 5FB

www.greatnorthernbooks.co.uk

ISBN: 978-1-914227-19-6

Design by David Burrill

Photography supplied by kind permission of:

Willoughby 'Gus' Gullachsen
ATV Network Ltd
Celador
ITV/Sony Television
Rankin
Hugh Whitworth – Extreme Railways
Capital FM
Brian 'Spikey' Turner
London Weekend Television

Tiswas picture research by Marc Neun

CIP Data
A catalogue for this book is available from the British Library

To Bernie
who had to read and type up
every single word of my ramblings.

CONTENTS

INTRODUCTION 7

THE LIGHTER ITEMS 18

A LESSON LEARNED 25

KIDS' TELLY? 28

THE DOYING FLOY 35

IN THE CLUB 38

THE HIT 45

CARSONITIS 51

FISHING IN THE TREES 57

TOP OF THE POPS 58

MATERIAL NO LONGER USED 63

SPECIALIST ENTERTAINER 65

EVERYBODY SING ALONG 71

CAROL CONCERT 73

THE PLACE TO BE? 75

SUMMER SEASON 77

SIGNING MY LIFE AWAY 82

DELILAH 89

THE NO SMOKING CAMPAIGN 91

POTS OF MONEY 95

THE MOUSE RULES 99

CHINESE WHISPERS 101

MASTER CHEF 105

BEADLE.. 110

IRRESISTIBLE TEMPTATION 116

A WHOLE NEW WORLD 118

ROCKIN' ALL OVER THE WORLD 127

CROWD CONTROL 131

ONLY THE VERY BEST GUESTS 135

FEARLESS? OR PLAIN STUPID? 139

WEIGHT WATCHERS 146

BREAKFAST IN AMERICA 149

TEL 154

THE INSURANCE MAN 157

A PARKING MISDEMEANOUR 159

MILLIONAIRE 162

NOTORIOUS 170

ROUND THE WORLD 182

TINY DANCER 191

CONGO 193

DON'T CRY FOR ME – ARGENTINA 212

HIRED GUN 216

WHO WAS I? 221

IN THE NUDDY 223

AREK 226

ENGLEESH ENGLEESH 233

BIG DADDY 239

SWEET CHEEKS 241

THE GREY LADY 248

"AND IN THE END THE LOVE YOU TAKE" 252

ACKNOWLEDGEMENTS 255

INTRODUCTION

This is not my autobiography. I'm not even sure I'll ever write one. My life has just been too complicated, but I have had an amazing life, a brilliant life, a rich life. I've travelled to just about every single country in the world. I've interviewed everybody I ever wanted to meet from Paul McCartney, David Bowie and Elton John to Bill Clinton, Jerry Springer and Robin Williams.

I have been privileged, I have been very lucky, I have worked hard, but I've been blessed and I can honestly say I've never ever woken up and just not wanted to go to work. I know so many mates who hate their work, hate their journey to work, hate their journey home from work, hate their boss, hate everybody around them all day, but they just have to get there to pay the bills. I genuinely have never ever not looked forward to a day's work in my life, and I have had so many laughs along the way. This book is about the laughs, the ridiculous situations, the ridiculous people and the wonderful people who have shared the journey with me.

****

"I am the face of the 70s, this is your last chance to snap me up." I still cringe when I remember that I really did write those words, back in the summer of 1971, and sent it to every single television company in Britain. There were nothing like the number of stations that there are today with all the satellite stations and so on, but there were still a hell of a lot. I know because I bought all the stamps, and in those days, it cost me what seemed like a lot of money.

I'd been working at the Royal Showground near Kenilworth in Warwickshire, and I saw some bloke arrive in a very nice looking sports car. He combed his hair in the mirror, probably blowing himself a kiss as he got out, and started what seemed like a very short, but very pleasant day's work. He did a couple of pieces to camera, standing next to a pedigree Hereford bull. He interviewed a couple of farmers, and talked to the crowd, who all seemed to know him and like him and think him a very nice man. He then did what seemed a fairly banal sign-off, and then got back into his sports car and drove off, waving at his admirers as he disappeared out of the showground, leaving his cameraman and sound man to pack up and load their much less impressive vehicles for the drive home, probably just catching the worst of the rush hour.

I thought, "That doesn't look like a bad life at all, doesn't look like a proper job," and of course it isn't.

I had no idea at the time just how much his lifestyle would become mine for decades to come.

So, I wrote this cringing, bumptious, arrogant letter to every television company in the UK: London Weekend Television, Southern Television, Westward Television, all the commercial stations and every single BBC station across the UK and Ireland. It was several pages long, all rambling on in the same vein, declaring myself to be irresistible to any employer in his or her right mind.

I did all this with two fingers on my dad's ancient typewriter, over and over again, put each one lovingly into an envelope with a first-class stamp, and off they went.

For a week or two I heard nothing, and then the replies started to come in. One after another they said, "Dear Sir/Madam, thank you so much for your application, which we all took the time to read carefully. Unfortunately, we have no vacancies for you at this moment, but we will of course keep your letter on file."

What any young prospective employee for any company needs to know from the off is that there is no such thing as a file. The file is a dustbin. I never heard from any of them again. However, ATV in Birmingham and Yorkshire Television in Leeds were the exceptions.

They did not put me 'on file'. They both invited me up for interviews, I think mainly just to see what sort of a lunatic actually wrote this absurd egotistic rambling letter.

Amazingly both of them offered me work. I knew Birmingham well, having lived in that splendid city as a student, and so preferred the idea of living there. It was also a lot closer to Mum for my washing.

So they offered me a week's work as a presenter on *ATV Today* which was the local 6pm current affairs programme. It would be a short-term, week-to-week contract, and I could start as soon as possible.

Now, this was October 1971. I was on the dole. I was living with my first wife, very happily, down in Weymouth. She loved the seaside, particularly in the winter months, as do I, but it was also very close to the Dorset Stour, at that time one of the best fishing rivers in England. I was drinking excellent Dorset beers every night and fishing, I think, every single day. We'd both given up jobs that we weren't particularly enjoying, and it was an idyllic period of our lives. I told the executives at ATV that I was writing a screenplay, which they seemed to accept. Thinking about it now, they must have been incredibly naïve. Of course I wasn't writing a screenplay; a screenplay of what? I was fishing. Something which, funnily enough, I hadn't mentioned in the interview.

Every few weeks they'd give me a ring and say, "When are you thinking of starting?" and I would always come up with some cock and bull excuse: "Sorry, this script is taking me a lot longer than I realised, but I do hope to come up and join you at ATV very soon."

I actually can't believe now that I was so completely blasé about what was undoubtedly a life-changing career opportunity, but I put them off and put them off for weeks on end.

Eventually, they were saying things like, "We're really going to have to give this job to somebody else, if you can't come soon."

I managed to hang on to this absurd "screenplay" nonsense until mid-March. When you consider the original offer of the job – an offer of one week's work made in the October of the year before – quite how I managed to hang it out that long is just extraordinary and idiotic.

It is also a terrible indication of my totally irresponsible attitude to any thoughts for my career. I could easily have thrown it all away, and just carried on fishing, but I seemed to have had no thoughts at all about the seriousness of being offered a job that most young guys in the country would have given their right arm for – and what was to become my life, my career, my total absorption and what was to become a very lucky, privileged existence for myself and my kids for the next fifty years. Put it this way, the coarse fishing season ends at midnight on March 14th, and my first ever contract with ATV Birmingham, that was to completely change my whole world, began on March 15th 1972. I was about to become the 'Face of the 70s'.

Well, that was the plan anyway.

I probably wasn't the face of the 70s, but I had a pretty damn good time along the way.

****

On the day I finally arrived, March 15th, I went quite nervously into the morning meeting, looking very smart, hoping I didn't smell of fish bait, met the team, and most of all met my new features editor, a lovely guy called John Swallow, whose job was ostensibly to show me the ropes. John's idea of showing me the ropes was to go immediately to The Crown pub in Broad Street, Birmingham. It was just after half past ten in the morning, they'd already opened, and poured pints of beer down my neck.

This became a normal pattern for most of the next ten years of my life. We would take what we always referred to as 'the livener', and then start our day's work. We would almost certainly have a couple more at lunchtime, and then there was the Green Room, open during the transmission of the show, and for an hour or two afterwards, where the trolleys positively groaned with free drink, beer, wine, whiskey, you name it. We named it and we gave it a damn good spanking, and then somehow went weaving homewards.

It was the days of a real alcohol culture. It was just what everybody did. There were bars in every TV station in Britain, including a very good one at the BBC and an excellent one in London Weekend Television. They've all gone now, along with a lot of the fun. A lot of the very best television ideas were dreamed up in the bars of television studios all over the UK.

I think all of mine were.

John Swallow became a lifelong friend, one of the nicest and funniest men I have ever met. Mike Warman, my news editor, was to outward appearances much more sensible, but actually completely mad. His younger brother Bob and I joined at more or less the same time, young, keen, thrusting reporters, and Bob is still there, fifty years later, still keen, and apparently still occasionally thrusting.

Mike was totally different, Bob was always smart, but Mike was absolutely immaculate. He looked exactly the same every single day of his life, perfectly combed hair, nice expensive glasses, always freshly washed and ironed shirt and tie, shiny black shoes, and always the pinstripe suit.

He was obsessed with punctuality. He always walked into the canteen at exactly ten minutes past eight in the morning. He loved his sports cars, and if he was even a minute early, we would actually watch him going around the block again, so that he came in exactly on time. He would also always have the same breakfast, a cup of tea, pasteurised milk please, not sterilised, and a poached egg on toast. He would put it on the plate, get his knife and fork ready, sprinkle on the exact same amount each morning of salt and pepper, and then manically smash the poached egg into a thousand bits. He would then cut the toast into cubes, with this runny mess all over them and lovingly devour the lot before he went to his morning meeting. This happened every single day.

****

One of my favourite directors of all time was a guy called Roger Thomas. He was always swathed in bright silver fur jackets, loved driving fast cars very fast and was ever so slightly odd. Come to think of it, he too was totally potty. But he had a brilliant sense of humour, a very quick wit and was always at war with the bosses of the company. He and I predictably got on like a house on fire. Our six o'clock programme ran till exactly 6:28:30, not a second more or less, five nights a week, and the timings were always on a knife edge. Because it was live, it was always frantically over-running. People would be screaming up in the directors' box, cutting items all over the place, and because there were a lot of items to cram into a short live show every night, it was always very fraught.

What was particularly ridiculous was that after all this chasing our arses every evening, to somehow come out on time, we then had to suffer a minute and a half of credits: for the presenters, whose names were pretty well known anyway, then the senior cameraman, senior sound man, PA, director, producer, and usually a long list of executive producers, several of whom none of us had ever met. Their credits were there night after night, meaning a lot to their wives and mummies, but probably nobody else.

Roger said to us one day, "Do you really want your credits at the end of the show, because it's a bloody bore and it would give us another ninety seconds to play with?" "No, not at all," we all agreed, "it really is pointless." So, the next day, the show had a much more relaxed feel, and at 6:28:30 we said Goodnight and went straight to an ATV caption, not a credit in sight. We were fine with it, but the executive producers, predictably, went absolutely berserk. Roger was dragged in, threatened with the sack, or possibly the guillotine, if he ever did anything like it again. The next morning Roger received a blistering memo, copied to all of us, the controller, the ATV managing director, our chairman Lew Grade, and probably the prime minister: "Dear Mr Thomas, you will never again run the programme without the credits at the end. In future you will give all the presenters their credit, then Senior Cameraman AN Other, Sound Man AN Other, Director AN Other, Producer AN Other, Executive Producers AN Other, AN Other, and AN Other. Any failure to comply with this will result with immediate dismissal."

So Roger looked bemused for a while and we all told him how sympathetic we were. I said, "Forget it, Rog, keep your head down and it'll blow over." And with that we all got on with our day.

But Rog didn't really do 'Keep your head down' …

When we came in to the Green Room that evening and sat watching the show, it all went pretty smoothly, although we were back to the usual panicky, very-tight-for-time feeling and our main presenter that night, Derek Hobson (Yes he, of *New Faces* and *That's My Dog*) had to race to the end of the show to allow time for the credits. But to Hobbo's credit he was a brilliant live performer and the credits went out as per normal, exactly on time, except that they read: "Presenters AN Other, AN Other and AN Other, Director AN Other, Producer AN Other, Executive Producers AN Other, AN Other, and AN Other."

Sitting in the green room we all stared in silent amazement, mixed with horror, but deep love for what Roger had just done. He was, of course, dragged in yet again, screamed at, threatened with immediate sacking, but said, "I only did what you asked me to do. Here is a copy of your memo." He also had the good sense to hand the memo to the shop steward, who of course backed him to the hilt, and told management he had only done absolutely precisely to the letter what they had instructed him to do. All of this meant nothing at all to anybody watching at home, but it was a wonderful television moment of pure, pure gold to everyone in the studios. Well, except, of course, for the executive producers. The normal credits did of course return the next evening, but they were considerably shortened, and it was a wonderful, wonderful day for the troops on the ground.

Timing on live shows is always a pain in the bum. Commercial breaks have to be hit exactly to the second and it often means really good strong items have to be hacked down and presenters' links suddenly become gobbledygook just to hit the ITN news on time. I have hardly ever used an earpiece. I absolutely hate the dreadful things. On the news programmes we just had really good floor managers who would count you down to zero. That's how I've always worked.

I hosted a live Friday show for a while which I loved. It was a mixture of live Midlands news, live music, live interviews with whoever was in town. I remember interviewing such varied folk as Victoria Wood, Larry Grayson and Jimmy Tarbuck, and the weekend sport with Gary Newbon, Nick Owen and Jimmy Greaves. One Friday Jimmy and I had the huge privilege of a live interview with Muhammad Ali, for me the greatest sportsman of all time. It left the whole team on a high and the next Friday we felt like we'd had a particularly good show as well. It seemed to have really motored along and we were getting to the end. I was just doing the weather and mentally getting ready for the Friday night pub. The floor manager, a very funny lady and a mate of mine, gave me the one-minute-to-go sign. I waffled my way through the highlights on ITV for the weekend. There weren't many, no change there. I got the thirty-seconds signal. The lager was imminent and then she suddenly, with a look of horror on her face, gave me nine minutes …

Nine? Nine? Nine? God knows what my face looked like to the viewers … they must have thought I was having some kind of seizure. After what felt like a year, but was probably five seconds, I just spotted dear Jimmy Greaves wandering about on the other side of the studio. "Jim," I said, "Come and sit down, mate. What do you think about Aston Villa's chances tomorrow afternoon?" Jim, who already had his coat on and was holding a cup of tea, rambled on wonderfully about the Villa, then we turned our attention to Wolves, Birmingham City, West Brom … In fact, by the time we'd filled about eight minutes we'd done Walsall and were up to Stoke City …

I thanked Jim for his in-depth analysis, did the weather again, and we came out exactly on time …

I breathed a huge sigh of relief. My heart was probably pumping fifty to the dozen, and I said, "Jim, that was brilliant. You saved the show." Jim looked at me blankly, and said, "Bloody hell, mate. I thought we were just chatting. I didn't realise we were actually 'ON'."

They were great days. Although, to be honest, it was all a bit of a lads' culture. I remember one afternoon the news team came weaving back from HQ (or The Crown, to give it its proper name) and found only one person in the office. This was about two hours before we went on air and dear Reg Harcourt, our political editor, was in the middle of what was clearly a very important conversation with a cabinet minister about appearing on the show the following week. For no reason that I can even begin to think of, we put Reg and his phone upside down in a large plastic dustbin. Reg, totally unfazed by our silly schoolboy antics, carried on his conversation with the minister, upside down in the dustbin, for another full five or six minutes. He ended the call by saying a rather muffled, "Thank you so much, minister. We look forward to seeing you on the show on Monday."

And, righting himself, emerged to wild applause from the whole office …

After a while, because I had long blonde hair and was a little, to say the least, 'off the wall' as a reporter, I began to get fan mail. Mostly it was very nice, just saying things like, "We loved the show,

Chris, like what you do, and would you please send me a signed photograph?" Which I always did and still do to this day, although it would be fair to say the requests are a tad thinner on the ground.

One or two could only be described as hate mail – perfectly understandable and thoroughly well deserved. One or two were slightly more raunchy, but one, that I've never forgotten, was totally explicit. She was a very nice-sounding lady from Willenhall. She explained to me her personal circumstances, that her husband had left her, that she lived alone, that she liked watching me on television, and that she would really like to meet up and buy me a drink, "but all I really want to do in the world is put my head in your trousers." This, of course, caused great merriment among my colleagues. There have been even more explicit ones over the years, including a wonderful lady from Leighton Buzzard, who said, "My husband's working nights, I'm usually home by 2.00, but if you get there before me, the keys are under the mat." Needless to say, I didn't reply to Willenhall, and I didn't go to Leighton Buzzard either.

The next week I was due to be on the news live, on the Wednesday afternoon, so I raced to the wardrobe where we all hung our clothes for the show and grabbed a clean shirt and tie. But in the place where my one and only suit in the world (Harry Fenton no less, no rubbish) should have been hanging, there was a jacket but nothing else. Some idiot had nicked my trousers, but I had no time to hunt for the guilty party. I was still in my jeans with holes in the knees. I just threw on a jacket, raced to the studio, and mercifully spent the entire half-hour sitting behind the desk looking a jolly smart boy! If only the viewers realised – I could have been wearing suspenders and stockings for all they knew or cared.

The next day at our morning meeting, I said, "It's no big deal, but somebody has nicked my trousers."

Mike said, "Oh yes, Christopher, that was me."

"Well that's ridiculous, Mike. You couldn't possibly get into them."

He said, "Oh, no, no, I didn't try to wear them, but I did reply to that dear lady from Willenhall. It went thus ..." (only Michael Warman would ever call me Christopher and use the word 'thus'):

Dear [sic] Miss Willenhall,

Thank you so much for your letter addressed to Christopher Tarrant. I'm delighted that you enjoy the show each evening, and Christopher's part in the whole magazine. He is a great new addition to our team, and I am delighted that you want to put your head in his trousers. Accordingly I have enclosed a pair of his most recent trousers and feel free to put your head in them at any time you feel the need. I hope this is a help.

Sincere best wishes,

Michael Warman.

Funnily enough, we got no reply.

THE LIGHTER ITEMS

It actually emerged quite quickly that I wasn't very good as a hard news reporter. In fact, I was pretty useless. My biggest problem was that I didn't like most of the people I interviewed – politicians, shop stewards, and so on – and I didn't seem to be able to hide my feelings.

I soon came to the conclusion that, with local politicians, union spokesmen and lord mayors, if their lips were moving they were almost certainly lying. This was a long time ago, and I have to say, I haven't really changed my mind much since.

ATV would have had every reason to get rid of me, but mercifully they started to give me the lighter items: interviews with naturally funny, ordinary people, and I absolutely thrived on it.

For about five years my job became interviewing eccentrics. Our research team used to find them, drag them into the studios and at 6.00 every night I'd interview one. It was amazing just how many there were about: light-bulb eaters, upside down beer drinkers, flea trainers, hedgehog jugglers, men who ate live frogs, men who ate live slugs, men who slept up telegraph poles, women who knitted polo neck sweaters for tortoises, women who'd met Martians in the chemist … I interviewed a man who had a pigeon on his head mealtimes, night-times, twenty-four hours a day for three days … a man who lived with his Shetland pony – nice enough man, lovely little pony, but the smell was appalling.

I got on the back of a rodeo horse. As I sat on him waiting in the stall, no saddle, no stirrups, just hanging on to the hairs at the back of his neck, he seemed a docile enough creature. "Don't worry, boy. We've got you a lovely quiet one," the main handler told me, with a strange grin on his face.

Well, it was nice and quiet … until the gate was pulled open and to howls of amusement from the handlers and my crew it went berserk. It reared up on its back hooves, then in a flash threw its head right down and went stomping round the area, bucking up and down, snorting with rage, until eventually I could hang on no longer and it hurled me off, somehow standing on my hand as I crashed down onto the filthy floor. I'd lasted a magnificent seven seconds and two of my fingers have never straightened since.

I went into one of those little cradles that window cleaners use at the top of skyscrapers. We were something like three hundred feet above the streets of Birmingham and, of course, the lads who go up in these tiny little open top coffins every day couldn't help giving the ropes a twist, making it swing and lurch round violently. When I brought the film back my producer said, in an almost caring way, "There was real fear in your voice." Trust me, there was real fear in my trousers.

I went into the wrestling ring with a terrifying looking woman called Hellcat Haggerty, the European ladies champion – a ridiculous title because she was certainly no lady. She beat lumps out of me for three rounds: Boston crabs, forearm smashes, piledrivers, the lot. She threw me round the ring like a rag doll. If there is a Mister Haggerty, I'm pretty sure he never dares to come home even a minute late from the pub.

My dear Mum and Dad still lived just outside Reading and so they didn't get ATV from Birmingham as their local news source. They got London, which was probably very lucky for them, but I'd obviously told them about my new job and a few friends had told them "your son's on the telly", so unbeknown to me they booked themselves into a hotel in Oxford, a city where they did get ATV and excitedly turned on at six to watch their son Christopher the fearless hard news reporter strut his steely stuff. Unfortunately, that particular evening I was covering a bloke on a charity walk from Worcester to Evesham, a distance of fourteen miles, with four ferrets down his trousers. After about two miles one of them bit him and of course that meant there was blood everywhere and the ferrets just feasted on his inadequately protected meat and two veg!

The item went from bad to worse when one ferret poked his little pink nose out of the bloke's flies and caused women to squeal with delight all over the Midlands and me to hand back hurriedly to the studio. Mummy and Daddy went quietly shaking their heads back to nice sensible Thames Television. Little did they know but over the next few years it was to get worse and worse and worse.

A few weeks later I was sent on another Mike Warman 'scoop' to interview a delightful old gentleman who claimed proudly to have bred wild fighting hens in his tiny garden in Northfield. When we got there he explained, "Genetically my team and I" (his team I discovered was his wife hiding in the front room) "have gone back through centuries of genetics and bred the warlike hunting hen that used to roam the earth after the Second Ice Age."

He said to me, "We can go out to see them, but stay well back, be very careful, and talk only in whispers. These are very dangerous creatures."

We put on special protective gloves and leggings and with our hearts thumping the crew and I, oh so slowly, opened the back door and went out into the garden. "Keep very still," he said, as two of the bigger birds came menacingly towards us. Holding a broom out towards them, he said, "Stay there Nemo, Prince get back," and then with real authority in his voice boomed out, "Get down, Satan!" Satan glowered at us for a few seconds, although it felt an age, and looked like he might attack. But then he ambled back across the garden and we all breathed a big sigh of relief.

We kept ourselves safely behind the boss, got our filming done quickly, and retreated into the safety of the kitchen. He was an amazing man and it was a pleasure to meet him and his 'team'. We handed back the protective clothing, thanked them both, and took our leave still hardly daring to speak. As we were loading our gear into the car, Roger, our very Brummy soundman, broke the silence and said, very earnestly, "Excuse me, yow lot, but weren't those just ordinary chickens?"

"Of course they were," I said, and we howled with laughter all the way back to the ATV studios.

But my absolute all-time favourite was the one-time world champion egg, nose and water jumper. I don't know who found him, but what a man. The bloke was a very nice, very logical sounding, 100% raving nutter, completely out of his mind. He was 63 years old, dressed in baggy football shorts, with really knobbly little knees, a string vest and a huge pair of black boots, the soles of which he'd literally plastered with boot polish, His props were an egg cup, an egg, a baby bath filled with water, a pile of sawdust and my nose.

He had a really strong north country accent and went into great detail about what he was hoping to do. "Now watch carefully lad. Sithee, what I shall be doing first is slowly circumventing that standard chicken's egg placed there and then at the right moment, hurl my body upwards just a fraction, but enough to kiss the egg on the surface, marking it with the polish that I've placed on the sole of my boots, without damaging the shell in anyway whatsoever."

As usual on live TV the seconds were ticking away so I said eagerly, "Can we make a start?"

"Aye, 'ang on lad, just get meself mentally attuned."

Now the whole item was supposed to last exactly three and a half minutes, so we didn't have too much time for mental attuning. Still, I waited patiently while he stuck his head down between his baggy shorts, turned around, peered manically at me from up between his legs and let out a couple of 'whoops'.

"Alright lad, ready," he said, and before I could ask him what on earth whooping from between his legs had to do with anything he did a series of mad bunny hops up to the egg cup, and instead of lifting just a fraction off the ground, took off about four feet above it, like a demented kangaroo.

"That was just a bit high," I said helpfully.

"No, that was a goodun," he assured me. "I just sort of caressed the top of the shell with both heels, lad."

Now the gap between his heels and the egg could have let a Birmingham bus through, but not wanting to go through it again, and comprehending that I was in the presence of a real five-star head case, I nodded. "Yes, just caressed the top of the shell," I agreed, and hurried him across to the baby bath.

"Now lad, I perfected this next bit as a result of studying the New Testament," he announced, as he busied himself piling up sawdust on his next run-up. I was about to mention something about not remembering anything in the New Testament about Jesus walking across baby baths, but thought better of it, and shut up. We could have been there all night.

And I was beginning to have a sinking feeling that we just might be.

"Watch carefully, lad. I'll take a good run-up, check my body and then with a half-walking, half-skating motion, take four steps across the water without disturbing the surface."

Now at this point there was a distinct snort from behind one of the cameras. Taking a quick look round, as this mad man was doing the whooping between his legs again, with a great trail of black shoe polish all over the studio floor, I realised that people were getting the giggles. All except in the far corner of the studio, where I could see a well-known MP, who was due on whenever I got this raving gentleman off, and with the usual politician's sharp sense of humour, was scowling, tapping his watch and frowning across at me, as if somehow this was all my fault.

I turned back just in time to see the champion go roaring up to the water jump, and instead of doing the promised four steps across the surface, he went skidding wildly on the sawdust and knocked the baby bath and its contents flying across the floor. At this point the studio erupted, the floor manager had lost it completely, the cameramen were snorting and trying to suppress belly laughs, and there was an angry bark of, "Oh, for God's sake!" from the prominent MP.

I gurgled out something like, "We'll take the water as read," and lay down on the studio floor, ready for the nose jump.

"Nay, lad. I can't do the nose until I've done the water," he said.

And I had to go through the indignity of getting up again, my back all covered in boot polish, and stand by like a giggling jelly while buckets were brought and the baby bath was re-filled. Then there were more whoops from his head jammed down between his legs and he raced up to the bath with some strange long-jumper style kicks in mid-air, and he cleared it by a great margin. He was nowhere near the water, not that he seemed to know any difference though, for as he landed on the far side of the baby bath he let out a great triumphal victory shout of, "Done it!" and rushed forth all around me punching the air with his fists like Stevie Gerrard winning the European Cup. It was complete chaos.

The floor was covered in cherry blossom, he was covered in cherry blossom, the director was screaming obscenities through people's headphones, a cameraman was holding his ribs and trying to draw breath in great gulps, the MP was hissing with rage at the floor manager, and I had completely lost it. I went to lie down, nose at the ready, sobbing with laughter.

"For God's sake, don't laugh, lad," he barked at me in total seriousness, which only made me worse, "or one of us could be killed."

I just lay there on my back desperately trying to keep my nose still, howling with laughter. With eyes closed I heard the 'whoops' again from somewhere down between his knobbly knees, there were a couple of heavy boot falls from just beside one of my ears, and then there was a great thump on the bridge of my nose, followed by the whole Stevie Gerrard routine all over again.

My nose felt as if I'd been hit with a shovel. It was pouring a mixture of blood and boot polish, somehow with him still fanning the air in triumph from somewhere behind me, and the strains of 'You'll Never Walk Alone' that the director had added as a final touch. I thanked the world champion egg, nose and water jumper and hurried off to see the nurse.

The interview was scheduled for three and a half minutes. It actually ran for just over nine. And the MP had to come back later in the week.

A LESSON LEARNED

B ecause I've always loved cricket, and have played it since I was a little boy, when I discovered that our studios at ATV were about a mile down the road from Edgbaston, I managed to sneak off several evenings in the summer and watch the matches.

I did mention to Mike, my boss, how much the game had changed in recent years. I'd become very aware of it one particular weekend, because the West Indies were playing England and the noise in the ground was wonderful.

This was clearly because there was by now a large, cricket-loving West Indian population in Birmingham. They loved the game, and at that time their team was the best in the world. So the match I had gone to watch at the weekend had been wild and raucous, the sun had even shone on Birmingham, the steel bands played and surprise, surprise, England were completely battered.

Mike said to me that I really ought to do a feature about how much the face of the game is changing with the more flamboyant crowds, compared to the more staid, old-school English ones.

So, I wrote a piece and recorded it that afternoon. I wanted to make the point that when I was growing up and watching cricket with my dad, the game was played in virtual silence, except for the occasional remark of "good shot", or an audacious bit of clapping when somebody scored a four.

Contrast this with last weekend's game, I said, when the crowd went wild with every boundary, screamed ecstatically when there was a six – regrettably there were a lot of them, all scored by the West Indies team, and also a certain amount of abuse shouted at one particular umpire when he made a decision that went the wrong way for the visitors.

Although it was a good-natured game, the superlatives used on the umpire were fairly shocking, even to me, and were laced with four-letter words. So I agreed with the director that I would say what the fans screamed at the match officials but we would bleep it out before the item went out on air. So we recorded it with me saying things like, "The umpire was a total blank, blank, blank, a complete and utter — and his Mother was a —."

We finished the item in three and a half minutes, and I thought it went well, but the director came down and said, "I'm really sorry, Chris. It just doesn't work, because even though we are bleeping it, it's very obvious from your lip movements that you're not actually saying the words."

"Well I can't say the actual words, can I?"

"Yes, of course you can. I promise you I will put bleeps on it."

"Well, my career's on the line here," I said, rather weakly.

"Yes, and so's mine," he said, reassuring me. "Don't be daft, say the words and I'll bleep them all out, I promise."

"OK," I said, and I did the piece again with the full gamut of four-letter words. It was rather weird saying them out loud, although I have to admit it was rather invigorating! For three and a half blissful minutes I was Billy Connolly and the crew were looking at me round their cameras, as if I'd finally gone mad. All was well though and the director was true to his word and bleeped all over the offensive language. The show went out, everybody agreed it was a good item, and I went home happy.

However, when I came in the next morning my boss wasn't happy at all. He said, "It's not your fault, Chris, and we don't blame you, but just look at all these complaints." There was a whole string of them, outraged letters that had already arrived by the first post of the morning, and many outraged messages left with the duty officer, all from various institutes for the deaf.

In their silent world, watching their televisions at home, this very nice man who was normally so amiable and wholesome had clearly gone mad and screamed abuse unnecessarily in what should have been a gentle item about cricket. They were outraged. They were shocked and stunned. And quite rightly. We had to cobble together some sort of a reply and an abject apology. I really was deeply sorry and ashamed, but it was generally agreed we hadn't got a leg to stand on.

It was a lesson learnt. It honestly hadn't crossed my mind or, luckily, any of the management's minds either, but it is one that I have never ever forgotten.

KIDS' TELLY?

Then my world was to change again. ATV's continuity announcer, a great chum called Peter Tomlinson, became increasingly bored and disenchanted with sitting through cheap cartoons and dreadful old black-and-white cowboy films like *Hopalong Cassidy* and *The Cisco Kid* as ATV's output on Saturday mornings, supposedly aimed at children. It wasn't peculiar to ATV. Most of the Saturday morning output across the networks was similarly drab. Some stations didn't even open on Saturdays till lunchtime. Just for fun, Peter one week did a competition for kids between the films, although in truth he was not at all sure who, if anybody, was out there. What happened made everyone sit up and take notice. Massive bags of children's competition answers began to arrive at Pete's tiny office. Clearly there was a whole untapped market out there.

By the autumn ATV had its own very cheap and cheerful Saturday morning children's show on air. I remember being thrilled at getting an extra twenty-five quid a week for three whole hours of live TV. As I said, it was very cheap, but we were very cheerful.

Initially I joined Pete and John Asher, with Trevor East doing the sport, for a brand-new show called *Today Is Saturday: Watch and Smile*, which quickly became shortened to *Tiswas*. It was produced and directed by a larger-than-life guy called Peter Harris, a wonderfully outrageous extrovert who just buzzed constantly with wild irreverent ideas for the show, and without whom undoubtedly I wouldn't have stayed in the industry. He went on to work on the

Muppets, *OTT* and *Spitting Image*, and is one of the few real geniuses I've ever worked with. Mad as a march hare but absolutely brilliant.

Within only a few weeks *Tiswas* ratings went through the roof and we knew we were onto something huge. The response everywhere was unbelievable. More and more of the networks took us. By the time Sally James and Lenny Henry joined us we were being nominated for every award and its success forced the BBC to try to compete with its own rather safe, drab little Saturday morning offering called *Multi-Coloured Swap Shop*, hosted by Noel Edmonds with his division-four footballers' haircut.

We all did personal appearances every Saturday afternoon and enormous crowds of kids and mums turned up. The whole *Tiswas* team once appeared at a large shop in Stoke-on-Trent. The security was inadequate and it was totally out of control. We had to hide in the manager's office until the police arrived, a whole clothes rail disappeared in the chaos and eleven lawnmowers were nicked ... Yes, *eleven*.

As *Tiswas* grew and grew, I was still doing my Monday to Friday stint on the news programme, and they started to talk about a 'credibility gap'. I'd be reporting on a bus crash on Friday evening and then I'd be throwing buckets of water all over people on a Saturday morning. "You've got to choose," they said, "buses or buckets?" certain, of course, that in the long term I would obviously go for buses. "Well, sorry," I said, to all of their amazement, "it's got to be buckets."

And I never looked back. I just loved it. A brilliant guy called Glyn Edwards took over for a while from Peter, who went off to be a muppet. Glyn was a great former seaside Punch and Judy man (Well, what other qualifications could you possibly need to be a TV director!) and I took over as producer. The show completely dominated my life for the next few years. I had no really fixed idea of what or where I wanted to take the show, I just hated *Blue Peter*. The other thing we began to realise was that *Tiswas* had built up a huge adult and student following.

At the height of *Tiswas* fame in the middle of the 70s, 58% of the audience were over 18. Pubs opened early on Saturday mornings with giant TV sets over the bar, it was obligatory viewing on all the sets in TV hire shops, and it was certainly on in every student union in the country, which I found a bit of a worry, even at the time. Now, having met many of today's captains of industry and Members of Parliament, who would have been students around this time, it seems my fears were justified. They will have been *those* very students.

In some ways this adult cult following was very gratifying, but in many others, it made life difficult. With my producer's hat on I was never quite sure what audience we were aiming at. In the end we copped out and just did whatever made *us* laugh, and since mentally we were mostly just big overgrown kids anyway, it seemed to work quite well.

A journalist from somewhere got the detail that I used to be a teacher and said, "Obviously this is where Chris got his love of children." Well, it's a good link, but to be honest teaching 15-year-old boys in New Cross wouldn't teach anyone a great love of children, and they were hardly children, some of them were bigger than me. Besides, I don't think *Tiswas* showed any great love of children anyway.

But we were constantly trying to come up with ideas that would somehow cut across all the age groups. Of course we had custard pies and buckets of water and the Phantom Flan Flinger with his wife Flanderella and their offspring the Baby Bucket Bunger, but the best idea of all was the Cage. In spite of the fact that it was supposedly a kids' show, we were forever getting requests from people who really should have been old enough to have more sense, but wanted to come and sit in amongst all the jammy-faced kids in the studio. We must have turned down thousands, until we hit upon the idea of allowing grown-ups into the studio, but kept them in a holding pen to the side of the set – and, of course, it just happened to be very close to where we kept all the buckets. Purely by chance? No, of course it wasn't.

If there was a lull in the proceedings, and some Saturdays the lull lasted the full three hours, we could pelt the grown-ups with anything we could lay our hands on. Admittedly it was a rather simplistic idea, and we intended to try it for one week only. In reality it ran for more than five years. The waiting list of grown-ups for the Cage was never-ending. At the beginning of each series we had enough for the whole run. I suppose that was harmless, although perhaps just a tad of a worry about where Great Britain was heading. Jeremy Kyle once told me that for each season they already had enough of those usually very angry guests to come on stage and scream abuse at each other for the whole series before the series even started. Now that's really worrying.

All we told the adults the first week was that they had been chosen to join a small selection of lucky Mums and Dads who would be allowed onto the studio floor during the transmission of next week's programme. They would be ushered into a 'private viewing area': "Oh, P.S. Please bring a change of clothes."

The next Saturday, about five minutes into the programme, Bob Carolgees and I got rather fed up with their grinning simpleton faces peering at us through the bars of the cage, so we pelted them with the contents of every bucket we could lay our hands on. There was uproar. The kids went wild with delight at the visions of their Mummies and Daddies completely coated in green and yellow gunge. The adults screamed in horrified disbelief, and the more they screamed the more we pelted them. Most ridiculous of all, once they were over the initial shock, the drenched grown-ups appeared to absolutely love it.

To this day I have no idea what bizarre raw nerve we touched on, but its effect was instant and massive. On Monday morning the office was besieged with phone calls, from supposedly intelligent adults who all wanted to come into the cage and get 'the treatment'.

It was presumably something to do with Warhol's theory of everybody wanting their fifteen minutes of fame – but it seemed a funny sort of fame to me.

By the Wednesday we had a waiting list for the Cage to last the series. By the next Friday we had a waiting list of bewildered grown-ups that would have lasted us the rest of their lives. Some of them I am almost sure are still sitting at home anxiously waiting to be chosen, even though the show finished in 1981.

So the Cage became a fixture. Each week a dozen or so lucky, lucky adults would arrive like lambs to the slaughter. It always amused me, that despite knowing what to expect, many of them would arrive dressed up to the nines – blokes in their best suits, women in specially purchased new dresses and immaculate hairdos – only to be splattered beyond recognition, often within seconds of the opening titles. One woman told me she later watched the whole show on video, and even she couldn't work out which one she was.

One of my less well-thought-out ideas was baby juggling. Not real babies, obviously. At least I thought it was obvious they were baby dollies. Lenny, in some sort of glittery showbiz suit, juggled one, two, then three baby dolls at a time, very skilfully and theatrically up into the air, doing somersaults and back flips and then back into his hands while we played a soundtrack of babies crying all over the item.

We thought it was very funny, but then the phone started ringing non stop with complaining parents. "Stupid, idiotic, irresponsible", were just a few of the cleaner things I was called. At first I was very defensive: "Oh, come on, for god's sake. Of course they weren't real babies," I kept saying, but then one irate mum told me that her 6-year-old son had started trying to juggle his two new baby twin sisters. I could only utter pathetic, bleating apologies. The game was up. It was a daft idea. I am "stupid, idiotic and irresponsible", and we never did anything like it again. Shame, though, because Lenny did it very well.

Apart from the occasional blip like baby juggling (not to mention mouse-washing) I was beginning to absolutely love it all. I was still in my twenties, as were Sally and Bob. John Gorman was only about

80 and Lenny would soon be 12. The show changed all our lives. We were rock stars overnight with all the perks and temptations that brings. I don't think any of us actually touched drugs, we were mad enough without any stimulants. We met everybody in the pop world at that time because it was the show that most of the bands wanted to be on, because as well as plugging their latest record or tour they had a hoot of a Saturday morning. Sometimes to their record companies' horror they were having such a great time they forgot all about what they'd come on to plug. I remember one Saturday morning I was rolling about in custard with Annie Lennox, Chrissie Hynde and Sheena Easton, thinking, "I'm being paid for this."

Early every Saturday morning the lads in the props crew were busily filling up the gunge buckets ready for that morning's cage dwellers – mainly water and green, blue and yellow foam, although they did tell me that they also made up extra buckets that they called 'their little specials'. They never would tell me what the ingredients of 'their little specials' were, but I had a few very nasty theories.

After a while we began to advertise for rather specialised cage occupants, usually restricted to the absolute pillars of society – headmasters, maths teachers and the like, just the sort of figures of authority that kids wanted to see get their comeuppance, *Tiswas* cage style.

We soon extended our criteria to the strata of society that *we* wanted to see get their comeuppance, and still there was no shortage of volunteers. Probably to the bewilderment of most of the children, we had cages full of tax inspectors, traffic wardens, policemen, bank managers, VAT men, solicitors, MPs, and even (oh, joy!) estate agents. The waiting list grew and grew and the props men happily prepared their 'little specials' in readiness.

One week, in a moment of madness, I decided we'd get together a celebrity cage. It seemed like a good idea at the time – on reflection it was one of the daftest ideas even I've ever done.

We had loads of mates from the music industry, who were

dying to come in the cage. Rick and Francis from Quo, of course, Rainbow, Cozy Powell and Co., Lemmy and Motorhead, a couple of The Pretenders and an all-girl rock band called Goldie and The Gingerbreads. We crammed them all into a special extra-large cage, added a few pop journalists to the mix and topped it up with John Peel, one of the most respected music buffs in the country.

It was a memorable morning. They got an extra special celebrity soaking, of course, but the atmosphere was great. About an hour into the show, I was in the middle of a sketch with Lenny Henry dressed up as David Bellamy, and a couple of pop stars, Phil Collins and Mike Rutherford in ill-fitting, obscene looking green leotards, dressed up as giant sunflowers. Nothing out of the ordinary so far.

All of a sudden, the unmistakable smell of marijuana came wafting into my nostrils from the direction of the Cage. Here's me, the producer of a supposed children's television programme, kids everywhere, parents everywhere, journalists everywhere, and one of my guests is smoking a joint.

I abandoned the sketch, much to Lenny's bewilderment, and rushed to the cage, completely drenching everyone in it with bucket after bucket of the Midland Water Board's finest product, the offending aroma disappeared, the spliff was no more. I have never ever revealed who was the offending miscreant who smoked pot on a children's television programme, and I would never do that.

Oh, ok then, it was Rick Parfitt, but it doesn't make him a bad person.

THE DOYING FLOY

Jasper Carrott had a very good idea. He had lots of ideas actually, most of them completely barmy, but in the middle of a meeting in the curry house that had become our weekend office, he said, "Why don't we get all the *Tiswas* team to do The Dying Fly, and get all the kids doing it as well."

"Wonderful," I said. "Just what we need. Brilliant. Genius. Er … what the hell is it?"

"The Dying Fly," said Carrott. "You must know The Dying Fly." (Bear in mind that Carrott, of course, pronounces fly 'floy' and dying 'doying'.) "Well, you sort of get your legs and you – oh sod it, I'll show you." So there and then, in a restaurant in Birmingham, after we'd just done a full morning of *Tiswas*, Carrott solemnly moves a few plates and knives and forks, lies on his back on the table and starts kicking his little hairless legs and arms in the air, like Bradley Wiggins who's lost his bicycle. "Of course, you would be wearing antennae on your head," he said, "and there'd be some music."

"Yes, Jasper, of course," we mumbled.

"It's also known as dead ants," he said, as if somehow that made it slightly more understandable. Anyway, because *Tiswas* was the sort of programme where you could try absolutely anything and, if it was a good idea, bask in the glory of it for weeks (like Spit the Dog), or if it was a really dreadful idea (like Bob's follow-up Cough the Cat), abandon it after just one airing never to be seen again.

Spit is still amusing people to this day. Cough the bright blue cat didn't last to the end of its first show. In fact, come to think of it, it didn't make it past the first commercial break.

So there we were the next Saturday lying on our backs in Studio 3, with little antennae on our heads, kicking our arms and legs like loonies, in time to a silly tune called 'The Typewriter Song'. It was ridiculous, and the doying floy became yet another *Tiswas* gift to a grateful nation.

All over the country the music would start up and people would get down on their backs and do 'The Dying Fly'. There were all-night 'Dying Fly' marathons, T-shirts with I'M DYING TO FLY on them, DJs in clubs would do attempts on the 'how many people can we get all doing the dying fly at once in one place world record'. We even made a record selling literally … dozens.

I was once asked along to a fancy-dress party at a ladies' college. Halfway through the evening, at the sight of all these 18-year-olds, mainly dressed in St Trinian's gear, gym slips and stocking tops, all getting down on their backs and kicking their legs in the air, for two minutes and forty-eight seconds, I thought, "Jasper, whatever have you started?"

It all ended rather abruptly, people started doing 'The Dying Fly' in the silliest places, like dual carriageways. It sounds ridiculous now, but that really is what happened. There were several near misses, and finally a really serious accident, at night on a busy main road near Cardiff and we were forced to abandon it before somebody actually died doing 'The Dying Fly'.

Every year, ROSPA (The Royal Society of the Prevention of Accidents) publish a list of the things most likely to cause accidents, and at the end of this particular year I received a very official looking bit of paper that read something like this:

Most dangerous practices for the last quarter ending 30th November:

1. Drink driving
2. Excessive speed
3. Poor car mechanics
4. Not wearing a crash helmet
5. Fireworks
6. Storing petrol without adequate safety measures
7. Weed killers
8. The Dying Fly
9. Faulty wiring
10. Unlicensed explosives …

IN THE CLUB

Fred Rumsey, a great England fast bowler who lived close to me in the Midlands, rang me out of the blue and said, "Do you fancy getting a *Tiswas* cricket team together to play the Lord's Taverners?" Now I have to admit, shamefacedly, considering how much of my life has been involved with this splendid charity ever since, that I'd never heard of the Lord's Taverners. My only knowledge of them came from Willie Rushton being asked live on Russell Harty's chat show, "What exactly do the Lord's Taverners do?" and Willie replied, "Oh, we get pissed for Jesus," at which Harty gasped and spurted out a whole glass of water down his best suit.

However, we got a team together and were told that we could play on the main pitch at Trent Bridge, which is really hallowed ground, and because of the huge following that *Tiswas* had we absolutely sold the place out, to thousands of Mums, Dads and their kids all proudly wearing *Tiswas* hats and T-shirts.

Most of the Taverners were very well-known actors and celebrities – people like Robert Powell, John Alderton, Dennis Waterman, Leslie Crowther, who had all come up from London for the day, and had never heard of us. They were in their best whites, and looked very smart. We were a bunch of rag-bag oiks in dirty jeans and, of course, the branded *Tiswas* T-shirts.

They did what they did best, which was try to play a friendly but serious game of cricket. We, on the other hand, did what we did best, which was throw custard pies at them, bowling soot bombs, bringing a huge gunge tank onto the pitch and also setting up special exploding stumps. And of course the Phantom Flan Flinger in his black cloak and mask, the blackest fiend in the cosmos, ran amok all over the pitch, covering friend, foe and umpire alike in green gunge. It was a riot, the crowd absolutely loved it, we absolutely loved it, the Taverners of course absolutely hated it, and on reflection who could blame them. They went off, grinning as best they could, covered from head to toe in soot, custard, and green gunge.

Fred did say to me afterwards, "Perhaps it was a mistake."

"I'm really sorry, Fred," I said. "I assumed they knew what we do."

He said, "Well they do now."

I agreed to pay for all their dry cleaning and we shook hands and parted.

To my surprise about six months later, I received a call from Taverners HQ saying, "Would I like to join the Tavs?" I was a little surprised to say the least, and I said so, but the nice man on the other end said, "Well, to be honest, we'd rather have you with us than against us."

And so began forty of the happiest years of my life. It is a wonderful charity that was started back in 1950 by His Royal Highness, Philip the Duke of Edinburgh. The idea was to get some prominent actors and musicians of the day to join him in cricket matches, but specifically geared to raising money for children with additional needs. The first ever meeting was filmed on Pathé News and was held in the Grosvenor Hotel where His Highness insisted that somebody provide a bat and ball and they played a game of cricket in the Great Room.

What went on from there has been truly amazing. The Taverners have now raised well over 80 million pounds since they started, and it's gone from strength to strength.

It was one charity very close to Philip's heart and he loved to see how well it had developed from his early pioneering days. He would often come to the grounds, particularly when we played at Windsor Castle. He was usually in great form, and very relaxed, but one particular afternoon he did seem rather down in the dumps. Encouraged, I think, by a couple of glasses of wine, I found the courage to say to him, "You seem a bit fed up, sir."

"Oh, yes," he said. "I am. I wanted to watch the cricket but I've got to go."

I said, "You don't have to go, sir, surely. You are the Duke of Edinburgh, you don't *have* to go anywhere."

"Yes, I do," he said. "It's ridiculous. George Bush is coming to meet me and the Queen."

And I said, "Well surely that's a standard part of your position, sir. You don't have to like him."

"Yes, I know that, but I want to watch cricket, and he's coming for twenty minutes, twenty bloody minutes," he said, with real emphasis. "What are we going to achieve in twenty minutes? World Peace? I don't think so." And off he went in his Range Rover, not the happiest of bunnies.

Sure enough about ten minutes later we saw three high-speed USAF jet helicopters racing towards the castle, and they could clearly be heard landing somewhere just behind the walls. One of them presumably contained George W Bush. Me and Mark Nicholas set our watches and said, "OK, let's see," and sure enough, twenty-two minutes later, the three of them went racing back towards Heathrow and Air Force One.

I don't suppose that did achieve very much, except George W could tell Laura when he got home he'd had "a long chat" with the Queen and the Duke of Edinburgh.

I became President of Lord's Taverners in 1990, joining a long list of high-profile previous presidents, including Prince Philip himself, John Mills, Sir John Barbirolli, Jack Hawkins, Colin Cowdrey, David Frost, Terry Wogan and Tim Rice. It was obviously a bit of a thin year when they chose me.

It's a two-year job. I went all over the British Isles to every single region, and it was truly wonderful to see how much difference to the lives of these young kids the presentation of one of the green Lord's Taverners minibuses could mean. It makes so many more things possible for them.

We try to raise the funds for at least one minibus a week for the kids all over Britain. They are not cheap, but we have managed to raise more than enough in recent years to find the funds to hand over more than fifty of these special customised coaches every twelve months. Anyone who has been to one of the official ceremonies of handing over the keys to these children, with a range of additional needs, will agree it's always quite a tear-jerking moment.

The charity itself is a hoot. Their motto is always 'Fun Through Fund Raising', and we have had enormous fun, and some wonderful nights, although the details of most of them I don't seem to remember too clearly.

Somehow, one evening, the Lady Taverners arranged for no less than Bill Clinton to fly over and talk to a packed audience about child poverty around the world. He was brilliant and spoke for an hour and a half without a single note anywhere in sight. He was extraordinary.

What was even more extraordinary was that far from tut-tutting his wicked treatment of Hillary and his hugely publicised antics with Monica Lewinsky and others, all over the papers just a few weeks before, every woman in the audience queued around the room and up the staircase to get an autograph and a photo posing with the arch fornicator before they would let him leave. Jane, my own partner, was all over him like a rabbit in a field of wet turnips.

I've played alongside most of my cricketing heroes, guys like Ian Botham, David Gower, Chris Cowdrey, Brian Close, Phil Tufnell, even Godfrey Evans and Bobby Simpson.

One of our big sponsors is a lovely guy called James Hull, who we always fondly call 'Lazarus' because he's been in hospital so many times, with dreadful things wrong with him, and every single time has defied the doctors and come out fitter than when he went in. Each time he comes out to prove how well he is feeling he seems to produce another child. He is a dentist, and he puts this team together called 'The Drillers' who are supposedly just a bunch of keen cricketers who all happen to be dentists.

So, one year when we were due to play The Drillers at Lord's, I was looking down his team sheet and saw the name Gibbs. "Who is that?" I asked him suspiciously. "Oh, don't worry about that, it's just one of the Gibbs toothpaste family. He's not actually much good."

"OK," I said. I should have known better when, half an hour later, striding to the crease was Herschelle Gibbs, one of the greatest South African batsmen of all time. He then proceeded to hit us all round the ground, and frequently out of the ground, until he got bored and went back to the bar.

The next year, among his 'dentists', I saw the name B Lara, and I thought, surely, not even Lazarus could have got hold of Brian Lara, the world-record-breaking West Indian captain. "Oh, yes," he said. "It is Brian Lara, but honestly he trained as a dentist." Yes, of course he did, and honestly, I trained as a heart surgeon.

When he came out to bat, for some reason, I had the misfortune to be bowling. I bowled the first ball, a full toss. He looked at it very suspiciously and just put his bat straight up, stopped the ball in its tracks, and went, "No, no run," to the guy at the other end. He was incredibly wary of my bowling, and he played every ball with enormous respect. When he got to the fifth ball and still hadn't scored a single run, my son Toby, who was also playing, came up and handed me the ball and said to me in a whisper, "Dad, he doesn't know how crap you are."

"I know, Toby," I said. "Let's not tell him, shall we?"

The fifth and sixth ball of the over were treated with the same trepidation by Brian, and somehow, I'd bowled a maiden over. Not a run was scored against me by one of the greatest batsmen of all time.

If only I had left it there, I'd be a hero to this day. However, there was another over at the other end, and then it was my turn to bowl at him again. He clearly had a bit of a think about my bowling in the meantime, because the first ball was hit savagely over the boundary for six, scattering a lot of ladies who were all having cups of tea and gin and tonics. The second ball he hit much harder and higher over the hospital at the top end of the ground. The third ball disappeared somewhere over St John's Wood tube station, and, as far as I know, the fourth ball is still somewhere in outer space.

Twenty-four runs in four balls, four huge sixes, and my captain actually took me off before the end of my over. It's not allowed in the laws of the game, but thank God he did.

Other great memories include the time I shared a stand of 80 runs with Andrew Strauss, although admittedly, he did get 79 of them. This is a bit like my good friend Chris Cowdrey, who always boasts that he and his dad, Sir Colin Cowdrey, captained England 38 times between them, but the tag line is that Sir Colin was captain for 37, Chris only the one.

I do remember once, we somehow got the great South African bowler, Allan Donald to play for us. He bowled four vicious overs at the poor, hapless batsmen at the other end, who somehow managed to survive without actually getting out.

My son Toby then came on and got a wicket first ball. Allan Donald ran across the pitch to give Toby high-fives. It was a wonderful moment for Toby, but above all, for a proud dad, it really doesn't get any better than that.

And, of course, we had to have a streaker. We were playing a game in Coventry and the crowd around the beer tent were getting louder and louder, until eventually one of them emerged completely naked, racing across the pitch. Now, one thing streakers normally don't have to worry about is how they get off the pitch and what to do with their clothes, because they are always arrested and go off with their willy hidden by the perfectly shaped policeman's helmet. However, with this being a Lord's Taverners game, none of us could care less, so to wild cheers, this bloke and his little tommy tinkler, came racing onto the pitch and we just stood there laughing at him. Somebody said, "Are you really going to take that funny little thing back to your girlfriend, mate?" And we just carried on batting. All his original pride slowly dissipated, he just looked rather pathetic. The only policemen on the ground looked the other way, and having come on to wild cheers and applause, he went off to derisory boos and slow handclaps. Worse still, when he got back to the bar, his mates had all disappeared and so had all his clothes.

THE HIT

Having given the Dying Fly to the world, Jasper Carrott re-appeared many years later on my *This Is Your Life*, and ridiculously, in spite of the dangers, did the dying fly.

I always said I'd avoid *This Is Your Life* like the plague, and also that anybody with even one brain cell would see the big red book coming a mile away. Well, I'm here to tell you it doesn't work like that.

The moment when the bewildered soul is confronted by Michael Aspel, or even in the early days by Eamonn Andrews, is called by the production team 'the hit', and they refer to you as 'the subject'.

Captain Hindsight here only realised any of this after being repeatedly referred to as 'the subject' by my driver on the way to 'the hit', as he was actually on the phone making sure events proceeded smoothly. All subjects have a codename, apparently mine was 'city' (for CT). Trevor McDonald was 'burger' and Robert Maxwell was 'house', presumably because he was the size of one.

When they got Mr Unsuspecting me, I was doing a simple handover of a minibus to a specialist kids' school called The Phoenix Centre down in Kent, where I'd been patron for a number of happy years.

I'd done my breakfast show in the morning, and was driven straight there. What I didn't realise was that all my mates at Capital Radio, my wife, my kids, my mother, my dad, and dozens of people I hadn't seen for twenty or thirty years, had all been making frantic secret calls to each other and the production team for over a month.

The splendid Les Dawson once told me that in the build-up to his *This Is Your Life*, he almost sued his lovely wife for a divorce because for weeks she had abruptly put the phone down whenever he suddenly walked into the house.

As I officially handed over the minibus, I do remember thinking why is that silly ambulance getting in the way at just the wrong moment, when the doors of said silly ambulance opened and Michael Aspel came flying out clutching the famous red book. It was one of the most unforgettable moments of my life. I truthfully hadn't a clue. I was like a lamb to the slaughter.

Once I got over the initial shock, I was raced across to Teddington Studios, and the show itself was predictably manic. All sorts of old chums came from way back. A great lady I'd taught alongside years before called Maeve, aka 'Maeve the Rave', talked about my teaching days when I lived outside the school in a minivan. All my old mates from *Tiswas* came on and talked about what I got up to when the cartoons were on. The boys from Genesis talked about the days when I stuffed the two of them into giant flowerpots and covered them in custard.

Years later I gave an award to Phil Collins, and he said, "The last time I met you, you were busy putting baked beans down the front of my trousers."

Lenny Henry talked about how difficult it was for a black man with short curly hair to be a head banger with the rest of us. Jeremy Beadle came on and took his trousers off for no reason that anybody really understood, and my little boy Toby, who was only five, suddenly appeared on film from his bed and explained he couldn't be with Daddy because that very morning he developed chicken pox – or, as he called them, chicken pops. He's now six-foot-five and the chicken pops have disappeared.

Silliest of all was when Jasper Carrott came on to remind us of the days of the dying fly. The whole thing ended with all of us, celebrities, uncles, aunties, teachers, and even the super smooth Michael Aspel, lying on our backs on the studio floor waving our arms and kicking our legs in the air.

Michael then, with enormous panache and athleticism, sprang from the prone position on his back up on to the balls of his feet, still clutching the red book, and delivered the immortal words, "Chris Tarrant, This Is Your Life."

The show ran for years, and there have been some great moments. Danny Blanchflower, the Northern Irish international footballer, was the first person ever to refuse point-blank to do the show. He left Eamonn Andrews and the crew standing there with their mouths opening and closing like goldfish.

Luckily, it's only happened a couple of times since, which is pretty good for a show that ran for well over forty years.

Everybody says they'd walk off, but of course they rarely do. Richard Gordon, the author of *Doctor in the House*, nearly did. In the days when the show used to be live, he said, "Oh balls," and walked off. Eventually he calmed down and was talked into it by frantic producers. All this time, of course, the show was running on air.

David Walker, the manager of my old chums, Status Quo, pulled the band out of the show at the very last minute, causing chaos for Thames Television. With the number of ex-wives, step-kids, and so on, it was getting too complicated, too close to the bone, and potentially just too nasty to be worth risking. David said, "We're a very successful band. We really don't need the grief of this."

Like Les Dawson, Ronnie Barker also became convinced his wife was playing away. It didn't help matters when one of the young researchers left her his card, and Ronnie found it, like Les's wife Meg. It was impossible for Mrs Barker to explain what her relationship with this man was, so Ronnie, still not at all convinced, rang the number. A man answered the phone, saying, "Hello, *This Is Your Life*. How can I help you?" The secret was out, and the show had to be cancelled. The production team were told from that day on, never ever to answer the telephone again with the words "This Is Your Life".

Colin Milburn, the brilliant England and Northampton batsman, is probably the only person ever to appear on the opening credits of *This Is Your Life* and never actually appear on the show itself. The subject of the show was the late brilliant Willie Rushton. Myself, Colin Milburn, Michael Parkinson, Nicholas Parsons, and a load of other Lord's Taverners, were taken up to the front of a pub, on the open top of a horse-drawn carriage, to take the focus away from the then presenter Eamonn Andrews who was hiding in amongst us all with a blanket over his head and clutching the red book. It was a bitter cold afternoon and there were a couple of very handy little hip flasks being handed around while we waited for the unsuspecting Willie to turn up. Milburn gave the hip flasks a spanking, but, having come down on the train from Newcastle, had had a few bevvies to help him through the long journey. By now, Mr Milburn, like Jeffrey Bernard, was distinctly unwell. It didn't help matters that 'the hit' on Rushton was going to be done in a pub. They cued the cameras and we bounced along happily behind the horses with Milburn still draining the last dregs of brandy from the flask, and Eamonn sprang out on an unsuspecting Willie Rushton.

Willie told us all later that he had absolutely no idea that he was going to be the subject of the programme, but he was the most calm and unfazed person I've ever seen appear on the show. When Eamonn popped out from behind the bar, shouting, "This Is Your Life," Willie just said, "Oh, there you are, you funny little leprechaun. I've been waiting for you for years."

Colin Milburn then bought an enormous round of drinks and proceeded to fall fast asleep in the corner of the bar. We all piled into a taxi, dragging Big Col with us. He woke up just in time to drink a large glass of hospitality wine before sitting as best he could on the seat in the studio. Colin was a very big guy and the seat was extremely uncomfortable and liable to eject him at any second. By now Colin was feeling no pain, and was chatting loudly to everybody. Eventually, after several calls of "Quiet" from the floor manager, so that they could start the show, the amiable Colin was asked if he wouldn't mind leaving. It was all perfectly polite and hassle-free, but off he had to go … slurring the words, "I'm terribly sorry, but I don't feel too good." He was quietly put into a car, helped back on to the train and was back in Newcastle before the pubs shut. Willie Rushton wrote him a very nice thank you letter for coming along to pay tribute, and I don't think Colin ever realised that he never actually quite made it to the show itself. Willie Rushton was one of the wittiest and most wonderfully irreverent men I ever knew.

I interviewed him once for *The Six O'Clock Show*, when there was a nasty rumour happily unfounded that the BBC's evergreen coverage of live test cricket, *Test Match Special*, might be taken off air. "Madness," said Rushton. "This would be the end of the empire as we know it. There will never again be an English summer day, the sky will ever more darken, the temple will be rent asunder. Whoever at the BBC dreamed up a such a disgraceful idea should be publicly disembowelled outside broadcasting house." It seemed a little extreme, but I got his drift.

"So," I ventured on, "what would be your perfect summer's day?"

"Ah," said Willie, clearly as always thinking straight off the top of his head. "It would of course be June. I'd be at Lord's, the sun would be shining, but not too fiercely and with a gentle breeze blowing from the members' end, *Test Match Special* would be playing in my ears, there'd be the lovely smell of newly mown grass in the air, England would be batting and destroying the Australians, I'd be drinking Pimm's …", and then he added, "and, of course, I'd be lying across a completely naked Tina Turner."

At this point the interview broke down into a series of uncontrollable giggles and snorts of laughter from the cameraman, sound man and, of course, me the hapless interviewer …

The one person who always seemed to make it onto *This Is Your Life* was Frank Carson. He appeared, welcome or not, in the life of just about every man, woman and child in the country. He was always available, or made himself available. He was always popular and he always had something funny to say about whoever the guest was. He probably appeared on the show more than anyone else in the UK, probably more than Michael Aspel or Eamonn Andrews. At one point he was on several weeks together and he used to sign off with, "That's it from me, Big Frank. Eamonn, I'll see you next week."

But Frank himself had never been the programme's subject. It was almost certainly because none of the other guests would have a chance to get a word in edgeways. Although he and Eamonn both lived in Dublin at the time, and they would see each other on the plane regularly to and from London, Frank himself was never 'The Life'. Whenever Frank saw Eamonn he would pretend to run off saying, "You'll never get me, I know you've got the red book in that briefcase." But of course, Eamonn hadn't. It was locked up in the studio in London.

This went on for years, until one day Eamonn was flying across to Heathrow from Dublin, and Frank came and sat next to him on the plane. Frank started going through his usual nonsense, with Eamonn saying, "Don't be so silly, Frank. We've got loads of much bigger stars lined up for the next five years," when all of a sudden, as they were leaving the aircraft, a film crew appeared out of nowhere and Eamonn produced the legendary red book from under his coat that he had hidden all the way across the Irish Sea. On the front of the book were the legendary words, 'This Is Your Life, Frank Carson', and Frank, for once, and probably the only time in his life, was absolutely gobsmacked. He was actually stuck for words. The silence lasted for nearly two whole seconds.

CARSONITIS

Frank Carson was the most relentlessly funny man I have ever met, Robin Williams and Billy Connolly were certainly funnier on stage, certainly more inventive, but Frank was unstintingly looking for laughs almost every single minute of every single day. As soon as he woke, he was cracking jokes: "It's the way I tell 'em." I saw his stage act, or certainly heard it, at least a hundred times. I knew most of the material, and yet still I couldn't help but laugh. It really was 'the way he told them', and the infectious cackling laugh at his own jokes never failed to get me and the whole audience going.

It seemed he was like it every minute of every day. He was like it in restaurants. I took him to a very smart London restaurant once – only the once. It was one of those where everybody spoke only in whispers. A very smart waiter discreetly asked, "Mr Carson, how would you like your steak?" And Frank replied in a very loud voice, "Just take its horns off and wipe its arse."

If he was doing two shows a day for a long summer season he was like it from the moment he came off stage to the moment he went back on again. I never saw him down. He was like it seemingly every second of his manic, wonderful life. He worked all the time. He said, "I'm like it all the time. I might as well be getting paid for it. I keep laughing at the money." Some of his humour was actually very Pythonesque when he was not on TV, but on stage he was very much an old-style comedian, never blue, but one of the very last of a kind, and one of the very best. He talked very fast with a strong

Northern Irish accent, but had very clear precise diction and always a huge grin on his face as he told his jokes for the thousandth time.

Also, he had this ridiculous language that he invented off stage, that seemed to absolutely take over everywhere he went and everyone he met. It was rubbish, it was nonsense, but it was somehow infectious – phrases like 'tubular scaffolding', 'Sanpan my giblets', and 'knick knack my cabarroes'. It was gibberish, but it left its trail everywhere that big Frankie went.

The first time I ever met Eddie Large, he said to me, by way of greeting, "Well Sanpan my cabarroes." Lenny Henry did it, Jim Davidson did it, Norman Collier did it, everybody did it – though none of us knew what the hell we were talking about.

If he had been somewhere for a long summer season, and he went to the same bars, cafes and restaurants every day, the waiters all had what we called 'The Carson Glaze'. They had this pallor and this look when he approached, like, "Oh, my God, here he comes again." They were all worn out.

I once went up to Great Yarmouth to spend several days with Frank, writing material for *Tiswas* and watching his summer show. I lasted twenty-four hours. He did two shows, but in between acts he must have done about twenty shows. I heard one joke about "Mick and Murphy going into a bar in Belfast" at least twenty times, but infuriatingly he still forced you to laugh, you just couldn't help yourself. He drove everybody mad, but we all loved him.

Some weeks I'd book him for *Tiswas*, some weeks I wouldn't, some weeks I'd pay him, some weeks I wouldn't, but he'd come in anyway if he was within a 100-mile radius. He'd say, "I was watching and it was dying on its arse so I've come in to save the show."

He liked a drink. In fact, he loved a drink. I drove him once to a place called The Sticky Wicket in Redditch, a cabaret club where he was booked to appear on a Friday night. It was the night before *Tiswas*, of course, but he'd been working in Portsmouth, and had clearly been drinking rather a lot in Portsmouth. Even though I was trying to get the show prepared for the next day, I felt strangely responsible for him. I knew Frank really shouldn't be driving, he was completely drunk, making even less sense than usual. I wanted to have a word with the compere of the club and say, "Can you at least get a few black coffees down him before he goes on, and maybe could he start a bit later."

However, while I was parking up, Frank jumped out of the car and disappeared. In a panic I raced into the club only to find that Frank, never one of those artists who hides himself from the audience until it's show time, was standing at the bar, slurring, and drinking lots of free lagers, bought for him by those that would be his audience in about twenty minutes' time. He was swaying and slurring. There was no way he could do a show, he'd have to cancel. But the compere would have none of it. Out of the blue I heard, "Ladies and Gentlemen, it's star time." The band struck up some sort of Irish jig. "Here he is from *Tiswas* and *The Comedians*, it's a cracker, it's the way I tell 'em, Mr Showbiz himself, Frank Carson."

He almost fell up the stairs. I could see the two of us being lynched, but he started his act, with his usual staccato fast-talking performance, did about an hour and a half, never slurred once, never repeated the same joke once and got a standing ovation. When he came off, he was as drunk as he was when he'd gone on, and I took him back to his hotel and helped him to his room. The next morning on *Tiswas*, after a giant breakfast, he was brilliant.

It seemed to be how some of those old boys lived. I suppose a lot of the bands have always done the same thing with drugs.

So back in Great Yarmouth we went from bar to bar between his two shows that evening. Everywhere we went they had the 'Carson Glaze' and I fell exhausted into bed at 2am. He booked us into a B&B, mercifully we weren't sharing rooms, but I was in the one next door to him. Through the night I could hear noises and voices coming from his room.

"The wicked old devil," I thought. "He's got a woman in there." I'd hear jokes being told, and I'd hear howls of manic laughter, and I heard "That's a cracker, it's the way you tell 'em, Frank," about seven or eight times through the night.

At six o'clock, bright and breezy, up he gets and the whole routine begins again. There was nobody else there, he'd been telling himself jokes all night and howling with laughter.

I rang my secretary Gail in Birmingham and said, "Gail, will you ring Frank Carson's agent and get a message to say I've got to get back to ATV urgently."

"No, no," said Gail, "you're there 'til Friday."

"No, no, Gail," I said, "I'm completely exhausted, I can do no more. I absolutely love him, he's wonderful, but I can't take any more of it. Please ring her saying I must get back to Birmingham, or anywhere."

He rang me once out of the blue, and said, "Chris, I'm staying in the Holiday Inn next week. Can you get me the ATV production rate on a room?"

"No, Frank. I can't do that. You're not booked on the show for a fortnight."

"No, I'll pay," he said. "But I'm doing a series of Irish nights at working men's clubs in the Midlands, so instead of paying £45 a night, could you just get me the room for £24 using the ATV rate."

"OK, Frank. I'll do that for you. As you're a regular I can get you the deal, but we're not paying."

So, I booked him in at the agreed £24 a night, £21 cheaper than the full rate, big double room with two beds and, to be honest, forgot all about him. We booked so many pop stars and comedians into the Holiday Inn, which was right next door to the studios, that they happily gave us the reduced rate.

Then I bumped into Frank in the middle of the next week, having breakfast in our canteen. I said, "Hi, Frank. How you doing? Everything OK?"

"It's going brilliantly. The shows are great every night and thanks for getting the deal on the room."

"That's no problem, Frank," I said. "But make sure it's not going on our budget. That's a very good deal at twenty-four quid."

He looked at me with a twinkle in his eyes and made the figures five and one from the fingers of his two hands.

I said, "What are you on about?"

He said, "I'm not paying £24. I'm paying £6 a night."

"You can't pay £6. It's £24 per night, not six."

"Oh, but it is," he said. "Two double beds. I'm sharing with The Bachelors."

I had this vision of Frank with The Bachelors howling with laughter, singing Irish songs, cracking jokes, and farting Guinness all through the night, with giant Irish trousers and unspeakable giant pants scattered all around the room. Who'd be a hotel cleaner, eh?

He turned up on *Tiswas* one day with a bloke called Bob Carolgees, who I'd never heard of. When I was doing a link all the kids around me started laughing and giggling and pointing behind me. Carolgees was entertaining them with a dog and a monkey.

"God, they're funny," I said. "Can you use them in the next link as well?"

"Yes," he said. "Of course I can."

So, Spit the Dog and Charlie the Monkey became regulars on the show for the next five years. Spit became a legend in his own toothbrush.

We were doing a charity fishing match in Ireland sometime in the 70s. It was some of the best professional fishermen in England against a team of celebrities, including Billy Connolly, Frank Carson, me, Gareth Edwards the great Welsh rugby player, and several others. We had an extraordinary week, but on the way home in the coach going to the airport, the Guinness had been flowing a little too well, and we passed a church, with what was obviously a very big Irish wedding going on. "Wouldn't it be a hoot?" whispered Carson, in a low volume for once in his life. "Let's go and stand on the end of the wedding and get in the photograph."

So, we crept out, me with long blonde hair, Connolly with a great flowing mane, and the impossible-not-to-recognise Carson. We didn't look anybody in the eye or say a word, just stood quietly on the end of the line for the family photographs. The photographer got everybody on the count of three, and we all smiled and quietly tip-toed back on the bus.

I did *The Late Late Show* once in Ireland, their big chat show, and I did mention our tagging on to the end of that family picture. I said, "Surely somebody out there must have a wedding photograph with three very recognisable gentlemen on the end. Please let us know." But strangely to this day we've never heard a word.

FISHING IN THE TREES

Incidentally, I once got invited to a big charity celebrity trout fishing match in Surrey. Lots of famous faces were promised to be there and I could take a guest, so I brought Fat Phil, my local tackle dealer, so-called because his name's Philip and he lives in the pie shop next door. We had the draw and Phil unfortunately got a bad draw right down the end of the lake in amongst lots of trees.

"Don't worry," I told him, "we all change round at lunchtime."

So off he trudged. He's not the best of casters and every time I looked up he seemed to be apologising to the poor guy next to him who seemed to spend his whole morning getting Phil's flies out of the trees all around him.

I caught two or three trout in the morning, but I was drawn on a big open lawn. When Phil came in at lunchtime, he'd caught nothing. "Yes," he said, "I kept getting caught up in the trees, but there was a smashing bloke next to me, really kind and patient. He spent most of the morning getting my tackle out of that big oak tree."

"What a nice bloke," I said. "Which one is he?"

"That one over there eating a sandwich. A diamond geezer. I know his face. I think he comes into my shop to buy maggots."

"Yes, Phil," I said, "he is a diamond geezer, and you do know his face, but not because he comes into your shop to buy maggots. You know his face cos he's called Eric Clapton."

TOP OF THE POPS

Meanwhile, back in the *Tiswas* office, John Gorman said, "Kids love smells don't they?"

"Well they have to in your house," I said. So taking that as some kind of endorsement he created the character of Smello, a horrible looking old tramp who basically stank, and the kids loved him.

And Smello's next big idea turned out to be a monster for all of us. In a former life John had been in the band Scaffold and he had written a lot of their hits, like 'Lily the Pink' and 'Aintree Iron', but this time he'd come up with a rousing marching number specially for us called 'The Bucket of Water Song', and for the next two or three years it governed all our lives.

It basically worked on the simple premise that when you came to certain key words like 'bucket' or 'water', for example, you and everyone else around you poured buckets of water all over your head, and all over the heads of anybody else within drenching distance. So we tried it out tentatively the next Saturday morning on *Tiswas*. It was a sensation.

The switchboard after the show was jammed with people asking where they could get the record, although, of course, at the time no such record existed.

By Monday lunchtime we had heard from people all over the country who had been drenching each other in time to whatever they could remember of the words. Not that it really mattered, what really mattered was that it provided yet another excuse for normally, perfectly sane, boring grown-ups to behave like great big overgrown kids.

By the time we repeated the song the next weekend, a whole new social phenomenon had been born: 'Bucketing'. From all over the country we heard reports of pubs, clubs and restaurants being flooded out by the occupants as they poured plastic buckets, tin buckets, fire buckets, ice buckets and probably even sick buckets all over each other in time to the marching music, and of course, because it was all our fault, we got it worst of all, for the whole of that lunatic summer, everywhere. Whenever we went out for a meal people came trotting up, either with receptacles of their own, intended for us, or at least as often asking very politely, "I know it's a bit of a cheek, and I know it's your evening off, but would you mind pouring the contents of this fish tank all over my head, please?"

I do remember a terribly well-spoken, well-dressed woman in Brighton coming up to our table one evening and saying, "I am awfully sorry, but do you mind if I do this?" and poured the entire ice bucket over Sally's head. Sally did that 'smile through gritted teeth' you do in moments like that. I remember quite clearly saying to the woman, "You're an idiot, please go away," and she was bewildered, saying, "But that's what you do, isn't it?" And I said, "Yes, that's what we do on Saturday mornings when we're being paid, but we don't do it every day of the week, especially when we are trying to have a bit of quiet time off." In fairness, we had sort of started it, but to hell with fairness, she was a very stupid person.

The record release on CBS was the next step, and although a lot of discos banned it, because of the trouble it caused in nice, posh, elegant clubs, it sold in very large quantities. And because we'd booked for a tour of British theatres and colleges that summer, with a rather hurriedly thrown-together entertainment for over 18s, the song couldn't have arrived at a better time. It became our anthem up and down the country. Every night the scenes at the end of our show for the encore were the same. We always had a huge tank of water and a large hosepipe organised at the side of the stage with a large range of buckets. Every conceivable electric wire, plug and socket were hastily protected with rubber and polythene sheeting, and then, once the electrical boys gave us the thumbs up, the music started and we would march back onto the stage and the entire audience would come running out of their seats and jam themselves against the front, screaming for a soaking. It was just ridiculous, the scenes were truly fantastic, and they became so commonplace to us, night after night, we just took them for granted as we threw bucket after bucket over the roaring audience. The screams were invariably the same: "Me, me, oh please, me." And the standard one that we heard at least once every night: "Oh please, please, I've paid £5 for this ticket and I'm still dry."

The record raced into the Top 40, but however well the record was selling, the BBC understandably were not keen to give it any plugs on any of their radio or television programmes. After all we were very much the enemy and why should they help us? However, because somehow it snuck its way into the Top 20, it had to be played on their weekly chart rundown on Sunday evenings on Radio One, and of course the more plays like that it got, the more the dreadful thing sold. About the third week after its release it shot up high into the Top 20 and *Top of the Pops* was hard pushed not to play it. The next week it shot up again and they realised with much unhappiness they really had to play it if it was to be a true representation of the charts.

Dave Lee Travis told us with huge amusement that, at one stage earlier in the week, there had been a serious discussion that Hot Gossip could dance to it, instead of us. "This is the song we lovers of water sing, two, three, kick." Even the Beeb saw the silliness of that, and eventually with tremendous misgivings this motley band of ITV wide-boys and girl were granted an appearance on *Top of the Pops*. From the beginning it was made abundantly clear that we were about as welcome as an outbreak of mumps. When one of us had the audacity to ask if we had a dressing room, one snotty little bloke with a clipboard said to us, "Just remember you're lucky to be here at all." Oh thanks, ever so welcome we felt.

Still, just to be able to say you'd been on *Top of the Pops* was worth going along for, something to tell your kids and grandkids in later life. Trust me, I've done this and none of them believe me. Then again, they have heard me sing, so no wonder they find it hard to believe. But however unwelcome we were, it was a great show to do just once in your life. *Top of the Pops* is an institution. But then so's Broadmoor.

So, there we were slotted between The Nolans and Hot Chocolate, and in rehearsals with empty buckets we actually felt almost like proper pop stars – well, almost, and anyway, the idea of throwing buckets of water all over the *Top of the Pops* audience sounded like terrific fun. We'd double-checked with our record company, CBS, earlier in the week: "Yes, no problem, agreed with the BBC, as long as we use a 'sensible amount of water' and keep it in agreed areas, fair enough."

So, imagine our surprise, when about half an hour before our tone-deaf quartet were due to go on, a bumptious little BBC researcher arrived clutching the obligatory clipboard, which I noticed was completely empty, and told us, "I'm really sorry, chaps, but I can't allow you to use any water in the studio."

"But it's called 'The Bucket of Water Song'," I protested.

"Appreciate that, old chap, but it would make an awful mess."

"But we were told that you'd put down some polythene."

"Out of the question, old chap. No time for that and anyway it's dangerous."

"But obviously we are not going to throw it anywhere near lights. We don't want to get electrocuted anymore than you do."

"No, sorry, out of the question."

I said, "Look, we've been doing this night after night in theatres, much bigger and more glamorous than this studio, and we haven't lost a single audience member."

"Not the point, old boy."

I was beginning to hate this person, more and more by the minute, and every time he called me 'old boy' I increasingly wanted to seize him by the windpipe. We'd been double-crossed by the Beeb and it was minutes before we went live or walked away.

"But not to worry … we've come up with something instead."

"What? Instead of water?" I asked. "It's called 'The Bucket of Water Song'."

"No, it's perfect, it will look exactly the same on television, but there'll be none of the problems of clearing it up afterwards."

And so it was that The Bucketeers made their one and only appearance on *Top of the Pops*, in front of millions of viewers, very obviously throwing four buckets of Christmas tree tinsel all over each other. No, it didn't look the same, it looked daft, and 'The Bucket of Water Song' became probably the only record in the history of the music business to get an airing on *Top of the Pops* and actually go down ten places.

MATERIAL NO LONGER USED

N ow this is a story I used to tell as part of my after-dinner routine. And it always used to get a big laugh. But for reasons that will become obvious I don't do it anymore.

I was taking a cab across town from Capital Radio one morning, going to a meeting at London Weekend Television. I jumped in the back and started to read the morning papers. The cabbie gave me one of those very strange, knowing grins in the mirror, that most of us so-called celebrities get used to. It's the 'I know who you are but I'm not going to disturb you' look. Every time I looked up from my paper, he was grinning away at me in the mirror and winking. Another strange thing they do, is that when you get to a traffic light, and there's another cab opposite, they do a strange backward heaving of the head and shoulders which means to all cabbies everywhere, "Look who I've got in the back of my cab."

This went on all the way across town, the grinning in the mirror and jerking the head routine continued, but he was harmless enough. When I got out, I think the fare was about four quid, (Yes, you can tell this was a long time ago) and I said, "Keep the change, mate," and gave him a fiver. But, unbelievably, he wouldn't have it – not just the tip, he wouldn't have any of it.

"No, no no," he said, "please keep it, mate. I just want to say thank you on behalf of me, my wife and my kids for all the pleasure you have given us over the years, all the marvellous shows on the radio, all the television, all the books you've written, we've got the lot, and the film you were in."

By now I was becoming very confused: radio, yes; television, yes; books, yes; film – er, no, not really. Then he said, "But above all on behalf of not just my family and me, but I think I speak for the whole nation … all that wonderful work you do at Stoke Mandeville."

Now, as I warned you at the top, I used to do this story as part of my after-dinner speech. It always got a big laugh and often a cheer. The cabbie, of course, thought I was Jimmy Savile, which was a very funny image at the time until he was exposed, all too late, after he'd died and couldn't be held accountable as one of the most vile predatory paedophiles of all time.

As I said, at the top, it's a bit of after-dinner material that I don't use anymore …

A man clearly two sandwiches short of a picnic.

New clothes
and hairdos
for their TV
appearance.

But why on earth bother?

The producer, but where's the respect?

Where's the love?

Rick Parfitt and Andy Bown with Michael Palin.

Lenny and I on Compost Corner ... "Compost Corner."

The Phantom Flan Flinger at home with the family – Flanderella and the baby Bucket Bunger.

The mystic Houdi Elbow.

A rare picture of Frank Carson with his mouth shut.

Lenny going berserk with a fire extinguisher.

I'm under the bucket.

Sally and I looking almost calm.

Seconds later she was
covered in custard.

Bob and Spit.
Spit's the good-looking one.

HRH Princess Margaret meets the Phantom Flan Flinger.

The album … The BBC hated it.

The beginnings of Bucketmania.

THE FOUR BUCKETEERS

OTT … We dare to go bare.

*T*arrant *W*ith *A* *T*elevision.

Proud dad
weighing new
baby daughter.

Another daughter
thinking she's Popeye.

Another daughter
bored stiff.

The publicity people told me I'd "look great."

They also told me a photo with a rat would "look terrific."

And riding a killer whale would be a "fun photo."

Matthew Kelly's just been told I'm a serial killer.

Looking very happy … What man wouldn't be?

Caught totally unawares by Michael Aspel.

In the presence of two legends – Jimmy Greaves and Muhammad Ali.

Jane all over the former President.

Who else was instantly recognised all over the world just from the back of her head?

Phil Collins, Annie Lennox, Dave Stewart, Kim Wilde, Me, Fluff Freeman, Kid Jensen.

SPECIALIST ENTERTAINER

Eventually it was time to move on. I loved *Tiswas*, they were some of the best years of all our lives, but I didn't want to be labelled as a 'children's entertainer'. I was also absolutely fed up with custard. I smelled of custard, my wife smelled of custard, my car smelled of custard, my kids smelled of custard. The switch to a late-night version was obvious, but certainly for me as the producer I was walking into a minefield. *OTT*, the late-night show I produced and presented in 1981, got more complaints than anything else I have ever done. Nudity, bad language, Alexi Sayle, Bernard Manning, it had all the ingredients of being thoroughly offensive to everybody. The controller had said, "Do what you like, but don't get me arrested," which seemed a wide enough brief.

The Sunday morning after the first show the vicar in one of the biggest churches in the Midlands went up into his pulpit and said, "My children ... my children ... I do not want to preach my sermon this day, instead I want us all to pray for Central Television to immediately axe that disgraceful *OTT* which was screened for the first and, we can only hope, the last time yesterday at midnight. Let me hear you say, 'Yeah.' All say, 'Yeah.'"

And *The Sun* wrote, "WHEN WILL OTT BE OFF?" Rather clever for them, in fact, by their standards – genius. But it wasn't taken OFF. It stayed ON, week after week, and still the mail poured in. Bearing in mind it went out at midnight on a Saturday night, I had one lady write angrily to me, saying, "I was so disgusted I sent my 6-year-old to bed." Madam, your 6-year-old should have been in bed hours ago.

Every Saturday it went out live and every Monday morning the controller wheeled me in for a damn good kicking all over his office for the next three hours. I scripted a snooker event on one show and, following a spate of streakers at sports events in the preceding months all over the UK, I thought what fun it would be to have a streaker run onto a snooker table. She did it beautifully. It worked perfectly. It was a total surprise to the audience in the studio and at home. She was called Candy, she had an absolutely beautiful body, and the item wasn't remotely sleazy. It was very well done and really funny. We loved it and were very pleased. In fact, we were proud of how well it worked, but come Monday morning the Fat Controller finally flipped. He lost it totally. "Now you've really done it. That snooker item was completely unacceptable, tasteless, disgusting, it's the lowest this station has ever sunk … I've a good mind to sack you." I think if he'd had a gun in his desk he'd have shot me. I was certainly relieved to walk out of the office.

I was enjoying the show, the writing, the performing, but I was getting tired of all the flak – some of it very fair, but also a lot of it very hypocritical. I continued to defend the snooker item and I found it weird how two people could be so far apart in their tastes. I liked him and, in spite of him getting on my back ever since the first show, he'd actually been very supportive. Up till then, anyway. The one other thing that kept us on air and kept me in a job was the simple fact that the ratings were enormous.

For a show that ran into the small hours of the morning, the viewing figures were like nothing seen in years. It was experimental, it was live. Some of it was very good, some of it was truly awful. Lenny Henry throughout was magnificent. From the young gangly boy who'd joined us halfway through the latter years of *Tiswas*, to try out a few impressions, he just grew and grew. He was a man very much his own man and he could do anything and everything. He was emerging as a huge talent.

And even as the complaints continued to come in – and this is so typically British – the biggest number of complaints weren't for offensive language or bare buttocks, but for an animal act. Put an animal on television and somebody somewhere will ring up to complain. In the course of your presenting duties, you could get bitten by a tiger, and somebody would write to the broadcasting authorities about unnecessarily blunting animals' teeth.

I couldn't, however, imagine people feeling sorry for rats – not until I met Ken the Ratman. That was his job, down the sewers – all day every day – catching them.

It can't have been much of a way of earning a living. I'd absolutely hated the nasty, disease-ridden creatures ever since I had one run right across my face once in the dark when I was fishing. Ken didn't loathe them as much as I did, but he wasn't making much money as your friendly local ratman, until one day down the sewers he had a eureka moment. Ken got the brilliant idea of supplementing his income by doing a cabaret act with them. He would strip to the waist, not a pretty sight, and let them run all over his body. Better still, he would stuff them down his trousers, and best of all, he would stuff them down the front of a pair of see-through tights so the audience could actually watch them running up and down his legs and disappearing sometimes between them.

A totally new concept in club entertainment! Brilliant. To say that bookings were on the thin side would be an understatement. People in the main didn't want to get their wife all dressed up with a new hairdo and sit her in the front row with a large gin and tonic, while some paunchy bloke paraded in front of her stuffing rats down the front of his tights.

Club managers didn't rush to book him, but when he did get a booking, Ken was a sensation. He had to top the bill, nobody could possibly follow him. Women fainted a lot and had to be brought around with smelling salts, only to pass out again because Ken and

Co were still on. It certainly wasn't a night out for anyone with a weak heart, but it was a sensation.

When I first saw it, in a club somewhere, I couldn't actually believe what I was watching. People all around were screaming, half covering their eyes, but between their fingers still continuing to peep in utter horror. At the end, Ken received a standing ovation.

"Great," thought Tarrant: "Scoop – I'll book him for *OTT*." After all, the show was supposed to make people sit up and take notice, wasn't it? It was supposed to be totally unpredictable, to shock people, so we booked Ken for the next Saturday night.

It was probably the stupidest thing I have ever done. And as you are almost certainly beginning to realise by now there's a long list. The first problem was with Equity, the actor's union. Ken – surprise, surprise – was not a member, and technically you are supposed to be a member in order to appear on television. So I had to have this ludicrous discussion with a very nice lady on the phone about what exactly his act consisted of, and whether or not by using Ken we would be "Depriving another actor of work …"

"Hello, is that Robert de Niro? Got a nice little number for you at the weekend. Five hundred quid, in cash on the night. It's stuffing rats down your Y-fronts. No, Mr de Niro, it's not *The Taming of the Shrew*."

Common sense prevailed. It was agreed that he wasn't depriving anybody else of work, because nobody else in their right mind would want the work, and Equity made Ken a member under the heading 'Specialist Entertainer'.

Saturday came. Rehearsals went fine. Ken did his stuff in time to the music, and the disbelieving crew applauded louder with each squealing little furry bundle that he popped down among his private parts. Lenny Henry kept banging his head against the wall in hysterics. "I don't believe it, I can't believe it. You're not serious, Tarrant."

"Oh yes I am," I said. "It's gonna be huge."

The big night. The piano played Ken's intro and in he came to face the unsuspecting audience at the end of the show. Stripped to the waist, his great paunch hanging over a specially bought new pair of particularly see-through tights, he started to stuff the live squealing rodents down his tackle box. The reaction in the studio was bedlam, complete uproar. One woman just stood on the top of her seat and screamed until long after the programme was over. She's probably still standing there screaming now. Another bloke was laughing so much, he actually bit a great chunk out of the back of his hand and had to be rushed to A&E pouring blood.

In the middle of it, with something like ten million people all over the country, well after midnight, watching in spellbound horror, Ken's nerve went. With about eleven or twelve rats already kicking and squealing about inside his tights, and biting like mad, because of all the noise and the hot lights, Ken dropped one. As it raced around the feet of the screaming audience, Ken panicked. He swiped at it, trying to step on its tail, and eventually, in full colour close up, gave it a great toe-ender back into its little box.

At that moment Ken had done something, that until that moment I would have thought was quite impossible. He had managed to get people feeling sorry for rats.

As we left the studio, the switchboard was jammed. I have never been able to fully understand the mentality of people who regularly ring television companies or radio stations to complain, and on this particular night we had some all-time classics. I can't really imagine what sort of person dials and dials and dials a television company until about four in the morning, but that's exactly what happened. The duty officer sat all night patiently logging each new complaint. As fast as he replaced the receiver, another call came through, and another, and another.

We were threatened with letters to the RSPCA, Mary Whitehouse, Lord Longford, Questions in the House, the lot.

Nobody cared about poor old Ken's privates – bitten to shreds they were – it was the rats that captured public sympathy. We all went out for a late-night Greek meal in our favourite restaurant that always stayed open for us to wind down in the early hours of Sunday mornings. And when we came back in the poor old duty officer was still logging irate calls. My favourite quote from a very long and increasingly silly night, was the still seething gentleman who finally got through to us at about 3.20am to dictate this message, in all seriousness I think, to our controller:

"Those magnificent animals should be free to roam the sewers and not forced down any man's trousers."

EVERYBODY SING ALONG

O ne wet Thursday night I was asked to give away the annual
prizes at an over-60s ladies club down in Sussex. It didn't seem
much of a night, frankly, for me or the ladies club, but because there
was a few quid in it, I happily agreed to go along. They were very
nice, all blue rinses, and dresses like tablecloths, and I have to say I
was made very welcome and was contentedly sipping Asda's finest
wine until it was my turn to do my bit. I managed a fairly gentle sort
of speech, gave away prize fruit bowls and hairdo tokens to nice
little ladies who had done the most knitting or made the best jam
over the last twelve months, and sat down.

The chairwoman thanked all the ladies for all their hard work,
somebody gave her a big bunch of flowers, thanked me, and thanked
the vicar who'd lent them the church hall for the evening, and then
while the buffet was being passed around, asked us to welcome the
folk group.

Now, to this day I don't know who these three lads were, but what
followed was one of the funniest things I have ever witnessed, and I
have to say we stole it shamelessly for The Bucketeers tour. It went
down a storm every night with our rather older, rougher audience.

They did a couple of folk classics and then they got us all ready to
join in the chorus of the next one. "This is good fun," agreed the little
old ladies. It was a gentle tribute to the great network of waterways
that crisscross our beautiful land, and after the first verse a whole
church hall full of totally innocent little old ladies dived eagerly into

the chorus, many of them standing on their chairs and singing, "Far canal, far canal, take out your dingy, do your own thingy, and sail up that far canal. Oh, far canal, oh far canal, sail up that far canal." And to cries of everybody and "one more time," and with me sitting there not daring to look anyone in the face, singing my chorus at the ceiling, one hundred dear little old Sussex ladies, all sang chorus, after chorus, after chorus, "Far canal, oh far canal."

Because of tenuous links with water, but mainly because it was just a wonderful hoot and a terrific sing-a-long, we immediately drafted it in to the next Four Bucketeers touring repertoire, and sung it night after night just before 'The Bucket of Water Song'. It was, of course, a triumph, and several times in places as far apart as Bishop's Stortford, Liverpool and Glasgow, we had to draw a line under it after about fifteen choruses. They sang their hearts out, "Far canal, oh far canal ..."

I think it was probably very good for the soul. It also prepared our theatre audiences for the soaking they were about to receive.

We were the Four Bucketeers, incidentally, because ATV were absurdly greedy. We wanted to call ourselves The Tiswas Team and put it on the posters outside and on the tickets. We would have been happy, of course, to pay a small fee for the use of the name, but we were told that if we used the *Tiswas* name on any advertising we'd have to pay ATV 75% of all money we took on the door. So we called ourselves the Four Bucketeers, sold out every night, and gave them nothing.

CAROL CONCERT

I've always been a big fan of Rod Stewart. I've bought – yes, bought! – quite a lot of his records. I've played a lot of his records on the radio. I loved him when he was in The Faces. I even loved him when he was Python Lee Jackson.

I think he's a proper bloke, and considering he's been making hits and making women squeal with his little leopard-skinned bottom since 'Maggie May' was a hit over fifty years ago in 1971, that is one amazing career, and he is still going strong.

I've seen him live in concert loads of times, and there's none of this pretentious 'here's a track off my new album that you've never heard of' nonsense. He sings all the hits, kicks a football into the crowd, forgets the lines of 'Georgie', does a full two-and-a-half-hour-plus encore and we all go home really happy.

I also like his wife, Penny, who I have met from time to time. She and I were once scheduled to do readings at Christmas time in a beautiful old church in Marylebone.

We were chatting beforehand, and I asked, "Is your husband coming?" and she said very quietly, "Yes, he'll be here." But as the church filled up and it was almost time to start, there was no sign of her old man.

Then, as the vicar got up to address us all, and share this yuletide with him, and the lights went down, an unmistakable spikey head moved in the darkness to stand in between Penny and me. It was great, he was very amiable, but each time one of the Christmas carols started, we all stood up and I thought, "Oh my God! Here I am singing 'Away in a Manger' next to Rod Stewart. I turned my head away to one side each time I sang a note and did quite a lot of miming and graciously he didn't mention how bad my singing was. My kids all say I sing like Mister Bean.

Then, when the nice vicar wished us all a Merry Christmas, Rod completely disappeared again, out of a side door, presumably to wait for Penny in his car round the corner. The great thing was that apart from people close behind, who must have been looking gobsmacked at the back of his spikey head, hardly any of the huge congregation knew that he was there at all.

THE PLACE TO BE?

One of the most successful but extraordinary people I have worked with is Greg Dyke. He has a brilliant brain, a really wicked wit and a strong London accent, with a voice that sounds not unlike Danny Dyer having just swallowed a dishwasher.

Greg went on to become Chairman of the BBC, and Chairman of ITV, which he left with 9 million quid in the bank as a 'golden handshake'. He once told me he "just put it into my local post office savings account, so my old mum could get at it." And knowing Greg, he almost certainly did.

When I first met him he was producing *The Six O'Clock Show* for London Weekend Television. Typically, he joined them as a researcher and, in a matter of weeks, was in charge of everybody.

He had a mission to try and prove to a young intelligent audience that current affairs could be fun, and in his hands, they sometimes really were. We were the most unlikely set of bedfellows. Headed by super smooth Michael Aspel, live every Friday, there were over the years Janet Street-Porter, Paula Yates, Jeff Pope, Samantha Fox, Fred Housego, Emma Freud, Danny Baker, and myself – and in charge of us all was the splendid, but loopy, Paul Ross. Hardly an ego between the lot of us, I'm sure you'll agree.

It was a hugely successful programme and the next time I caught up with Greg, he somehow blagged me into joining him when he took over as the incoming controller and saviour of the ailing *TV-am*.

The famous five, David Frost, Angela Rippon and Co, had been and gone in a wave of adverse publicity in a matter of weeks. When I joined, as well as teaming up with my old mates from my Central TV days in the Midlands, Nick Owen and Anne Diamond, the only other name they had booked was broadcasting legend Roland Rat.

After the nightmarish episode with Ken the Ratman a couple of years earlier on *OTT*, I wasn't too keen, but this rat was only a stuffed rat, and David Claridge didn't put the dreadful thing down his trousers. Between us we all somehow turned the station around, it hung on and even made a profit until 1993, when it lost its franchise and was replaced by the almost identical *GMTV*.

By then Greg, Nick, Anne, Roland and I had long since gone, and running things in Greg's place was Bruce Gyngell, an amiable but strange Australian, whom I had first worked with in the Midlands back in the 70s when he was Lew Grade's number two in Birmingham.

I don't know quite what happened to Brucie while he had been away down under, but when he resurfaced at the *TV-am* studios in Camden he wanted everybody to wear pink. He had a plaque mounted in the foyer that said, "TV-am. The place to be, the winning team for '93." As the staff came into the foyer in the closing months of the station, they were all supposed to touch, rub, or even kiss it, and chant the slogan out loud and proud. It was a precursor to the Chinese Republican Party a few years later.

Sadly, they weren't the winning team, sadly the authorities didn't think *TV-am* was the place to be, and sadly it wasn't the winning team for '93 – and Eamonn Holmes and Anthea Turner took over.

My twelve months at *TV-am* turned out to be one of the happiest years of my working life. At any second the station seemed likely to go broke, nobody got paid for months and months, and there was no question of industrial action, let alone strikes. But the atmosphere among the crew, presenters and management was a tremendous camaraderie all pulling together just to survive another day. Miraculously the thing stayed on air and for a while actually went from strength to strength.

SUMMER SEASON

Never work with children or animals, is the old adage. And it's absolutely true. Over the years my dealings with animals on live TV have included breaking two ribs, when I fell off an elephant, being bitten by a python (OK, so they are not poisonous, but a snakebite is still a snakebite), being bitten on the very top of my leg by a ferret, and having my fingers stomped on by a rodeo horse.

Silly stories, including kids on TV, are endless. One of my favourites is still the little 5-year-old boy who live on *Tiswas* wanted to say hello to his teacher. "OK," I said, "go ahead. What's she called?"

"Mrs Carter," he said, sweetly, "but we all call her 'Stinky Farter'."

So, they're right, you really shouldn't work with kids or animals.

You also should never get roped in to choosing the winner of a baby contest, as once happened to me. They all look like Winston Churchill and whichever one you choose all the other mums hate you. But somebody should also have added, "Don't work with Freddie Starr or 80-year-old super athletes, especially on a live programme."

So, I was working for *TV-am* and I was out and about on the great British seafront. It was a brilliant few weeks. We went all over the UK, and we had a great time, but the schedule was ridiculous. Every night we would arrive in a new seaside town, more or less throw together a show for the next morning, have a few beers, occasionally rather a lot of beers, and go to bed.

Bear in mind that, at that time, *TV-am*'s survival – and this was only weeks after the abrupt exit of the famous five – was constantly hanging by a thread. Each morning, just finding that our cameras still hadn't been repossessed by a finance company, and that there really was a large crowd waiting for us on the beach, was very gratifying.

What the large crowd didn't know was how very thrown together the whole thing was, and all items and guests had been booked in a mad panic only the day before. This had been the pattern from day one of *TV-am*, when the famous five got together for dinner before the first broadcast, and suddenly realised they hadn't got a guest. I think it was Michael Parkinson who frantically rang John Cleese, who appeared on the show in his pyjamas.

Anyway, even though the famous five had gone, the preparation continued pretty much like before for the next twelve months, because everybody was under frantic pressure. Because we were going from a different resort day to day, most of the arrangements for the next day were done over the phone as we travelled throughout the British Isles.

In Blackpool, we somehow got the Mayoress dancing on the beach, in the arms of a man in a gorilla suit, who then caused chaos by goosing one of the dancers, as men in gorilla suits are likely to do.

In Scarborough, we booked a very nice classical orchestra, who even agreed to turn up at 6.15 the next morning in dinner jackets, bow ties, the lot, only to find that halfway through their live performance the tide came roaring up Scarborough beach and washed music and musicians away. Apparently, Mike, our production manager, had misread the local tide tables and was an hour out.

In Brighton, during the final round of a 'Miss Lovely Legs' competition, a gentleman who had escaped form a local asylum, but who was luckily completely harmless, appeared wearing a long mac and carrying a string bag full of plasticine models and joined in among the parading beauty queens. He was taken away, kindly but firmly, still clutching his shopping bag, and put into a panda car which could just be seen with blue light flashing as the ladies continued to strut their stuff.

In Rhyl, in North Wales, the nice locals warned us, "Sometimes it can get a bit rough in the evenings." I'll say it could. As we took a quiet stroll along the high street the night we arrived, the scene suddenly transformed into something more in keeping with Dodge City in the days of Wyatt Earp. A large bar stool came flying out through the window of the first pub that we passed, swiftly followed by a very fat man wearing a blood-stained T-shirt, and who for some unaccountable reason, went running back in.

There was glass everywhere, there was blood everywhere, and everybody seemed to be hitting everybody else. Police cars with flashing sirens came racing onto the scene and took offenders away in one of the several Black Marias that arrived. It was no big deal in itself, but bearing in mind we'd only been in Rhyl about a quarter of an hour, it made us a little wary of what might happen the next morning on live TV.

In actual fact, Rhyl went almost smoothly by *TV-am*'s standards. There was a particularly fine singing dog item, a hypnotist who managed to burn somebody's fingers with his cigarette lighter, a volunteer who clearly wasn't in as deep a trance as the hypnotist had believed, and the whole show closed with a 'How much do you look like Roland Rat?' competition.

All very exciting stuff, first thing in the morning, and how nice to be back on the cutting edge of current affairs.

Whoever worked out our itinerary clearly hadn't got a map. They'd booked us to arrive in Great Yarmouth at the end of the same day we'd started in Rhyl. Which is about as far across the UK as Moscow is from Johannesburg.

So we said our fond farewells to the good people of North Wales and raced across Britain to Norfolk with our researchers on their new-fangled mobile phones, which were the size of house bricks, and kept losing the signal (no change there, forty years later), trying to set up some sort of show for the next morning in Yarmouth.

To give the producers and researchers their due, they didn't do a bad job at all. They managed to book Freddie Starr (who was appearing in Great Yarmouth's summer season), the local beauty queen, a Punch and Judy person, and one of those pillars of society, who seem to exist in every seaside town in this country, an old gentleman who goes swimming in the sea every single day of the year, come rain, hail or snow.

This remarkable old gentleman was 84 years old, brown as a berry and had swum in the sea off Great Yarmouth every day, including Christmas Day, for over forty years.

So the show sounded particularly promising, even by our rather easily pleased standards.

The next day, I said, "Good morning" to Nick Owen and Anne Diamond back in the studio, the crowd that had already turned up at half past six on the Great Yarmouth seafront gave a big cheer, and Freddie Starr ran around goosing the over-40s aerobic dancers who were trying to follow the manic instructions of 'Mad Lizzie', our resident keep-fit fanatic.

It was all good fun and going worryingly well, until the point where I cued the 84-year-old swimmer to dive into the sea. I mumbled something like, "And now racing down the beach here beside me at Yarmouth is a remarkable old, super-fit octogenarian, who has plunged into the sea at sunrise every morning for the last forty-three years."

This remarkable old gentleman got this cue and off he went towards the sea. Unfortunately, in our conversations with him, all hurriedly done on the phone the day before, nobody checked out whether or not he had both legs. So, suddenly at 6.35 on a mid-summer's morning, the whole of Britain was treated to the extraordinary sight of a totally focussed, one-legged man hopping down the beach as best he could, with just an unmistakable flap of skin showing out of the other rather empty swimming trunk leg as he bounced towards the waves.

It was made extra disturbing for the viewers who were just about settling down to their breakfast, by the cameraman going in for a great big close up of the one leg protruding from the ocean as he made his magnificent dive. The crowd went into a shocked silence, and Freddie Starr roared past me goose stepping, pretending to be Adolph Hitler, and stuck his tongue in my ear.

The director hurriedly cut back to Nick and Anne in the studio, who were looking gobsmacked at the pictures coming up from Great Yarmouth. The switchboard, meantime, was jammed with complaints, about "typically, tasteless Tarrant and Starr behaviour."

I have to say in fairness to myself and Freddie, it was a genuine mistake because nobody had actually met the man before the morning of the show and hadn't even seen him change into his swimming costume until seconds before he was cued, so nobody had any idea of his disability. In the event he was a remarkable, fascinating character, who thoroughly enjoyed his moment of fame.

But if nothing else, the whole episode did contribute yet one more golden rule to the trainee 'TV researchers' guidebook', in how to keep your job.

From then on, every single conversation I overheard from the guys in the background fixing up items and guests for the rest of the summer shows would begin like this:

"Hello, it's *TV-am* here, and our outside broadcast cameras will be on your beach tomorrow morning. Now, before we go any further, I know it sounds like a silly question, but have you got both your legs?"

SIGNING MY LIFE AWAY

I don't know how many autographs I must have signed in the fifty years since I first started out on the telly, but it must be thousands and thousands. It's really no big deal. I think that if you gave a stuffed bear its own TV show every day it would start to get fan mail and requests for signed photos before the end of its first week.

Over the years, one way or another, I've signed all sort of things: nice neat autograph books, postcards, bits of school exercise books, family allowance books, chequebooks, T-shirts, brassieres – large, small and enormous – bus tickets, bog rolls, arms, backs, stomachs, and far, far worse ... more of which later.

And, of course, in recent years it's been selfies, which are OK, except they give you a bit of a crick in the neck. The one thing I will say that is annoying is when they have no idea how to work their camera, so you have to stand around like a lemon while they work out what to point and what to press on their brand new iPhone. I suppose, at least selfies last unless you choose to wipe them, whereas I'm sure the great majority of autographs are lost or thrown away within days or even minutes of signing.

There haven't been many occasions when I've refused, possibly less than the fingers on one hand, but I do remember the first time I *wouldn't* sign one. I was doing a live TV show at The Royal Showground near Kenilworth, and once we'd finished, I was happily signing away for a bunch of 9- to 10-year-olds and their very friendly teacher, when suddenly a great shaven-headed oaf of about 17 or 18 pushed straight through all the kids, stuck a bit of paper under my nose, and said in a loud, leering voice, "Sign that, tosser."

Needless to say, I didn't feel that I was absolutely duty bound to sign it. I'm six-foot-two, he was about five-foot-six, so I lifted him off the ground, stuck him firmly back where he came from, at the very, very last place in the queue, and made him lose a lot of face in front of the younger kids. He actually stood there for several minutes looking red-faced and embarrassed, and then did a runner. To be fair, he was an exception. In the main, people are very nice and polite.

Signing autographs is also quite a good way of getting feedback from your audience, of learning what they like and what they don't like, about whatever show you're currently doing. I remember the first weeks when Spit the Dog had started appearing on *Tiswas*. I went to an open-air carnival the next afternoon and signed hundreds of bits of paper. All the mums were moaning at me because their kids had been making nasty spitting noises at their brothers and sisters while cleaning their teeth in the mornings. Of course, I couldn't appear to approve, so I apologised to them all profusely, and tut-tutted dutifully, but secretly I knew we had a big hit on our hands – or, to be more precise, a big spit.

I'll never forget that particular afternoon, because the carnival organisers had me sitting at a nice table with a couple of beers in the sunshine, while a long queue of kids and their mums patiently waited for 'the man' to sign their programme. I was chatting to most of them as they came up, about this and that, mainly it seemed about Spit the Dog, and one dear little boy of about five came up with his mother.

"Hello, little man," I said. "What's your name?"

"Simon," he whispered, and tried to hide behind his mum.

"OK," I said, and signed, 'To Simon, best wishes', etc, on his bit of paper. "And who's this?" I said, to the shy little boy. "Is this your mummy?"

"Yes."

"And is she nice?" I asked.

"Yes," he said, and then added in a much louder voice to the delight of the eavesdropping crowd, "but my daddy says she makes smells in bed."

The poor woman went absolutely scarlet.

Then, of course, there were always the mums and dads who came up pretending the autographs were not for them. "It's not for me, it's for the kids." "It's not for me, it's for my friend at work."

My favourite was when a bloke who, with a totally earnest face, said to me outside Capital Radio a few years back, "It's not for me, honest, I think you're crap."

Although I've said I never mind signing autographs, or doing 'selfies', and honestly most of the time I don't, but sometimes I am in a hurry and it can be a bit of a nuisance. I was on my way to Lord's a couple of years ago to a big cricket match between England and the West Indies. At the close of play on the previous day it had become very exciting, so I couldn't wait to get there on time for the start the next morning. I finished my radio show at 10.00, made a few calls, sorted out a few emails, and jumped in a taxi for Lord's, which is only about fifteen minutes up the road from our studios.

The traffic was busy, and I got there a few minutes after the start. I could hear wild applause coming from inside the ground, just as I arrived, so obviously something had happened. As I got out of the taxi, outside the ground, a bloke spotted me and went, "Hello, Chris Tarrant," and I went, "Oh, hello, I'm racing in to watch the cricket, mate."

He said, "Yes, OK, just sign me this bit of paper before you go, please, for my kids Daniel and Karen."

"OK," I said, but even as I signed it, I was aware of a little crowd starting to form, a couple of women arrived, then a schoolgirl, then a couple of others, and clearly my cricket watching time was getting reduced by the second. I kept hearing wild roars and loud applause from inside the ground, but I dutifully signed all the various bits of paper, chatting and smiling, but inwardly getting very frustrated.

"Oh yes, and this is for my mum, Karen," said the schoolgirl.

"OK. No problem." And then another hand appeared, and with another piece of paper, and without looking up, I said, "What's your name, mate?"

And he said, "Paul."

So I wrote, 'To Paul, Best Wishes Chris Tarrant,' and as I looked up, there was someone very familiar standing in this little queue with his finger on his lips, with a 'Shush, don't say a word' sign.

"Thank you very much, Mr Tarrant," he said, and very politely got into the back of his car and carried on.

He has a house just around the corner in St John's Wood, very near the Abbey Road Studios, which was handy for him because *he* was Paul McCartney.

He thought it was very, very funny. Which of course it was.

Nobody else knew the big secret, I signed a couple of more bits of paper and went shaking my head and smiling into the cricket ground.

Paul McCartney's autograph is currently rated on average at over £3,000 a time. It is the most expensive autograph in the world, and he tiptoed away with mine, for nothing.

I've met Paul on and off quite a few times over the years, going back to the *Tiswas* days, when he was attacked by Spit the Dog. I've always found him very easy going, and I do think he is much maligned. He can't help being still good looking, into his seventies, hugely talented and ridiculously rich, and I think most of his critics are, almost certainly, deeply jealous. I think he tries as best he can to just be an ordinary bloke.

We were offered an interview with him exclusive to Capital Radio a few years back, when he had a new album coming out, and I said I'd love to go down there to his studio, just outside Hastings, meet up with him and record it. Now usually on these occasions there's a sound engineer available, but this time the guys were all out and McCartney was only available for an hour or two. So I said, "Don't worry, I'll drive down and do it. As long as somebody shows me how to work the machine before I leave, it'll be fine."

So, I was given some ancient looking Uher tape recorder, that I think went out with the days of *The Goon Show* and The Light Programme, and off I went.

We had a lovely afternoon, he was in great form, talking about The Beatles, about John, and just about day-to-day life if you happen to be one of the two surviving Beatles. Linda, bless her, kept coming out with more and more sandwiches, and cups of tea, and we had a thoroughly enjoyable afternoon, in the presence of a song-writing genius.

I thanked him and raced back towards London very pleased with what had been a very good interview. As soon as I got around the corner, I stopped in a lay-by and tried to play back the tape, only to realise it was one of those ancient machines where there is no playback. They always seem to work fine, but you never actually know until you put it on in the studio whether you have recorded anything at all. As I drove fast back to London, I was becoming increasingly convinced that there was nothing on the tape, that I hadn't pressed the right record button, or whatever. I couldn't possibly ring McCartney and say, "You know that very good interview we did yesterday afternoon? Well, could we do it again today, please?" The shame would be too much to bear.

When I got to the studios, I raced in with my machine and handed it in a panic to Mike Osboy, my long-suffering engineer, who'd been with me since the very beginning on the breakfast show. I said to him, "Mike, please, for God's sake, tell me I've got the interview."

He put on his headphones, put the tape in and listened. Then, with a mournful face, said, "I'm really sorry, mate, there's nothing on there."

"Oh, no," I said, "I don't believe it," and the air was black with expletives.

"Oh, sorry," said Mike, grinning. "There is just a bit of you talking to Paul McCartney."

There was about forty-five minutes of me talking to Paul McCartney actually. I love Osboy, but I could easily have shot him with a twelve-bore.

Anyway, do you remember me saying that I've signed all sorts of things, like arms, backs, stomachs … and worse? Well, back in Great Yarmouth, when we arrived there the evening before we filmed *TV-am* on the beach, Mike Purcell (the unit manager) and I decided we'd go out for a couple of quiet beers, and maybe meet a few good old Norfolk locals.

However, when we opened the door to a nice looking old tavern, we found we had walked into the pub from hell. There was not a sign of good old Norfolk locals, presumably they'd all drunk up quickly and done a runner hours ago, because the pub seemed to be packed with the entire population of Glasgow. We learnt, too late, because we were in and had been spotted, that up in Scotland it was industrial holiday fortnight and it seemed that the whole lot of them had come swarming down, over Hadrian's Wall, and coach after coach had arrived at this tiny bar in Great Yarmouth.

And, of course, they were absolutely legless. I'm quite large and so is Mike, but everywhere we looked there were huge hairy tattooed, drink-crazed Scotsmen towering down on us and calling my name. They were drunk and they were big, but some of the women with them were even drunker and bigger. It was terrifying. The crowd more or less carried the two of us to the bar and forced pints of McEwan's down us. We shook their hands, we politely, but very carefully, kissed their women, purely upon the cheeks you understand, trying not to offend anyone or quite look anyone directly in the eye in case it all went horribly wrong.

I signed beer mats, I signed raffle tickets, I signed big hairy arms, anything just to stay in one piece. It was one of those situations that seemed like a great laugh, but any second could suddenly have switched to a flash point and ended up with a bottle in somebody's forehead – most probably mine, which is never a great look for a TV presenter, which I was due to be the very next morning.

When a lady came up, lifted up her top and produced her naked breasts for me to sign, I thought, "This is it, I'm going to die." At that moment her enormous hairy husband came out of nowhere and instead of head-butting me and nailing my three-piece suit to the dartboard, he positively insisted that I sign his very nice wife's bare breast – or her 'tut', as he so quaintly called it, which I obligingly did to the wild whooping applause of the dangerously drunken crowd, all chanting, "Sign the tut, sign the tut."

"That's it," I said to Mike. "Let's drink up quick and do a runner."

But the baying Scottish throng were having none of that. They had one more little demand before they decided to let me live another day. A particularly savage looking Jock with a great un-combed mane of red hair loomed towards me, slopping Tennent's everywhere.

"OK," he said, "you've signed that, now sign this."

It is not an episode I am particularly proud of, but there are times in this life when you just have to do what needs to be done to stay alive. Which is why, in front of the by now completely hysterical crowd, who were shouting "Sign, sign, sign" at the tops of their voices, like some nightmarish scene from *Lord of the Flies*, and without touching anything except my biro (how I wish I'd had a fountain pen), and, with both eyes firmly shut, I signed a Scotsman's willy.

DELILAH

People have a very strange attitude to meeting well-known faces. When I was doing *Tiswas* I do remember vividly going round to a few mates' houses, who had small children, and when I walked into the room they would run off screaming and crying. Totally understandable, I hear you say.

At first, being a sensitive soul, I felt rather perplexed and saddened about the situation, but then I realised that the average television screen is probably about eighteen inches tall. I'm over six feet, so to them this small figure from their TV screen suddenly coming looming through their front door, would be the stuff of nightmares. Of course they were terrified and ran off screaming at my approach. My eldest daughter still does it now, and she's 41. It's a bit like if your goldfish, that had been swimming happily around in circles for years, suddenly hopped out of its bowl, grew to a height of over six feet, and came ambling into your kitchen.

My two youngest daughters used to watch Daddy on *Tiswas* but, apparently, when we went to a break, they would both run around the back of the set, and try and work out where Daddy had gone, until I reappeared at the front of the set a couple of minutes later. It sounds very sweet, but it is actually quite dangerous, and we had to insulate all the plugs and the wires at the back of the set and ask them to please not go looking for Daddy during the commercial breaks.

One of the weirdest reactions to fame was told to me by the late, splendid Barry Mason. I met him at an annual songwriters' dinner that

I occasionally get invited to, although I have never written a single note of music in my life. But it's a chance to meet great songwriters like Tim Rice, Andrew Lloyd Webber, Graham Gouldman, Tony Hatch, Don Black, Justin Hayward, and even Paul McCartney.

Barry Mason's claim to fame is that he wrote 'Delilah', which became of course a huge hit for Tom Jones. To be more specific, and this is very relevant, he wrote all the words: "She felt the knife in my hand and she laughed no more …", but his good friend Les Reed wrote the music.

So, after a good lunch and meeting up with a lot of his peers, Barry needed to go to the gents. As he walked in a bloke was already at the urinals holding his little tommy tinkler, and quite clearly whistling the tune of 'Delilah'. Barry moved in, stood next to him, undid his flies and commenced quietly relieving himself. He then turned to the bloke, still whistling happily next to him, and said, "This is a really weird coincidence, but I wrote that."

The bloke looked at him, clearly not at all impressed, and said, quite aggressively, "No you didn't, Les Reed wrote it."

"Yes," Barry said, "quite right. Les did write the music, but I wrote the words."

The bloke then, instead of saying, "Well, how nice to meet you," or, "What a small world," said, even more angrily, "I wasn't whistling the fucking words," and stormed off out of the loo, slamming the door behind him. Now *that* was a really weird reaction.

THE NO SMOKING CAMPAIGN

One day, when I'd quietly popped into the office from the seaside to do my expenses (which were, of course, vast but perfectly reasonable), Greg came flying out of nowhere and grabbed me. One of the many great talents that Greg has, apart from using language that would make Billy Connolly blush, is that he is one of the greatest motivators of people I've ever met.

He's only tiny. I'm looking down on his shiny head, but he still managed to eyeball me and said, "Tarrant, I know it's your day off, and I know you're not supposed to be in here, but tomorrow is National No Smoking Day and *TV-am* wants you to champion our British Stub It Out campaign. Now get a camera, get a fire bucket, and grab a pair of scissors."

With this, which was probably the most comprehensive and detailed brief I ever received from Greg, without a bodyguard or a safety net in sight, I went out onto the streets of Camden. It seemed to me that I had every chance of getting a damned good kicking, but I have to say the collection of dinner ladies, commuters, prostitutes (yes, we did wander a bit too close to King's Cross, after all), and a lone wandering Franciscan monk (I swear) that we encountered, were all very reasonable. In fact, the ridiculous thing was that they were almost too reasonable.

Greg's great idea was for me to go up to complete strangers and say "Good morning Sir/Madam, it's National No Smoking Day and *TV-am* is mounting a stub it out campaign. I can't help but notice you are smoking a cigarette. Now you can either stub it out in our bucket of sand or face the forfeit, which means that I will cut your cigarette in half with this here very sharp pair of scissors."

So those were the two choices. In reality there were actually a couple more. Bearing in mind that this was being filmed first thing in the morning, they could just carry on smoking their cigarette, which they were perfectly entitled to do, and walk away as fast as they possibly could, puffing happily.

Or another alternative, was that they could smack me in the mouth. What was unreal about this item, which turned out to be a strangely watchable piece of television, was that nobody went for options C or D. They clearly saw it as a straight neck and neck mental battle for them, between option A and option B. Lots of them went for the bucket, several of them went for the scissors, but none of them went for the 'ignore' or 'smack the flaxen-haired fool in the mouth' alternatives. What was really bizarre was that as everybody walked away from the camera, either with their cigarette extinguished by being stuck into my handily provided bucket of sand, or being completely ruined by me having it cut it in half with my extra sharp scissors, every single person, without exception, turned smiling to camera, and their last words were, "Thank you."

"Thank you." What the hell for? It was your first and possibly only cigarette of the day and some gangling fool with a camera and a microphone cut it in half. Why on earth are you thanking him?

I honestly think if we set up a guillotine somewhere in central London and put a camera next to it, somebody would be quite prepared to be the first person ever to be beheaded live on TV.

As the head landed in the basket, it would turn on cue to camera and say, "Thank you." I remember thinking this sometime early in the 1980s. Now, after being subjected to far too many years of reality television, my early forebodings were clearly spot on. And I'm spoiled for choice whose head I'd love to be the first to land still grinning vacuously in the basket.

I think it's all something to do with Warhol's fifteen minutes of fame. Again.

The item was really rather good, and I had to, begrudgingly, admit to Greg it had been one of his better ideas. This, of course, was the worst possible thing I could have done, because he said, "Great, next week is the second week of the National No Smoking campaign." I'm still sure that it was only an original one-off idea for a single day, but Greg was now convinced that it was good for a fortnight, certainly as far as his ratings were concerned, anyway.

So, on the spot he dreamed up 'Stub It Out Part Two'. "Hang on, Dyke-ie," I said, "we've cut their cigarettes in half, we stuffed them in buckets of sand, what the hell else can we do to these poor people who are happily enjoying what is probably one of the few pleasures left in their lives?"

"We'll take the forfeit a stage further," said Greg, completely unmoved by any moral qualms or any sheer cowardice on my behalf. "What you need this time is a bucket of sand, and a bucket of water." No scissors, no mercy.

Seven days later I found myself back on the streets of King's Cross, again with no bodyguard, just a wimpy cameraman and an even wimpier sound recordist. This time between the three of us we were juggling a bucket of sand and a bucket of ice-cold water. It was 6.30 in the morning. People were going to work, they were not awake, they were not alert, and above all they were not happy. They were just enjoying their first cigarette of the day, when suddenly they were confronted by a tall, peroxide-blonde interviewer, saying, "Excuse me my good man/woman, it's the continuation of 'National Stub It Out fortnight'. You are on *TV-am* and you can either let us stub out your cigarette or pay the forfeit."

As I said the words "pay the forfeit" my brief was to leer ominously towards the bucket of cold water. Most people, in fact nearly everybody, had the very good sense to stub their cigarette out in our bucket of sand and do a runner, not before having turned to camera, of course, and saying, "Thank you," and presumably lighting up a second cigarette as soon as they got around the corner hidden from our prying camera.

Again, the fact that they didn't actually have to do either of these options seemed to be forgotten, nearly everybody went for the bucket of sand alternative, nobody went for the carry on smoking, and give me a fat lip possibility. Only one gentleman, a nicely dressed, clearly not particularly wide-awake guy from Camden, failed to realise that the alternative between the bucket of sand and the bucket of water was really not an alternative at all, either way your cigarette would end up ruined.

One way it was just your ciggie, the other way it was your ciggie, yourself and all your clothes. To my horror, he went for option B, "No, no," he said, "I don't see why I should do that. I'm not stubbing this cigarette out in your bucket."

"Oh, sir, surely A makes a lot more sense. You really should go for option A."

"No, I'm not going to do it, you're depriving me of my rights."

"OK then, sir," I said to camera, "I'm afraid you have to pay the forfeit," and I completely drenched him with a bucket of water. This was a mere fifteen seconds, not fifteen minutes, of fame, and it consisted of a completely drenched man looking at me with murder clearly the only thing in his heart and sheer bloody hatred in his blinking water-filled eyes. His cigarette was ruined, along with his clothes, and – surprise, surprise – he was the only one who didn't say thank you.

POTS OF MONEY

I was walking slowly along the far end of the King's Road in London one afternoon, the bit they call World's End. It's an area where there are some very strange elitist shops selling things like Belgian chocolates, Persian rugs, truffles, copies of *Mein Kampf*, vegan socks, that sort of thing. I find it quite therapeutic just wandering along window-shopping, but I spotted a big earthenware pot in one doorway, and I thought it might be just the job for my garden. The bloke behind the counter gave me a nod of half recognition and I took a good look at the pot. It was about five foot tall, brown and solid looking, and to my delight there were two of them. Perfect, I thought, put some compost and trailing plants inside and they'd look great either side of my front door. I just hoped they wouldn't be silly money, so I tentatively asked him, "How much?"

"Well," he said, "if you are only taking one I'd have to ask you for two hundred, but if you took both I'd let you have the pair for three hundred."

That's not bad, I thought, three hundred quid and they'd look great. "Would you deliver?" I asked, cheekily, "we're out in the country in Berkshire."

"Oh yes, of course," he said. "We'd wrap them very carefully and deliver them right to your door. After all it's not every day we sell two items for three hundred thousand pounds."

I tried to look very nonplussed and matter-of-fact, but inwardly I was gasping. Three hundred thousand? Was he mad? I might have gone to four hundred quid, but that would be my top figure and even that seemed high. I was sweating, but tried to act nonchalant.

"Great," I said, and somehow mumbled, "I'd better just go and check with my wife," even though at the time I didn't have one. I turned and made my way as coolly as I could manage out of the shop, then ran like hell as soon as I got round the corner.

This was about eight years ago and whenever I walk along World's End, as I get close to that shop, I always cross over and keep my head down. The really daft thing is, even eight years later, they're still there in his front window. For three hundred quid he could have got rid of them both.

All of which leads me on to Mike Morris. He was a lovely guy who used to present the *TV-am* breakfast programme for quite a long time. He was a really good lad, but did seem to be in fear of the bosses upstairs, whoever they were by then. I think most of us rather lost the plot. There were so many comings and goings in the early days of *TV-am*.

One day he came bouncing into the office, saying that the most expensive vase in the history of British auction houses was coming up for sale in somewhere like Sotheby's the next day, and we were allowed to actually show it and talk about it in the studio. Mike was very excited, but he was also paranoid about it, particularly about a great clumsy lump like me knocking it over. It was worth hundreds of thousands. And it was too priceless to even think about insurance.

I went down to the studio in the afternoon to have a look at this irreplaceable wonder and one of the props blokes said, "It doesn't look much, that vase, does it?" It had all sorts of padding round it and it was carefully placed well out of the way behind a great barrier in the props stores at the side of the studio. It was to be carefully wheeled out the next morning, just before we went on air, and would sit in front us for the whole show. To be honest, considering how many hundreds of thousands of pounds it was worth, it wasn't particularly impressive. It seemed to us to be just a great earthenware pot with a few ancient diagrams on it. I think they were Egyptian, but they might have been Chinese.

"I reckon we could build one of them," said one of the props men, "but make it easily breakable."

"What on earth are you talking about?" I said, not comprehending.

But slowly, the wicked plan emerged. They would construct a pot the same height, and looking pretty similar, but that would shatter on impact. Mike Morris, of course, the presenter of the next day's programme was to know nothing about it, and the really bad news for him was that for the first hour of the show I would be sitting beside him.

The next morning came and I don't think the props lads had ever worked so hard in their lives. But the end product was truly fantastic. It really was almost identical, except it was made of something like sugar glass. "All you need to do," they told me, "is tap it, and it will shatter."

So, the next morning the show started live at 6.30am, as always. There was nothing much happening in the world, or nothing much that we'd covered anyway, and then the magnificent pot was wheeled in front of us, with Mike making 'just be careful' looks at me with his eyes. He then said to the camera, "After the break we are all looking forward hugely to talking about this stunning vase which goes on auction in London this afternoon, almost certainly fetching the most money that has ever been paid for such a beautiful item. Join us in a couple of minutes."

"Oh, that's great," I said, "how exciting," and tapped it with a coin that I had put between my fingers. It smashed into a thousand pieces. Mike looked aghast and we went to the break. During the commercial break, the longest two minutes of Mike's life, the boys swept the studio clean and wheeled in the real vase. When we came out of the break, Mike was still white and shaking, but the whole thing happened so quickly, probably just a nanosecond, before we went to the commercial break, that virtually nobody in the audience (although, to be honest, there was virtually nobody in the audience), or the bosses (but they, of course, were still fast asleep) had any idea that anything so naughty had taken place.

These are the moments that lift the spirits of broadcasters everywhere and keep them going for year after year. In my case, year after year after year after year.

THE MOUSE RULES

O ne December I was asked to front one of those nice Disney at Christmas programmes. Lots of cartoon characters, lots of music from people like the Pointer Sisters and Tom Jones (a hero of mine, who at that time I'd never met). It was to be shot in Bavaria, where the original Magic Kingdom Castle can be found, over a weekend by an all-American Disney crew. It was a really tough schedule with seventeen different nationalities all presenting their versions of each take one after the other. The first thing I learnt to my alarm was that as the UK representative I'd have to record the first take of each scene so we could iron out all the problems in English before we passed it on to the French, German, Dutch, Russian hosts in turn. The second thing I learnt was that I wasn't going to meet Tom Jones or even a single Pointer Sister. I would just say, "Hey kids, there's Tom Jones and Mickey Mouse," and I would wave in the general direction of Christmas and Tom would wave back and start singing. Tom was actually in a snowy looking studio in Italy.

Making sense so far? Me neither. The weather was bitterly cold, we were getting further and further behind schedule, and things were getting very fraught. The biggest problem was that the schedule was just too ambitious. The other sixteen presenters were kept topped up with glühwein, but the thing that was really slowing us all down was the horrible brat they'd cast as Mickey Mouse. He was a precocious little Yanky 10-year-old who just kept whingeing. He was cold, he was tired, he wanted a chair to sit on, he was hungry ... We were all working our arses off, but this kid was slowing us all down. All Mickey had to do was wave a lot, make silly squeaking noises, and his entire script for the weekend was to say, "Happy Christmas, kids," and, "Hallo, Pluto," twice. Not too demanding for his weekend's work, was it?

With the Disney director beginning to scream at everybody I felt I had to have a word. "Sorry, Richard," I said, with my terribly reasonable voice, "but it's not the crew or the presenters. Everybody's giving it their all. It's that bloody kid in the Mickey suit. He keeps stopping for quarter of an hour at a time and we're just getting farther and farther behind schedule." Richard took me very gently to one side and gave me inarguably the most stupid piece of advice I've ever been given.

"Hey, Chris, I love you man, but don't ever forget … we're all working for the Mouse."

Somewhere over the years Richard has lost all contact with the real world.

And I still didn't get to meet Tom Jones.

CHINESE WHISPERS

I was doing a radio interview a while back, and the young guy presenting the programme mentioned that he, like me, had studied for three years at the University of Birmingham. For his opening question, he asked:

"Chris, as we are both from Birmingham University, can you tell me, is it true about the goose?"

"I'm sorry, mate," I said, "but I've absolutely no idea what you're talking about."

"The Goose," he said. "Apparently, you were at Birmingham a few years before me, along with people like Rik Mayall and Victoria Wood, and everybody knows that you climbed to the top of the Old Joe Tower, sometime after midnight, carrying a goose with its wings tied together and threw it from the top of the tower. Chris, what on earth made you do it?"

I knew where this story had come from because it had been going on for years, but this was the latest version of it, and by now it had clearly got out of all proportion. Old Joe Tower is the tallest free-standing clock tower in the world. It's over 300 feet tall. As far as I know it has never ever been climbed by anybody, even in daylight, let alone in total darkness, and certainly not holding a goose. I also really didn't like the idea of this poor goose having its wings tied together so it couldn't fly. I really wouldn't ever do that to any living creature (well, maybe Donald Trump or at least one Jedward), but I was quite shocked that the story had now come this far from the truth.

I almost didn't want to tell him the original story, because by comparison it was so feeble, but I thought it really was about time to put things on record.

My first year at university I stayed in a huge skyscraper inventively called High Hall. All of my mates' rooms and mine were on the seventeenth floor. I think the authorities wanted us as far out of their sight as possible. There was an eighteenth floor, but that was very much for private functions and mostly closed. It was terrifying enough anyway up there on floor 17 if you were ever silly enough to look down, and the altitude clearly affected our little brains, because my best friend Malcolm, aka Big Malc and I did all sorts of stupid and very anti-social things, particularly at dinner time when all the students from all seventeen floors got into the lift and went down to the canteen to eat. At teatime there was a separate queue just outside at the front of the building, way down below. We did things like throwing eggs out of our window onto the students' heads, seventeen floors below, and then racing down the stairs to see them coming in screaming abuse and covered in egg yolk. Another time it was worms. The really dastardly one was setting off the fire extinguisher in the lift on the seventeenth floor, jumping out just before the doors shut and seeing how far down it would go, spinning wildly and throwing out disgusting brown sludgy foam all over everybody on each floor when the doors opened. I can tell you now, it went down to floor 11, before it mercifully ran out of foam.

We raced down the stairs, probably about the only exercise we ever took as students, to watch one bedraggled student after another coming in for tea with just their eyes peeping out of the gunge.

It's possible now that the germ of a later children's television programme was hatched in those moments.

So, all in all, I was a thorough nuisance, and so were most of my closest chums. Like is attracted to like and we all seemed to gravitate towards each other.

We had what the hall authorities called a 'social evening' at the end of one term. It wasn't very social, because it was all blokes and they wouldn't let the girls from the hall next door in, so basically, we all sat around drinking and when the bar eventually shut, I thought it would be a good idea to climb over the bar, where I was found later by security, with my mouth open lying under an open tap of Banks's Ale.

They then had a second social evening, this time with girls, which should have made me a lot happier. I think I was for a while, and then I seemed to lose the plot altogether, and hurled a beer glass through some very expensive looking thick glass windows at the top of the eighteenth floor. Of course it was a stupid thing to do, but I'm afraid I did rather a lot of them at that age, many of them I still haven't even got the nerve to tell my own kids. I honestly think from between the ages of 17 and about 22 I was completely unhinged. Some may say nothing's changed.

So that's where the story started. And pathetically that's what actually happened. I was wheeled in the next day by the authorities, and they said to me, "Mr Tarrant, last time we had a social you were a thorough nuisance and got into trouble. Last night we had a social and you were a thorough nuisance and got into trouble. Can you promise us, that if we have another social at the end of the summer term, that you won't behave in an equally stupid and irresponsible manner?"

I looked at them and said, "I'm sorry, I really can't promise that. I think you ought to let me go." And they did. I was thrown out, and I lived in digs, some of them pretty grim, some of them absolutely awful, all over Birmingham for the next two years.

The university actually lost touch with me and thought I'd left, but I turned up one day ready to do my finals, and they said, "Oh you are still here. We've got you down as no longer at this university."

So, I'd thrown a beer glass through the window. Two years later, a guy I shared digs with asked, "Is it true about the fridge?"

"What fridge?"

"The fridge full of beer you threw through the window of High Hall."

"No," I said, "it wasn't a fridge full of beer, it was a beer glass with nothing in it."

"Oh," he said. "That's a bit of a let-down."

But it then started to get sillier and sillier. I then heard that I'd thrown a whole piano through the window of High Hall. By the time my son Toby got to the same university as his father, the legend had become that I'd thrown not just a piano, but a piano with a man playing it, still sitting on the stool, through the window of High Hall. Things were now getting ridiculous. And then just as Toby was leaving, he said to me, "Dad, it's not a fridge full of beer anymore, it's not a piano with a man sitting on the piano stool, it's now become a live goose."

Now where the hell I would get a live goose from, at a fine gentlemen's and ladies' social evening at Birmingham University, God only knows! And why and how would I ever manage to throw it through a plate glass window?

So that was the last I heard of it, until I did this radio interview. So, for the record, anybody who has been to university in Birmingham, in the shadow of Old Joe, or is going there in the future, I almost hate to admit this, because it sounds so utterly feeble: it was never a goose, with or without its wings clipped, I've never been up to the top of Old Joe, and as far as I know nor has anybody else who lived to tell the tale, it wasn't a piano, it wasn't a piano with a man still playing it sitting on the stool, and it wasn't a fridge full of beer. I'm afraid to say, it was just an empty beer glass, and I'm sure I've just let down my own legendary status for thousands of disappointed students, but I think it's about time the true story was told.

MASTER CHEF

My cooking is not great. I can just about cook for my own simple needs, I don't set light to the hairs on my chest, and I don't blow myself up very often. Come to think of it, I've never really blown myself up at all. Although I have been blown up on a canal boat, but that's for another day and another book involving an ex wife.

I'm still the only person I can completely trust to make the perfect bacon sandwich (with mustard and Marmite, of course), and I do a mean toasted cheese. I can just about grill a steak, but I can never get chips right, and my poached eggs are a disaster. On the plus side, I can grill a trout in a pan, but don't seem to able to get them right on a barbecue. I have caught lots of trout all over the world and I've been stuck in the middle of some godforsaken wilderness in Alaska, Iceland, or even Northern Russia enough times, with just my day's catch between me and starvation, to have had to learn how.

In Canada, up around Hudson's Bay, the shore lunches after a hard morning's fishing are one of the great highlights of the day.

The wonderful Indian and Eskimo guides up there, a long way above the 49th parallel, have methods of cooking up freshly caught lake trout that taste superb.

A lot of it is, of course, to do with the fresh air and the magnificent scenery all around, but they appear just to chuck them into a really hot frying pan full of butter and add a few onions. They make it look all too easy, and in theory it is, but if you try it on your own, or more specifically, if I try it, the fresh trout, with a bit of butter straight into a pan routine, all ends up in a sticky black goo on the bottom of my frying pan.

It was back in 1983 when I'd been contracted to make the series of summer shows for *TV-am*, and a reporter girl friend of mine on *TV Times*, said, "Chris, we've got to do a promotion piece about 'Tarrant's Summer'. Let's do your favourite BBQ."

"I don't have one," I said. "I only do toasted cheese sandwiches."

"No, no, no. That's no use at all," she replied, never one to let a single grain of truth stand in the way of a good story. "You're a fisherman, we'll find you your favourite way of barbecuing trout."

"But I really don't have one," I bleated. "I just chuck 'em in a frying pan and they come out all burnt and tasting like something you find on your lawn the morning after Guy Fawkes night. I only do toasted cheese sandwiches."

"Don't be a wimp," she told me. "You do a BBQ trout. And you do a very good one. In fact you do a whole exciting variety of them. Now, get a silly loud shirt on (God knows you've got plenty of those), and get around here at 12 noon sharp. I'll book a photographer."

So sure enough with some tenuous link to the series of summer shows that I was due to start the next Monday, there appeared a picture of me in a loud Hawaiian shirt, looking in total control behind a sizzling sumptuous BBQ. The article alongside was about how much I loved cooking trout and salmon, with no less than ten of my favourite recipes.

But not only that, not one of the ten was 'bung it in a frying pan, cover it in a pound of butter, leave until it's as black as soot, and give it to the nearest cat.'

There was no mention of my best technique at all, but we got away with it – or so I thought.

So I did the series of early morning reports for *TV-am* from all over the UK, including an extraordinary item I've forgotten to mention so far from a picturesque hotel in the Highlands of Scotland, where they had a 'trust the guests open drinks cabinet' after midnight. Anyone who ever offers a 'trust the guests open drinks cabinet' to a film crew anywhere in the world, is clearly a very well-meaning human being, but sadly away among the pixies and almost certainly heading for bankruptcy.

Anyway, we thought we had just about got away with this piece of harmless but obligatory publicity nonsense, until I got home and started wading through my postbag. There were requests from all over the country. There are always the usual ones like 'Ere Tarrant, why don't you eff off and die?' But a lot of them were along a whole brand-new theme:

"Dear Chris, I was so interested in the article about your ways of cooking trout in the *TV Times*. Have you got any more recipes?"

Or even worse:

"Dear Chris, I was fascinated by your recipes for trout, but will they work equally well with mackerel?"

For God's sake! I don't know. I was just doing a contractual obligatory photograph.

To compound my misfortune, I'd left *TV-am* by then, and all these letters were being re-directed to Capital Radio. I stalled them all for weeks, and then one arrived that said, "If you don't reply to my letter and send me a recipe by return of post, I'll ring Kenny Everett who will denounce you as a charlatan."

Now this was a nightmare of nightmares. Dear Kenny, who was a seriously good cook, was also dear wicked little Kenny, who knew my skills as a chef were on a par with my abilities as a dressmaker and would have had a field day. It would have given Cuddly Ken radio material for months. In a desperate quandary I went to see nice Norman, a delightful gentleman in our press office who I believed to be a very fine cook. I told him my plight.

"No problem," said Norman. "I love to cook. Any queries, send them on to me and I'll do a reply. You just sign it. That'll keep them all happy."

And so it went on, week after week, people wrote in with all their queries, nice Norman replied and I signed it. Recipe after recipe was sent off, with or without my blessing.

I was even offered a weekly cooking spot in a national newspaper, which I declined.

I was even offered my own cooking spot on a well-known daytime TV show, which I also declined.

There was talk of a 'Cooking with CT' book deal.

It was a ridiculous scenario. It was absurd, but manageable, until horror of all horrors, nice Norman left.

Still the correspondence kept coming in, usually in response to some cooking article that Norman had ghosted for me. His recipes were mouth-watering but totally beyond me. Here's a typical example.

Truites Jurassienne
Preparation Time: 15 mins
Cooking Time: 35-45 mins
Serves: 6

Clean 6 medium trout, leaving the head and tails. Lay them side by side in a buttered oven proof dish. Peel and finely chop 2 shallots and sprinkle over the fish. Pour over half a pint of rosé wine and cover the dish with buttered grease proof paper or foil. Cook in the centre of a pre-heated oven at 300F (gas mark 2) for 25 minutes.

Meanwhile make the hollandaise sauce by boiling 3 tbsps of white wine vinegar and 1 tbsp of water with 6 black peppercorns and 1 bay leaf in a small saucepan until reduced to 1 tbsp. Leave to cool. Cream 3 egg yolks with half oz of butter and a pinch of salt. Strain the vinegar into the eggs and set the bowl over a pan of boiling water. Turn off the heat. Whisk in 5 oz of butter (quarter oz at a time) until the sauce is shiny and has the consistency of thick cream. Season with salt and pepper and add nutmeg to taste.

When the trout are cooked, lift them carefully onto a cloth and remove the skins. Strain the cooking liquid and reduce it by fast boiling until there are only 2-3 tbsps left. Let this cool slightly, then stir into the warm hollandaise sauce. Finally, stir in 1 tbsp of double cream and garnish with bread croutons and chopped parsley.

They were incredible, detailed recipes, and almost certainly delicious, but a lot more complicated than a toasted cheese sandwich, and still the mail kept coming in.

Just towards the end of the summer, I received yet another letter from a nice lady called Mrs Hunter from Padstow in Cornwall. It said, "Thank you so much for your marvellous recipe for Truites Jurassienne. My husband came home with two trout the other evening and I cooked them as you instructed. They were absolutely delicious, but a little too spicy for both our palates. Do you think I may have overdone the nutmeg?"

I didn't know how to break this to Mrs Hunter, but I hadn't got the foggiest idea. I think we rang Norman at home in a panic, got a suitable reply about the correct amount of nutmeg, and then did a generic letter to all concerned, saying:

"Thank you so much for your letter. Unfortunately Chris is too busy to keep up with the constant requests for his secret recipes that he gets on a daily basis, as he is now fully tied up with his other television commitments.

"Many thanks for your interest, I'm sorry we can't be more helpful.

pp CT."

BEADLE

I don't know why, but I'm always attracted to silly people. Jeremy Beadle was one of the silliest of all. We became good friends over years shared together that, in the end, were all too short.

He produced a TV programme that I presented down in Southampton. It was a pop show, but to be honest, although I knew him and got along with him quite well socially, I wasn't at all sure about him as a producer. He was the presenter of *Game for a Laugh* and had no real experience of producing, but I couldn't have been more wrong. He was brilliant to work for, he was meticulous about every detail of the show, about my presentation, and all of the various celebrity contestants who came on. He was a pleasure to work with, and at the end of each day's recording we would race off into the nearest and best Chinese restaurant in Southampton, bizarrely called 'Pearl Harbour'.

We then spent a wonderful week, coming back from New York to England on the *QE2* with both our families, and the splendid, incredibly likeable Richard Whiteley of *Countdown* fame. Richard had just written a book called *Himoff!* When I asked him what had inspired that seemingly strange title, he said, "It's because members of the public never seem to know my name. I think I've got one of those faces that looks like an awful lot of other people, but whereas you get 'Hello Chris' and Beadle gets 'Hello Jeremy', I get people coming up to me and going, 'Oh it's you, you're 'im off ... and eventually I have to fill in the blank, with the word *Countdown*, followed by them going, 'Oh, yes'." Or a couple of times, they said to him, "Are you sure you are?" or, "No you're not, he's taller." Which is a worry.

Apropos of nothing, Terry Waite is about six-foot-ten and once got mistaken for Ronnie Corbett, which is an even bigger worry.

The whole *QE2* sailing from New York to Southampton was basically a PR jolly. We only had to do a one-hour audience presentation each during the week and for that they flew us from wherever we were in the world – in my case, with my wife and kids, from Mexico City, in Beadle's case with his tribe, I think from Hadley Wood, and Richard Whiteley and his girlfriend were flown down from Yorkshire. We all stayed in New York for a few days in a very nice hotel right next to Central Park, everything was paid for, and then we eventually made our way back to the UK on the *QE2*. So what was not to like?

I don't think there was a fee, fair enough, as we didn't do a fat lot, but all our flights and accommodation were paid for. The only thing they didn't feel they could finance was our drinks bill, which was very fair and very sensible. Whiteley, Beadle and I drank enough to sink the *Titanic* all over again.

Incidentally, a couple of years later, Jim, my trusty driver, was asked if he would collect Richard Whiteley from Heathrow, take him to a function in Park Lane, London, and then take him back in the afternoon to catch a flight up to Leeds, where he was based.

Whiteley being Whiteley was rather late coming out of the lunch. In fact it was nearly teatime, but Jim always waits patiently, found Richard to be a very nice man and said, "I'm sorry, we've missed the first flight, but there is another one at eight o'clock this evening."

"No problem," said Whiteley. "It's my fault. I'll catch the eight o'clock," and fell fast asleep in the back of the car.

Jim had a nice new shiny manual Mercedes, and off they went towards the airport. However, after about half an hour, Richard woke up to discover they hadn't gone very far at all, and the normally unflappable Jim was looking rather anxious.

"Everything alright?" asked Whiteley.

"Not really," said Jim. "I'm afraid the car is stuck in second gear. I didn't want to wake you. What I could do is ring for another car to take you on for the rest of the journey to the airport."

"No, no, no," said Richard. "Don't worry about it. We'll get there when we get there," and went back to sleep.

Miraculously he did catch the eight o'clock flight that evening by the skin of his teeth, having been driven all the way from central London to Heathrow in second gear. I'm just telling you that to demonstrate what an extraordinarily nice man he was. Carol Vorderman would always agree.

The next time I tied up with Beadle we were doing a sleep-out for a homeless charity in London, where we had to sleep in the streets of Covent Garden for twelve hours on a bitterly cold night. Beadle, being Beadle of course, arrived without a sleeping bag, and said to me, "Never mind, I'll climb into yours." We spent a ridiculous night, somehow, two big blokes in one sleeping bag, giggling a lot and hardly sleeping at all. It really didn't help, that, entrapped in a shared sleeping bag, Beadle kept farting.

Jeremy always had the most vicious, poisonous press. The adjectives 'cruel' and 'unkind' were always used about him in print, and yet he was one of the kindest, most generous men I have ever met. Generous of his spirit and generous of his time. He worked tirelessly for several charities, but the one he spent thousands of hours, unpaid working for, was 'Children with Leukaemia'. He travelled the length of the country raising funds for them, so much so, that leukaemia amongst children was almost wiped out, although sadly it is still a horrific disease for far too many adults. Because of Beadle's tireless work the charity is now renamed 'Children with Cancer'. It's estimated that he raised in excess of 90 million pounds for them, and it was only after his tragic death, horribly, ironically caused by cancer, that the press suddenly realised what a great bloke he was. All a little too late.

It was because a lot of his TV work featured members of the public looking very silly, but then again lots of members of the public are very silly. *Game for a Laugh* started it, and then his series *Beadle's About* featured some of the funniest sketches starring real people, ever seen on television. The woman who honestly believed that a space alien had landed on her lawn and invited him in for a cup of tea, and the white van owner, whose van appeared to be driven into the harbour, are still two of the great ground-breaking moments of television people shows.

I suppose it all started with *Candid Camera* many years ago, but Beadle took it to new heights. It's amazing he never got thumped, but he didn't because people just liked him.

His wedding was, without exception, the funniest wedding I have ever been to. It was almost like one of his own Beadle stunts. I arrived at a very posh hotel in North London, parked up, and a very worried looking hotelier came out to meet me, saying, "I'm really sorry, Mr Tarrant, there's a big problem."

"Oh, God," I said. "What's that? Is one of the Beadles ill?"

"No, not at all, but we've had a power cut."

"OK," I said, "so what does that actually mean to us?"

"Well, at the moment all the guests and the Beadle family are downstairs in the bar drinking (this was just after ten o'clock in the morning) and I'm afraid the electric till doesn't work."

"Oh, God," I said. "That sounds awful. Does that mean that nobody can pay for their drinks."

"Exactly. It's a nightmare."

"I agree," I said, and raced down to join the nightmare.

When it got to the actual wedding, we all weaved our way upstairs into the room that had been put aside for the ceremony, with about two hundred of us, all crammed in to what was quite a small room not much larger than the free bar we'd all just come weaving out of. The worried looking registrar came in, and said, "Hello, ladies and gentlemen. My name is Kevin," and I don't know why, but probably because we had all consumed rather too much, with the electric till not functioning, the name Kevin got a huge burst of laughter, which probably didn't help the poor registrar's nerves at all.

"I'm afraid we still have this power cut," said Kev. "So we can't have any music."

"Don't worry," we all said. "We'll sing everything."

And sure enough, when Sue Beadle came in we all lustfully sang 'Here Comes the Bride'.

The first hymn was 'Onward Christian Soldiers', which we sang at the top of our voices, but then because there was quite a large Jewish contingent of their friends they all shouted, "Hang on, what about one for the Jewish fraternity?" And all started dancing in the aisles to 'Hava Nagila'. Kevin, by now, was looking deeply alarmed.

Unfortunately, we were all beginning to love it too much. I was standing next to the splendid journalist Richard Littlejohn, and he said, "This is brilliant. When it gets to that bit where they ask, 'If anybody here knows any reason why Susan should not marry him,' let's you and I put our hands up."

"Good plan," I agreed.

When it came to the moment, and Kevin said, "Does anybody here know of any reason why Susan should not take Jeremy in holy matrimony?" I looked at Richard Littlejohn, we both nodded, and were about to go for it, when what happened, uproariously, was that the whole of the congregation put their hands up, and all two hundred of us started shouting dreadful allegations at once, about why Beadle would make an unfit husband. It was a riot, Kevin looked aghast, Sue was just numb, and Beadle, stuck and shocked at the altar, was looking around waiting for someone to jump out from behind a camera. But of course nobody did because the only person who would have done exactly that was stuck and shocked at the altar.

The entire congregation was convulsed with laughter for several minutes. Littlejohn and I both had that wonderful feeling when you laugh so hard that your lungs actually ache before poor old Kevin somehow brought us to order and solemnly declared that Beadle could now kiss the bride, whether Sue wanted to be kissed or not.

The reception was even sillier, because the power cut had affected the whole of Hadley Wood. So we trooped back from the hotel to Beadle's house, and we all had to climb over his very spiky electric gates. Many of the women were in elegant, expensive, long frocks, and some of the sights, as they climbed over the gate, showing all sorts of thongs, suspenders and panties, will live with me forever.

Oh, and of course there was no food cooked because the oven was off.

Luckily, Beadle had a splendid collection of alcoholic drinks waiting for us, so having started at ten in the morning, without the electric till, we were still drinking at five o'clock in the afternoon, when eventually the power came back on, and some sort of meal arrived as long overdue blotting paper.

IRRESISTIBLE TEMPTATION

O ne week filming down near Ledbury was a total washout. The weather was diabolical, bitter cold and pouring with rain most of the time, which made life pretty miserable and filming downright impossible. After about four days of hanging around our hotel getting smashed out of our brains every night and plodding through the same menu every evening, luckily, I was invited by a very nice lady that I was supposedly going to interview, a retired school mistress, to have dinner with her and her husband to chat through what we were going to talk about on film if it ever stopped raining. I said, "Yes please," at once to her invitation, just to break the monotony.

I got myself spruced up and knocked on the very large front door at 7.30 on the dot. Patricia came out smiling, produced a large scotch from a beautiful antique cabinet and motioned me into the lounge. "Charles is in by the fire," she said. "Go in and say hello while I serve up, but whatever you do, don't touch his nose."

I stared at her departing back with my mouth opening and closing. What? Don't touch the nose? I mean, it had never crossed my mind. Why on earth would I go up to some complete stranger and touch his nose? I went into the lounge and there, beaming amiably in front of the fire, was Charles who came across to shake my hand with his great big hand. He was a big bear of a man, about six-foot-six, used to play rugby for his county, was terribly well spoken, and kindness itself.

"Nice to meet you Chris," he said. "Got a drink, have you? Good man. Now come on in and sit down." Now all this polite chatting and handshaking was all very well, and I made suitably polite replies, but really and truly all I wanted to ask him about was his nose. What was wrong with it? Why couldn't I touch it? I kept staring at it. It looked alright, a little large perhaps, but not broken or anything, no bandage. Then the food arrived which was absolutely delicious after the meagre fare we'd been getting in our hotel and for a while I forgot all about Charles's hooter. Perhaps I'd misheard?

The wine flowed freely, and all three of us got on like a house on fire. Charles has a really silly sense of humour, and his wife is great. But all the time in the back of my mind I was hearing this one warning voice ringing in my brain again and again: "Whatever you do, don't touch the nose." The whole thing was absurd. Perhaps she had said 'rose' or 'hose', but that was even sillier. No, I hadn't misheard, and although nothing was further from my mind when I walked into their house that evening, by the end of that dinner I wanted to touch his nose more than anything else in the world.

The brandy came around and the cigars came out. Charles and I sat alongside each other roaring with laughter, until eventually, at about 1am, I could restrain myself no longer. As Charles sat rocking in his chair with laughter, I reached across the table, gently took hold of both his nostrils between forefinger and thumb, and gave it a damn good tweaking. There was a scream from Patricia, and a crash of broken glass. Charles let out the roar of a wounded bull elephant. There was a great flash in front of my face, and I vaguely made out the shape of a huge hairy fist coming towards my face. The next thing I remember was lying on the floor under the dinner table, tasting blood in my mouth and a terribly apologetic Charles looming over me, saying, "I'm really, terribly sorry, old boy, but Patricia should have warned you ..."

A WHOLE NEW WORLD

R adio really was a whole new wonderful world for me. After all the union struggles getting television programmes on air, just going into a radio studio with a pile of records, talking nonsense in between them, wishing everybody a nice day, and then going home was a wonderful thing. I'd got a call out of the blue from a lady called Jo asking if I would like to do some radio in London at a place called Capital. I was doing some promotion for *Tiswas* on radio stations all over the Midlands. I had done one that went really well as a Christmas special for Coventry Radio which they'd syndicated on various stations, including Capital in London, which is where Jo Sandilands had heard it.

I'd never really heard of Capital Radio because I was based in the Midlands and still working for Central Television. I knew Michael Aspel and Kenny Everett socially, and I did know Capital was the place where Kenny used to post his legendary Captain Kremmen weekly series, because he lived quite close to me in the Cotswolds. I'd seen him work there in his studios a few times. He lived in an old converted pub called The Red Lion, in Little Cherington, with his wife Lee. He'd drink a few large glasses of brandy and coke and then disappear wearing white gloves into a room with hundreds of tapes. They were all cut into different lengths by razor blades and hung up all around his studio with Sellotape.

Kenny was unquestionably a genius, and it's a real sadness that he died before the digital age that we all now live in, because Kenny would have absolutely loved the technology. What he used to create the old-fashioned way with Sellotape and razor blades, like Captain Kremmen and his amazing, award-winning jingles that used to take him half a day to make, would now take him half an hour.

He used to send his radio show off to London, to this Capital Radio place, popping it into the post box at the end of his road saying, "Here it is, my darlings. Here's the latest masterpiece." And off it would go.

He'd make it on about Wednesday, post it on a Thursday and it usually got there in time for Saturday morning. Presumably even Kenny had some sort of master tape somewhere, but that's how he worked for years.

I was quite sniffy at first about doing radio. I didn't really understand it, and I wasn't sure that I liked the idea of it. I am one of those peculiar people who did television first and then discovered radio, rather than almost everybody else's normal route, which was radio first and then TV. But because I had come to it afresh, I absolutely loved it. I loved the simplicity of it. I loved the immediacy of it.

There was none of the ridiculous overmanning that was happening more and more on television programmes because of the sheer power of the unions. I used to go out to film a three-minute interview, quite frequently with an eight-man crew, all of whom had to have a hot lunch for probably an hour and a half. On ATV News once, we went out to cover a big fire in Wolverhampton, but because union rules meant we had to stop for an hour's lunch on the way, by the time we got there, the fire was actually out.

And if we ever went to somewhere equally heavily unionised, like Longbridge car factory, we could waste an hour squabbling about who would be allowed to put the plug in the wall for our lights.

And it wasn't just outside filming. Things in studios had also got lost in a fog of their own, guaranteed to kill all spontaneity.

A director I was once working with on a series for ITV, one

afternoon during rehearsals, said, "OK, Chris, you'll make your entrance through this archway here. The audience is there. Your camera is over there. Now, what's your first ad lib going to be?"

"I've no idea," I said. "But isn't that rather the point of ad libs?"

I took to radio immediately. It is undoubtedly the best fun. I think I had more fun at Capital Radio than anywhere else I have ever worked. I have lots of mates from those days who I still see a lot socially.

For someone who wasn't that keen on radio, I then spent the next twenty years of my life at Capital. The first show I did went out on Sunday lunchtime, under the wackily titled *Lunday Sunchtime*, which wasn't very funny, but then nor was the show. I was learning, though. All the time I was beginning to see the potential of radio and I was loving it.

When I took over the breakfast show three years later, although it meant getting up at five o'clock every morning, it certainly was one of the best and happiest periods of my working life. After my first week, one critic wrote, "This dreadful, loud, unfunny new man on the breakfast show at Capital Radio won't last the month." So, when I left seventeen years later, I wondered whatever became of him.

Radio was so relaxed, it was live, it was honest, and it was immediate.

Breakfast radio presenters want to be the first to tell you everything that has happened overnight while you've been fast asleep. It's not just the funny stuff, like 'a lady in Chingford had a space craft land on her lawn, where she was taken in by aliens, impregnated and then put back on Mother Earth'. This was supposedly a true story, although if her husband really believed that, I think they probably deserved each other.

Or while you were all asleep, 'Freddie Starr has eaten somebody's hamster in a sandwich'.

Of course, we loved bringing those first, but it wasn't always the silly stuff that you wanted to share with your audience. There was the night of the great hurricane. When I woke up at 4.30am, I couldn't believe the devastation caused to London as I carefully drove into the studio. There were trees down everywhere, there were cars flattened, there were sparking lamplights, and the window in dear old Fluff Freeman's office had been smashed in by the sheer power of the wind. All his treasured albums, collected over many years, had blown off down Tottenham Court Road. We managed to get quite a few of them back, but tragically a lot of them were lost forever.

Another time, as we came on air, there had been a horrific fire in King's Cross underground station, and the bodies were being brought out as we started our programme with the 6am news. But I suppose most memorable of all, tragically so, was the news that shocked not just London, but the whole of the UK, and the whole of the world – that overnight, Princess Diana had died in a tunnel in Paris.

Diana had become a great friend of Capital Radio. She would sometimes quietly sneak into the studios, and was a wonderful patron for our charity 'Help a London Child'. Her patronage brought in extra tens of thousands to disadvantaged kids all over London.

The long week after she died, we could not conduct the usual loud, irreverent radio show at all. Radio that week became a therapy for us and everyone listening. Grown men were coming through on the phone lines in tears, and on the Saturday we had to do the radio warm-up for that emotionally raw, unforgettable funeral at Westminster Abbey.

I had to go to Ireland straight after the show that morning, and as I drove away from the studios towards Heathrow, I have never seen London so empty in all my life. Not at any time, day or night. Apart from all the people lining the funeral route, there was virtually nobody else out on the pavements at all. It was very eerie, as if there had been a nuclear attack. It was just one more expression of how much the world loved her.

The thing I loved about live radio, was that you could have a good idea driving into the studios at a quarter to six, you could do it live on air at quarter past six, and by quarter to seven realise it was one of the stupidest ideas you'd ever had.

The great thing about doing anything, however silly, at quarter past six in the morning, is that none of the management will have heard it.

My own radio heroes include Kenny Everett, obviously (I think the best disc jockey of all time), Noel Edmonds when he did the breakfast show on Radio One, Michael Aspel, Steve Wright, Les Ross, the late Ray Moore, the late Terry Wogan, and a guy I worked with when I first arrived at Capital, Roger Scott.

Roger Scott was hugely respected as a man and loved his music. He was obsessed with Bruce Springsteen; he had every record that Springsteen ever made and went to see him if he could wherever he was performing in the world.

When Bruce Springsteen did his famous 'Three Hours Live at Wembley' concert, Roger was, of course, in the front row, and when he brought out his *Three Hours Live at Wembley* album, Roger couldn't wait to play it. Now, just to show how much music policy has changed in recent years, where more and more stations are obsessed with playlists – from which disc jockeys only dare to deviate at their peril – Roger went into the studio, turned all the lights down and played the entire Wembley album for the whole of his three-hour show.

I'm all for DJ choice, and in fact I was given a lot of freedom myself at Capital, but this was obviously the extreme example of where it really doesn't work. I like Bruce Springsteen, thousands of people like Bruce Springsteen, but three hours non-stop was a bit much. By the end of about an hour, people were throwing themselves on their own swords, mice were throwing themselves on the traps, and even Bruce Springsteen was going, "Oh, come on Rog, give us a break."

I remember when I first listened to radio in New York, thinking,

"God, how can so many weird people be on the phone lines? But once I started working at Capital, I realised there was just as many weird and wonderful people living in London, just waiting for their own little radio home. Well, rather like what happened at ATV, I became that little radio home.

I remember a guy called Andy rang me up to say how much he loved the M25. "Going on the M25 is like going into a West End play, we should enjoy it and be grateful for it." Can you imagine how popular that phone call was, with commuters stuck all the way round the motorway on a busy morning.

There was a bloke who rang up and asked me, in all seriousness, if I would buy him a new radio. He had been caught by his girlfriend making love to another women at a party. She had stormed off and when he got home all his furniture, including his prized radio, had been thrown out of the window and was smashed to pieces. Why he thought it was up to me to replace it, I don't know. Funnily enough, I didn't.

And then there was a woman who rang up to say "Capital had ruined her image by changing the Car Sticker," which she had proudly tattooed on her left buttock. Would we pay for a change to her tattoo? We used to have a little bird as our car sticker, flying the music around London, and then we changed it to a bright shiny sun. The PR people came into the studio, with yet another one of their great publicity ideas, so for no reason that I can think of, I agreed to go to a tattooist in Soho straight after the show with this lady and a *Sun* photographer. She was wearing a tiny G-string and *The Sun* ran a feature of me watching her tattoo being covered over with the shining sun tattoo. It was a harmless enough bit of press. In fact, it was almost tasteful by tabloid standards, but it didn't help at all that there was blood pouring out of the new tattoo as he worked on her bare left buttock. Our press department, of course, thought it was a wonderful thing. Personally, I think it's one of the daftest things I have ever agreed to do. She was a really nice woman, but there was something seriously seedy about the whole thing.

We introduced an item called 'Party Pieces' which demonstrated, in a quite eye-opening way, the lengths people will go to, to make complete fools of themselves on the radio. Bear in mind, it was all on the phone, people went off into flights of fantasy for their moment of glory and they came through on the lines, day after day.

One bloke rang me and said he wanted to jump out of his window on the count of three, and then land on the tarpaulin roof of a market stall beneath.

I said, "OK mate, you're on your own, 3, 2, 1."

And from the dying scream and the unmistakable thud that came down the telephone line, it was obvious he'd really gone and done it. We laughed a lot, then went to another record and forgot all about him.

About quarter of an hour later, an irate market trader from Bethnal Green started shouting abuse at me over the airwaves. "Oi," he said, "some idiot has jumped through the roof of my market pitch, and he said Chris Tarrant put him up to it. Well, Chris bloody Tarrant better pay for it."

I took no responsibility at all and politely wished the market trader well. His reply was a little muffled, but I seem to remember the second word was "Off."

We did all sorts of things on April Fool's Day and, as always, people in the morning were so gullible. On April Fool's Day in 1995 we did our most successful prank of all. It fell on a Saturday that year, so David Briggs, my long-time friend and executive producer (whatever one of those is) said, "Why don't we come in on Saturday, do the normal time, send up the flying eye, etc., do the weather and the traffic and tell everybody it's actually Friday 31st March."

I remember at the meeting somebody said, "Don't be silly, nobody is going to fall for that." But by now we knew better and said, "First thing in the morning? – oh yes they will."

We had hundreds and hundreds of calls from people who were

completely bewildered. If the nice man on Capital Radio tells you it's Friday, then it's Friday, even though when you opened your eyes you were sure it was Saturday.

One bloke with a terrible hangover from his weekly Friday-night bender got as far as the kitchen convinced that it was Friday morning, felt really rough, rang his boss and left a message to say he was going to be late. One woman set off for a meeting she had already attended the day before. But my favourite was a very high-powered lady who drove into her central London office from Gerrards Cross. It did occur to her that the Friday morning traffic was a bit on the light side, and she was very pleasantly surprised to see a lot more room than usual when she got into the car park. Also, there was no security, the barrier was already up, and she sat alone for an hour in a big open-plan insurance office just along the Euston Road, where there were normally three hundred people working, before she realised she had been well and truly had.

I remember being handed some sort of radio award by no less than Prince Philip, Duke of Edinburgh. He asked me, "What time is your show on?" and I said, "It starts at six o'clock in the morning, sir. You really ought to try it." He looked at me in stark amazement and went, "Not bloody likely! Six o'clock in the morning? Are you mad?" and went wandering off shaking his head.

Going to the loo first thing in the morning is obviously a fraught affair on breakfast radio, because there is always the danger of the record running out before the DJ gets back to the microphone.

In the 60s that was a real problem because the average length of records by Elvis Presley, Cliff Richard and Co, could be something under two minutes. So calls of nature, for people who obviously drank a lot of coffee to keep them awake, became a frantic breakneck race out of the studio to the loo and back again. If you took too long, in the early days of playing vinyl records, there was an unmistakable noise, that only disc jockeys knew: the sound of the record ending and the needle playing the rubber mat.

By the early 70s the records were slightly more comfortable at three minutes plus, and by the 80s records of four minutes or even five made life a lot easier. Sometimes going to the loo promoted silliness, like the crew locking the studio door, so that the screaming DJ couldn't get back in.

So, I'd been at Capital for about four years and had already achieved a kind of fame (or should that be notoriety?) through *Tiswas*, *OTT* and the breakfast show, and getting really good ratings. Anyway, I dived into the loo one day while five minutes of David Bowie was playing, and found myself at about seven o'clock in the morning standing next to one of my all-time heroes, the brilliant director and actor, Richard Attenborough. I was a huge fan of his work, but of course he was in that day because he was also one of the founding members and chairman of Capital Radio.

In fact, there is a famous true story about 'Dickie' that, after the first year on air, Capital Radio was really finding it tough financially to stay above water. It seems bizarre now because it is one of the wealthiest radio groups anywhere in Europe. But the first year was a real struggle and Richard Attenborough took two of his prize paintings (one was an original Monet) in the boot of his Rolls Royce, parked it outside the bank, and showed the very impressed bank manager the priceless paintings that he would put up as the collateral against the loan to keep the radio station afloat for another year.

He was an amazing man, he became a great friend, but clearly at that point, I hadn't made much of an impression on him, despite the ratings, because smiling he looked across at me and said, "Oh, hello there. How's it going, Kenny?" and wandered off smiling to chair his meeting. I reminded him of this several times during the years that followed, and he always showed mock humility. Secretly though I know he thought it was very funny, and I still do.

I always used to wonder if he ever stood next to Kenny Everett having a wee and called him Chris, but probably not.

ROCKIN' ALL OVER THE WORLD

Outside broadcasts were always great fun on radio. I did some on television, and in the main they were no fun at all. I remember once doing a live OB for ATV, back to the studios from Dudley Zoo in Worcestershire. For some reason the director placed me in front on an orangutan's cage, and as I uttered the immortal words, "Hello, good evening, we're live from Dudley Zoo," I was hit in the back of the neck by an enormous pile of orangutan dung. He'd clearly seen some of my work over the years and was less than impressed. Fair play.

I don't know what they'd fed the orangutan that particular day, but there was lots of it and most of it went all over the back of my neck. He kept it up for the whole programme.

The *Capital Breakfast* show came from almost every corner of the world, from Los Angeles, from Hawaii, from New York, South Africa, Thailand, Kenya, all over Europe, including several weeks from luxury yachts moored along the Riviera coast, and we came from Australia more than a dozen times.

My longest serving producer for most of the time I did the breakfast show was Annie O'Neill, who was always carrying armfuls of plastic bags around with her everywhere. She became known to the listeners as 'The Bag Lady from Hell'. People would come up to us and say, "Hallo Chris," and then turn and say, "Is this the Bag Lady?" If you're thrown together for year after year, stuck in a studio, working in the dark and cold of winter mornings, you really have to work with people you like. Actually I do know of one very well-known breakfast show couple who actually loathe and detest each other and only speak when the microphone is on, but that's very unusual. I've been very lucky. I've usually only worked with mates. Annie became one of my closest friends and she still is. My kids loved her too and we travelled the world together. I do remember once chasing her round the deck with a live fish during an outside broadcast, on a yacht off the coast of the south of France. She had been silly enough to tell me she loved to eat fish, but was really squeamish about live ones.

Mike Osbourne (Oz Boy, the engineer) and I sometimes used to fish off the side of the boat when the records were playing. This does sound a bit disrespectful to the artists, but we would have heard all the records at least a hundred times before.

We came from Australia more than any other place in the world. We were sponsored by Foster's, the Amber Nectar, so the routine was we'd be live on air from Sydney on a Friday and live from London again first thing Monday morning.

My boss used to say, "Chris, it sounds great. Capital is the radio station of the world," and I'd say, "Very nice, but I'm completely knackered, and I don't know where I am, who I am or whether or not it's Monday or Wednesday."

The very first outside broadcast that we ever did was live from Tenerife. We went on air at 5.30am. Now by that time in Playa de las Americas, everybody was still making their way home from clubs that had stayed open for most of the night. This meant that the audience who came down to watch us were noisy, lively and 95% drunk.

As I said "Good morning, this is Capital Radio live from Tenerife," there was a huge cheer from the assembled crowd and a can of McEwan's hit me squarely on the top of my head. It was probably somebody related to the orangutan at Dudley zoo.

By about six o'clock, as we soldiered on, a minibus full of

extremely nasty looking Canary Isles policemen appeared, with some even nastier looking guns, and started menacing the crowds. I thought, "This is all going to go terribly wrong." Luckily, the drunken crowd began to wilt, and by about 7am they were all fast asleep on the grass and in the flowerbeds, and not a single shot had been fired.

It was our first outside broadcast, and we'd had a lot of technical problems, with the line back to London constantly cutting out. By about the Wednesday though, all the problems seemed to be sorted and Peter Ockelford, our OB engineer, said, "I've got a system now. There won't be any more problems."

It was only when we were flying home on the Friday afternoon, I asked Ockel what the system was that had completely fixed the earlier technical problems.

"Well, what we did," he said, "was shin up a telegraph pole and link up to a German gentleman's phone line."

"Good God," I said. "Didn't he mind?"

"No. Not at all. It's his holiday home, and he doesn't go there much 'til about the end of July."

Quite how huge the German gentleman's phone bill was for the second quarter of the year, we never found out, but it was emphasised to Ockel, that maybe, although it worked well in the short term, it wasn't a system we could really count on for future outside broadcasts, unless we all wanted to spend the rest of our lives in a German prison.

One of the problems with doing OBs is the variations in the world clock. So, although it sounds great that you're coming from LA or Hawaii, the reality is that for a six o'clock breakfast show in London, in LA you have to go on air about midnight. Anywhere West was a problem, and obviously it got better and better when you went East. My favourite was always OZ, where we would frequently go on air at seven o'clock in the evening, having had a nice lunch, a bit of a swim, a few beers, and then stroll down to do a breakfast show just as the sun was going down on Bondi Beach.

Doing the American shows meant that we were frequently struggling in the middle of the night to get guests to come and talk to us. We did do one show from a nightclub in Los Angeles called 'The China Club', so instead of trying to get guests to come along live at two o'clock in the morning, we thought it was a much better idea to go to where the guests were.

It was a great buzz in the club, lots of people were available for interviews, lots of celebrities, Rod Stewart was in there, John Travolta popped in, a couple of The Doobie Brothers, and legendary country artist Kenny Rogers.

Kenny was there with a lot of friends and some enormous scary looking minders, because it was his 50th birthday. He was one of the most successful country singers of all time, had sold millions of records and was one of the wealthiest men in America. He was happy to be interviewed, we chatted about his songs and about working with Dolly Parton, wished him Happy Birthday, and then myself and a couple of our crew grabbed a leg each and tried to give him the bumps. Now, Kenny is a very easy-going, laid-back kind of a guy, but apparently in the USA, they don't have a tradition of the bumps. In fact they'd never heard of them, had no idea what I was doing, decided I had completely flipped my lid, and five or six enormous bodyguards dragged me off a bewildered Kenny and made it very clear to me that the interview was over and that I had better put Mr Rogers down if I wanted to live to see the sun rise.

CROWD CONTROL

The crowds were always a problem at outside broadcasts. We did find, for example, that if we were out in Australia or Cape Town, we had to be very careful about reading out the English weather, or the audience would overreact. Doing outside broadcasts in the winter from sunny climes can really irritate people sitting stuck in traffic on an icy morning on the M25.

The first time we ever came live from Sydney it was February, the middle of their summer, and a huge crowd of Brits came along to see us. It was, of course, evening over there at the end of yet another long, hot day and most of the crowd were in shorts. As I read out the English weather, which was minus four and absolutely freezing, they all let out a huge cheer, which quite understandably infuriated listeners back home. So from then on we learned to play down the UK weather, and whenever we came up to a weather forecast we did it away from the crowd with all the outside microphones switched off.

We had problems sometimes with where we were broadcasting from, particularly in the USA. One night in LA we discovered that although our studio was fairly well protected and cut off, we were in the middle of an area notorious for drug gangs and drive-by shootings. When I foolishly went outside to do some street interviews I was brought back in very quickly by a large LA sheriff with an enormous gun at his side, saying, "Sorry, sir, but if you go out there, you are crazy and we can't be responsible for your life."

Funnily enough, we locked the studio door and stayed inside for the rest of the show.

I suppose the best gig of all for us was flying Concorde to New York. Concorde was the most beautiful plane and a feature of everybody's lives in London for many years. My daughter Sammy's first words were, 'Mummy', 'Daddy', and 'Concorde', which she heard every morning lying in her pram in the garden as it flew over our house at almost exactly half past ten.

Concorde was never that roomy or luxurious inside. After all, it was basically a rocket. But the great thing was that you got to New York two hours before you left. This meant I could do two breakfast shows in a single morning. So we did our normal show until ten o'clock, got a helicopter straight to Heathrow, caught Concorde with minutes to spare and were off to New York.

It was clearly a bit thin on celebrities that morning. In fact the only other people I recognised were Naomi Campbell and her mum, but Annie got very excited because we were sitting in seats 1A and 1B, and she said to me, "Can you imagine all the famous bums that have sat on these seats?"

I tried as best I could to clear any thoughts of famous bums from my head, got on with some work, but had completely gone off my breakfast.

The captain then invited me up to the cockpit, which was very exciting. I remember doing the link from 60,000 feet, travelling at twice the speed of sound, back to the studios in London where I could quite clearly hear Pat Sharpe talking to somebody's granny in Tulse Hill. I remember thinking this is surreal.

When we got to the coast of Newfoundland, they invited me back into the cockpit again (how times have changed since 9/11) to see if I'd like to watch the landing in New York. "Fantastic," I said. "Thank you so much," only to discover that as we got close to New York, about twenty minutes later, the nose cone came down and I couldn't see a bloody thing. Nevertheless, three hours and four minutes after we'd left London we were on the ground in New York, and whisked by helicopter straight to a New York studio, where I went straight on the American equivalent of *This Morning*, which featured Regis Philbin and Kathie Lee every morning with a live studio audience.

Like all American audiences they were great, very welcoming and very noisy, and because Regis had become the host of *Who Wants to Be a Millionaire?* over there, we had a great conversation. I'd met him before when he came to Elstree to watch us recording the show. He was that rare thing, a nice American game show host. His audience, though, were aghast that they, America, the country who invented the big money game shows, had been beaten to it by the Limeys in creating what was inarguably the most successful game show of all time. I proudly told the audience that it came from Britain, that we made it, and that we owned it.

It seemed that the US producers had sort of forgotten on purpose to tell America – where the show was a huge hit and was number one in their ratings for months – that it wasn't actually American.

We then went into another studio to do our second radio show where Regis, among others, was a guest, and then flew back later that night after a truly frantic and wonderful day. I was still on a high at the weekend when, relaxing quietly at home with the family, I managed to break my leg.

At first, we thought it might be just a bad sprain, but an X-ray revealed that it was in fact a bad break at the bottom of my left leg. They put me in heavy plaster from my ankle up to above my knee and told me that I would have to keep the plaster on for six weeks. I rang my boss that evening and told him the news. He pretended to be sympathetic, but was actually horrified. "Six weeks!" he said. "For God's sake, six weeks!"

I said, "I know, but there's nothing I can do about it. I can't drive, I can't stand, and they are telling me it's at least six weeks before the leg will have healed and the plaster can come off."

I think my colleague Neil Fox took over the programme the next morning, and although I got a lot of sympathetic cards and messages of goodwill from the listeners, there was no goodwill coming from the bosses at Capital. I settled in for my first day of sitting around the house bored stiff, drinking cups of tea, and later in the day a few beers, watching all sorts of rubbish on the television. It was the same routine on the Tuesday and the Wednesday, hobbling about with a crutch under my left arm, thoroughly fed up. It got to early evening on the Thursday and my mood became black. Eventually I picked up the phone and rang my boss. "I'm coming in tomorrow," I said.

"You what?" he said. "You're supposed to be off for six weeks."

"I know, but if you can arrange things your end I think it'll be OK. Jim can drive me in. If you can get me up in the internal lift to the studio and give me some sort of a chair with a few cushions on, I honestly think I'll be fine."

"I'm delighted," he said. "Of course, but do you think it's a good idea?"

"Yes, it is. And I'll tell you my main motivation for getting off my arse and getting into the studio. It's not that I'm missing you or my mates or even doing the show. It's because I'm actually beginning to care about what happens tomorrow on *Home and Away*."

ONLY THE VERY BEST GUESTS

Considering that I was not at all keen to sign a radio contract in 1984, it became a huge and very happy part of my life for the next twenty years. The breakfast show became a massive success. Before our arrival British people were used to just one single voice doing their morning radio, on virtually all stations, and usually a man. Michael Aspel, Terry Wogan, Noel Edmonds, and Les Ross on my local Midlands station BRMB, all ran their shows single-handed.

We listened to some tapes of what the Americans called 'zoo format' and adapted it to the UK market. This meant there was one central figure, a sort of circus ringmaster, but all sorts of other voices, from traffic to phone-ins, to weather forecasters, to larger-than-life newsmen, and obviously music and guests making up a much more frenetic sounding breakfast show. We weren't initially sure how well it would take off in the UK, but it became an absolute monster hit in London, so much so that this style of zoo format breakfast radio is pretty much what you hear now, certainly on the commercial stations, all over the UK.

At one point our breakfast show was getting bigger ratings than all the other morning shows in London put together, and of course we were loving it. We were very careful only to get the highest calibre of pop guests on the show. Although we played lots of music, we mostly did without bands and pop singers altogether. I'd met a lot of young bands over the years, particularly on *Tiswas*, and to be honest, apart from moaning about life on the road being exhausting, after they'd only done about a year of it (compare this to The Rolling Stones, Elton, or The Who) they really had little else to say, so we only ever had the likes of Phil Collins, Paul McCartney, George Michael and David Bowie as our guests.

I didn't know what to expect from Bowie. I'd never met him, but he strolled in all on his own, no big PR machine with him, and was one of the nicest, easiest-going blokes I had ever met. He said, "All I want to do is plug my album, because I'm obliged to, and get on a plane back to New York and see my new daughter grow up."

I said, "Do you mind taking a few live phone calls?"

"No, I'll do whatever you want."

So, we opened the lines, and a bloke came on and said, "Hello, Dave."

I interjected, "'Dave', for God's sake! This is Mr Bowie to you, or even Mr Stardust."

And totally ignoring me, the caller went on, "Dave, I remember spotting you, a few years ago on the number 27 bus coming out of Streatham Garage."

"Oh, yes," said Dave, aka Mister Stardust, "I remember that. I used to use that a lot. I also used to use the one that went from Crystal Palace down to Thornton Heath."

We then got a lady on, saying she'd seen David Bowie on a bus going out towards Hackney.

"Oh, yes," he said. "There's a studio over there. I used to use that bus route quite often as well." The lines were quickly jammed, so we then had a wonderful, occasionally hysterical morning of people ringing in with their memories of David Bowie on their local bus. Even a conductor called, who'd sold him a ticket. He loved it and went happily back to New York, presumably on a plane, as bus routes across the Atlantic aren't too reliable.

George Michael was another great favourite. He was very much a local boy, with a big family of Greek origin all living in North London. However huge a star he became he never forgot his roots.

He was extraordinarily upfront about everything, good or bad, that had happened in his life. He was booked as our star guest at our annual Capital Awards ceremony at a posh hotel in London, but because he had just, that week, been arrested for indecency in a public lavatory in Los Angeles, it seemed unlikely that he would turn up. Most artists' managers would absolutely forbid it, and the star would be told to keep their head down until it all blew over.

But George was made of sterner stuff. He turned up at the awards, smiling and shaking hands with everybody, signing autographs for all his many fans and he did the most amazing speech, talking very much upfront about what had happened and asking for his fans to forgive his indiscretion.

Of course, we did, and the wild applause he received made it clear that everybody still loved him.

He was also extraordinarily generous. We used to do our big 'Help a London Child' marathon fundraising weekend every Easter. All the money went direct to kids' charities in London and we were live from Saturday morning to Sunday at 4pm. One year, as we got late into the Sunday afternoon of the broadcast that had been going since nine o'clock the previous morning, we got close to raising a million pounds for the first time. But the minutes were ticking by, and by about half past three I looked at Annie and said, "We're not going to make it. We're going to end up with 900 thousand and something, no matter how hard I push the phone lines. If only all these people pledging money now had come in at any time earlier in the weekend. We're just not going to be able to get to the total we want." The money was pouring in, but at four o'clock I knew we had to hit the full radio network for another show, no matter how well it was going or how close we got.

At 4.55, with me running out of time and patience, and haranguing London to donate more money faster, Annie said to me, "Take that call there on line three."

I hissed at her, "Who is it?"

She said, "Just take it."

I took it. It was George Michael. He said, "Hello mate, how are you doing?"

"We're doing good thank you, but we really are tight for time, George."

He said, "Yeah, well, how close are you getting?"

"Well, we're just about up to £920,000, but I don't think we are going to make a million this year. Perhaps we can do it next year."

"No," he said. "You'll make it. Whatever the shortfall is, I'll make it up to a million," and put the phone down.

And the next morning at Capital we received a cheque from George made out to 'Help a London Child' for £80,000. A great bloke.

FEARLESS? OR PLAIN STUPID?

I got up at five in the morning for seventeen years to host the Capital Radio breakfast show. Nobody likes getting up at 5am day after day, especially in the cold dark English winter months, but I sort of got used to it once I was there. I loved it and, of course, I was very well paid for only four hours' work. And what's real 'work' anyway about playing Pink Floyd and talking bollocks.

In spite of my refusal to ever go to bed early I was only late four times. One time was in the early days when I still foolishly drove myself. I had a puncture in the pouring rain. So, at 5.30 on a black February morning, I had the Mercedes jacked up and I was underneath it completely soaked, changing the wheel, and some bloke really did come up for a soggy autograph for his wife. "Sorry, Chris," he said, "I can't stop and help. I'm late for work." It was so outrageous that instead of hitting him with a tyre wrench it actually made me laugh.

It was on another bitter cold February morning that I met the world's worst mugger. I parked up in the St Martin's Lane car park and made the short five-minute walk down to Leicester Square, when a skinny, red-haired bloke came out of a doorway and said, "Hey, you! I want your money."

I was still half asleep, but I can still clearly remember how very cool and articulate I was, probably for the very fact that I was still half asleep. At the time, it just seemed to me such a preposterous idea.

"You what?" I said. "Are you for real?"

He came closer, I think in an attempt to be more menacing: "You don't seem to understand. I want your money, man."

"No, *you* don't understand," I said. "I'm cold, wet and miserable. It's still pitch black and I would so much rather still be in my nice warm bed with my wife and have breakfast with my kids. I'm only here to make money, so why the hell would I give it to you before I've even started? Now f**k off before I break your legs!"

At which point he raced off across Leicester Square and disappeared into the dark streets. It was after a few more steps that the shock kicked in, and I realised he could have been carrying a knife, or anything, and I got the shakes.

I told the story later on the radio. The police came round and achieved nothing, and all the media latched onto was the completely irrelevant fact that he had red hair. One paper, and I'm sure you can imagine which one, ran the ridiculous headline:

"COULD IT HAVE BEEN CHRIS EVANS TRYING TO SABOTAGE TARRANT'S SHOW?"

Chris would not be jumping out of doorways at that hour. He would have been over the other side of London in his nice warm radio studio, or still happily in bed with Billie Piper.

Capital Radio Christmas parties have always been legends of misbehaviour. A private room full of disc jockeys, producers, production staff, and a mixture of assorted pop people, all winding down for Yuletide, with a free bar open all night, inevitably leads to all sorts of naughtiness, and thank God for that.

It's probably best to draw a discreet veil over the Kenny Everett, Roger Scott, Michael Aspel early years of Capital, except to say that it is a well-authenticated fact, that one well-known disc jockey, (neither Kenny, nor Roger, nor Michael, by the way, before you start guessing,) was caught with his willy in the office bulk eraser.

In my own years the Christmas parties were equally riotous, although as far as I know we managed to steer clear of sexually molesting any of our office equipment.

There was the year that Irish Betty from the canteen consumed enough Guinness to have kept the whole of the west of Ireland drunk for twelve months, then managed single-handedly to knock down the entire cloakroom and pass out with a great crash in the middle of the dance floor, to wild applause. Somebody plucked up the courage to give her the kiss of life and she was rushed off on a stretcher into an ambulance.

There was a wonderful moment when our personnel lady, Sue, watching the departing form of the unconscious Betty, said, "But why does everybody jump to the ridiculous conclusion that it must have been alcohol. It could just as easily be a stomach virus."

Yes, of course it could, and the moon is made of Camembert.

At Christmas time all radio station studios are swamped with freebies. Most of it is rubbish: T-shirts that you don't want, silly hats with a name of some obscure band on, and, of course, mountains of records, most of which will never ever sell.

However, there were also some very, very nice bottles of wine, whiskey, brandy, sent by the music companies to thank us for playing their records all year, and hoping that we were going to play lots of their records again the next year. The reality was, of course, that it really didn't make any difference. If the records were crap, no matter how good the brandy was, they still never got played.

I do remember vividly one year somebody sent me a case of twelve bottles of Blue Nun. Not my favourite wine and it stayed on my desk for several days in the run-up to Christmas. We had one of our particularly excessive Christmas parties when, by midnight, people were drinking bottles of paint stripper and sniffing dry cleaning fluid.

The offices at Capital were open-plan and anybody and everybody could walk through. The Christmas party came and went, the Blue Nun was still there.

I did a Christmas Eve breakfast show and then I was live until 1pm on Christmas Day – something I really enjoyed doing – and then, because I'd given up my Christmas, the company always gave me a few days off, so I didn't go back in the building until January 4th.

The office had been trashed, none of the cleaners had been in since before Christmas, and there were all sorts of strange half-open presents, half-eaten mince pies and assorted undergarments scattered all over the office. But – surprise, surprise – all twelve bottles of Blue Nun were still there.

I also remember that particular year, because I decided to demonstrate my lambada skills, and crazed with a mixture of Newcastle Brown Ale and Famous Grouse, decided to make the dance even more impressive, by picking up a huge twenty-stone producer mate of mine, Paul Pink, and carry him in my open arms across the dance floor as I tripped the light fantastic. Tripped was the operative word. After about four steps I went down like a sack of spuds, with the huge bulk of Pinky right on top of me, neatly landing with my elbow straight on top of a beer bottle.

I needed several stitches, and then had to press all the jingles and put on the records the next morning with only one working arm.

Of course, the thing about having a Christmas party at a radio station is that all the time the party is going on there is some poor DJ in the studio next door live on air, still desperately trying to hold himself and a radio show together.

Like most stations, Capital pumped it out live twenty-four hours a day, 365 days a year, so as the party got more and more out of control, there was always somebody thinking, "Oh, God! I'm on air in ten minutes. Oh well, I'll just have the one more beer."

This was also the same year, as I recall, when one senior member of management was caught pleasuring a female member of staff on the boardroom table. But I digress. This particular Christmas I decided not even to try get home for a couple of hours' kip before the breakfast show and took a room in the hotel right opposite the studios.

Having had a serious skinful, I fell into my room around three in the morning, only to find several of the girls and a couple of DJs had also decided to use my room as a handy place to put their heads down for a few hours. I was due on air at 6.30 and Richard Allinson, who was as drunk as a skunk, was due on at 4.30, in about an hour and a half's time.

I somehow set the clock for 6.20 and dived into bed fully clothed. I think I even had my shoes on.

The alarm screamed into my ear after what seemed like only five minutes, but there was no mistake, the clock said 6.20am. I felt like death. My tongue tasted like the bottom of a rhino's cage, and somebody appeared to be hitting me over the head with a shovel.

The room was full of people, several of whom I was sure I'd never seen before in my life, all sprawled comatose in various corners of the room.

Bewilderingly, I was stripped to the waist, even my shoes had disappeared, and horrifyingly, my jeans were completely soaking wet. "Oh, my God!" I thought. "This is the worst day of my life." Having drunk gallons and gallons of beer and whiskey last night, my bladder had finally thrown in the towel sometime in the small hours of the morning. My decrepit body had finally caved in. I was incontinent. From now on I would be a rubber trouser job.

I had no change of clothes, so I dried my trousers as best I could with a towel. Somehow I picked out a T-shirt and trainers from the motley selection of garments strewn across the floor, and soaked and ashamed, raced over to the studio which was two minutes across the main Euston Road. By the time I got there we were into the commercial break.

Allinson had been and gone. God knows what his show had sounded like. I suspect a lot of music with just the occasional slurred time check. The whole place stank like a brewery. I fired a jingle, cued the news, and I was on.

The next three and a half hours felt like an eternity. My diction was surprisingly clear (well, about normal anyway), despite the coating of fur on my tongue. My head stopped pounding after about an hour, several coffees, and a bit of The Eagles' 'Tequila Sunrise', which I actually played twice.

But all the time I was sitting there, still soaked and filled with shame, knowing that after years of appalling abuse, my body had finally given up on me. I kept hearing a voice saying, "You are now officially incontinent, you are a rubber trouser job."

People came popping in and out of the studio, handing me the usual bits of paper. Nobody said anything, but I was sure that they knew. I was certain I could see them twitching their nostrils as they passed me in the heated studio. And still the voice came, "You are a rubber trouser job."

At this point, Richard Allinson came in looking like death. He was unshaven, distinctly green around the gills, and his bloodshot eyes were peeping out of their sockets like two pregnant prawns.

"God you look dreadful," I said, forgetting my own disgusting state for a second. "I've never seen anyone look so dreadful."

"I feel dreadful," he said. "I've never drunk so much in my life." Then, rather sheepishly, he added, "Look, I'm really sorry about the bucket of water."

"What bucket of water?"

"Well, you know, *the* bucket of water. At about four we threw a bucket of water over you. I don't really know why we did it now, but it seemed a good idea at the time, and the amazing thing was that you never even stirred. We took your T-shirt off, but thought it best to leave your trousers on. You were completely drenched. I'm really, really sorry, it just seemed like a fun thing to do."

It was possibly the best news I'd ever heard in my life. I grabbed the bewildered Allinson. I pumped him by the hand. I gave him a huge bear hug. I may even have kissed him. I couldn't begin to explain to him how happy his mumbled apology had made me.

The rest of my radio show was a breeze – a sweet-smelling

breeze, I'm delighted to add. I was not a rubber trouser job at all. The listeners must suddenly have found me inexplicably chirpy. I put on Bill Withers' 'Lovely Day', followed by Andy Williams' 'The Most Wonderful Time of the Year', wished everybody a very merry Christmas and left the studio with my head, and my trousers, held high.

WEIGHT WATCHERS

We did quite a few live gigs from cruise ships. They were great fun. But, as I've already said, if you went on air from anywhere West the downside was that the show that started in the UK at 6am would probably mean going on air around midnight or into the small hours of the morning USA time.

We did a show for a week on a cruise ship in the Caribbean, which was great. I love the Caribbean. I saw lots of islands that I had never seen before and our quarters where we did the show from were great. The ship was one of those enormous Carnival cruisers that have about 3,500 guests, nearly all of them American, a few French, a few Italians, one or two Japanese, and not one single Brit. Which was good for us in one way, because they didn't know us, but the real problem was that we used to go on air at 1am from the ship for 6am UK London time. So, for the first hour, when most of southern England were just crawling out of bed and feeling distinctly delicate, the early part of the show was broadcast with a raucous background of drunken Yanks who had just come out of the bar, the disco and the casino, and were feeling no pain, shouting in the background. Also, it was mid-winter. Sitting in a car on a freezing cold icy morning, it must have felt very surreal at least, or probably more likely thoroughly irritating.

Then, of course, when we got up to the main rush hour time of between eight and nine in the morning in London, most of the Americans had gone to bed or had fallen drunkenly asleep and were sprawled around the decks.

One guy though, Dave, was an incredibly loyal fan. He just loved music and the English banter, and he always stayed with us for the whole show. His wife Maisie would wander in and out with a supply of drinks and sandwiches, and Dave just sat there munching away, happily listening to live radio and music being broadcast back to London. He was a really nice bloke and very funny, but it has to be said he was hugely overweight. He must have been close to thirty stone. He referred to it a lot. "Chris, I just can't seem to shake these pounds off." But it was clearly caused by overeating and the thing about these cruise ships is that you really can eat and drink twenty-four hours a day. He was a total salad dodger, he had clearly never said no to a second helping in his life, and his wife Maisie was not much smaller. They were lovely, but they were very unhealthily overweight, and it wasn't just them. The whole ship was full of American gentlemen and ladies of a similar size. I don't know how we stayed afloat.

America has more health advice, more health channels, and more health warnings on all their products than any other country in the world. Lots of Americans are obsessed with health. They jog every morning or walk everywhere at high speed, with those funny mileometers strapped to their wrists, don't have an ounce of spare fat on them and live seemingly for twenty-four hours in Lycra. It is a very health-conscious nation. But there is also an enormous proportion of Americans who choose to totally ignore all health advice and absolutely stuff themselves day after day.

The guys are usually the largest, but the wives are often large as well, and in most cases the children are also very large.

There was a jogging deck which was a sight to behold every morning. There were a few super-fit ones who pounded around the course for an hour or more every day and then went down, presumably, for some ghastly weight conscious breakfast of budgie food and lettuce leaves. The others, though, groaned and gasped all the way round the jogging deck, and frequently went purple in the face. I was always expecting at least one heart attack every morning. They would then undermine any good they might have done by going for the most enormous breakfast: sausage, egg, bacon, absolutely coated with ketchup, fried bread and/ or pancakes, hash browns, grits (whatever they are), and maple syrup over the whole lot.

Dave and Maisie were like that. He would listen faithfully until the end of each breakfast show, go for a little sleep, and then he'd get up and go for a nice big breakfast washed down by the first beer of the day.

He'd often say to us things like, "I think this excess weight is just hereditary. My dad and mum were big." Somehow I just bet they were. "In many parts of the USA it's almost obligatory," Maisie added. "We have done a lot of exercise on this trip, but it just seems to make no difference."

I'd make suitably soothing noises, but I was thinking, "Dave, Maisie, if you didn't eat so much food every day, washed down with so much alcohol, and put maple syrup all over your sausages, you might notice a difference."

One teatime we were making our way towards the studio to record a couple of things for later that night, when Dave was sitting there in a suit and tie with the most enormous burger. It was not a Big Mac, it was a Huge Mac. It seemed to be a triple of everything. There was a mountain of meat, three or four separate layers of buns, chips of course, and ketchup. He almost certainly had maple syrup on it as well. He munched happily away, we got on with setting up our outside broadcast rig, and he was halfway through a conversation about how much he liked Genesis music, when Maisie came in looking very smart, and said, "Hi, boys," and then turned to Dave, and said, "Hi, honey. Can we go in now?" Dave wolfed down the remainder of his mega burger and, arm in arm, they strutted their stuff into the restaurant. He was actually eating a burger while en route to his dinner.

And he wondered why he was a tad overweight.

BREAKFAST IN AMERICA

David Briggs and I spent an extraordinary week studying breakfast shows in America. I was the morning guest of the day on breakfast radio shows right across the States. I was introduced in various ways, including, "The man who sits at the wheels of steel every morning in London town playing the platters that matter" (streuth!); and "the hottest thing to come out of London, England since The Duchess of York." Could have been worse, I suppose. It could have been the Duke.

I was in another world. In fact, I was on another planet.

On a bitterly cold morning in New York at WPLJ, we were asked to come in no later than 3.55am, for God's sake, and Scott Shannon, the number one DJ in New York, was already in the studio with his breakfast show team, going through the papers, dreaming up ideas for the phone-in that day, and even writing and recording radio sketches at 3.55am. They weren't even on air until 6am. But this seemed to be how it worked all over the USA. I can't imagine any sketch being remotely funny at 3.55 in the morning, and to be honest, when they went out sometime after 6am, they still weren't.

But it was extraordinary how hard they worked, compared to people like me and Wogan and Evans back in England. Even the men in suits are there at that ridiculous time of day. They have pre-breakfast show meetings, and when they come off air at 10am, they have yet another meeting, and some days perhaps another meeting after that.

The competition for ratings is so savage, and there are so many stations, lots of the DJs are absolutely wrecked and have nervous breakdowns. Some are also totally dependent on a range of stimulants to get them through.

I had never arrived at a studio at four o'clock in the morning in my life, and nor had any of the grey men in suits – they usually arrive just in time for pre-lunch drinkie-poohs and then disappear until about teatime. They usually then leave to beat the rush hour. This is purely what some of the other DJs have told me. I was already long gone by then.

If I was parking my car as I heard the opening news jingle start playing at 5.59 and thirty seconds, that seemed to me about right. I would stroll in, wait for the end of the news, say something vacuous and play a tune while I got my brain together. And if my brain still wasn't together I'd play another one and I'm sure I speak for all the breakfast DJs in Britain.

If you ever hear a DJ say, "I'll let the music speak for me this morning," it means he's got a hangover.

I do remember once listening to Kenny Everett who'd made a very funny first twenty minutes of his show, recorded, as a standby in case he was late. It said things like, "I'm still not there yet, my darlings. I'm still on the Westway, or possibly in bed with my plumber." It was very funny, but of course when he actually was late, it would mean he'd have to record another one. If he had done that in America, he'd probably have been hung from the roof of the White House.

I did meet just one American DJ who didn't hang around for yet another meeting once his show was over, and that was the morning man at KKDA Dallas. He was a lovely guy called Tom Joyner. He did the breakfast show in Dallas, but then raced to the airport and flew straight off to do the afternoon show in Chicago, and then back to Dallas for a bit of sleep before the whole routine started all over again. That's a bit like me signing off at ten o'clock and saying, "I'll see you tomorrow morning at 6am, I'm just off to Moscow."

The rewards in America were very high, even then, and this is probably more than fifteen years ago. Fifty or more of America's main morning DJs earned more than five million dollars a year. Nowadays, for the lucky few, it's much nearer ten million.

There are new stations opening up all the time and there are old ones going skint all the time. The pressure is horrendous. Some of the sponsors they get are equally extraordinary. In Washington, one quarter-hour segment was sponsored by the local cats home, on another station the news was brought to you by "the best funeral parlour in this great town."

The best-known disc jockey in Los Angeles for years, Rick Dees at KIIS-FM, had a huge billboard of himself at the top of a skyscraper, almost as big as the famous Hollywood sign on the hills, and daily it would carry the message, "Did you hear what Rick said today?"

One station's brilliant idea was to hire a huge video screen over the main road into town so you could actually watch the DJs in their studio while listening to them in your car. This was abruptly ended by the traffic police, after a multi-car pile-up was caused by all the drivers staring up at the screen.

At the cheaper end of the market, Washington WRXQ, had their traffic guy out on the pavements with a sandwich board around his neck, with the name of the station in big felt tip, recruiting any new listeners that he could, and getting them to ring the studio live and tell the DJ where there were any traffic jams.

The promotion never stops. One FM station in Los Angeles gave a lady a million dollars for knowing her birthday. But of course now ITV give people a million pounds just for being able to work their telephone. It has become ridiculous and there is no skill factor whatsoever.

A lady in Atlanta, Georgia, won a golden retriever, although she kept squealing, "I'm really a cat person." And a man in Tennessee won a free carwash for life, even though he couldn't drive.

Then there were stations giving away liposuction, tummy tucks, facial Botox and breast implants. And this is a wonderful true story: one lady only got one half of a two-part question right, so presumably she now proudly sports just one huge silicon breast and the other one is still as nature intended. In the words of Mr Littlejohn, "You just couldn't make it up."

I sat in on the breakfast show at WGCI Chicago, where the main morning man was a big amiable bear of a guy called Doug Banks. He ate more during the breakfast show than most people eat in a month and was getting listeners to guess what flavour soup he was eating that morning. He made lots of revolting slurping noises over the microphone and, if anyone got it right, they won large sums of money.

It sounds ridiculous, but it worked mainly because Doug was actually very funny. There was a wonderful moment during his show when he announced the number of the car of the day. "If that's your car just dial WGCI inside thirty minutes and you can win 1000 bucks," only to have a worried policewoman ringing the show, saying that she had been listening, had checked her computer, and discovered that the car of the day was actually stolen.

The pace of these radio shows is verging on madness. A guy in Georgia had signs propped up in front of him, presumably written by someone in management, in big letters saying, 'Energy, Enthusiasm, Excitement, Keep it up, NON STOP'.

Over here that would make perfect toilet paper.

I did love their slogans. One said, "We are the fine dining station – for those who eat their young."

Another, "We are the frequency of delinquency."

And my favourite: "If you are in the car with someone who doesn't want to listen to KR and R, make the Mother get out and walk."

Marvellous!

There was a station coming out of Martha's Vineyard, one of the really wealthy areas of the USA, and it described itself as: 'Martha's Vineyard, where the billionaires go to get away from the millionaires'.

There is something for everybody in every town in America: Top 40 stations, Christian stations, Country stations, Dusties (which, apparently, are very old records with dust on), Easy listening, Reggae, Gospel, Non-stop rap, Hard Rock, Soft Rock, Hispanic Middle of the Road, whatever on earth that is – even non-stop 24-hour traffic reports.

Talk radio is still huge all over America, and is equally extreme. The strangest phenomenon of all on American breakfast radio for years is Howard Stern at XRL New York. He talks non-stop every morning. I don't think I heard him play a single tune, and he offended just about everybody for his whole show. He abused everybody on all other stations, all other disc jockeys, and everybody who was anybody on television.

He also makes a television show of his radio show, featuring non-stop four-letter words. Anybody silly enough to go on live is insulted. There are frequently serious fist-fights in the studio. Oh, and he is obsessed with oral sex and talks relentlessly about the size of his willy.

His best idea of fun is slagging off people with serious illnesses, like cancer or any sort of physical defect. I've listened and watched lots of Howard Stern, and I've never ever found him remotely funny. But I'm clearly out of step, because while we were there, Howard Stern was for the umpteenth time voted the number one DJ out of all 120 stations that were on air at any one time that year in New York. He's now on a five-year, 500-million-dollar contract.

The talk radio hosts seem to have no bounds; they offend everybody. They are almost beyond censorship. Politicians, sexual and racial minorities are all fair game. They literally rant away over their microphones, people are attacked often in totally unfair and unfounded ways that would have any station taken off air here in the UK. But America being America, it does have its own very aggressive form of censorship. Over the years several of the more extreme talk show hosts have been shot dead.

TEL

O ne of the true gentlemen I have ever met, and did shows with on occasion, was the late, splendid Sir Terry Wogan, one of the kindest and wickedly funniest men I ever met.

A dear friend of mine, Howard Mann, died very unexpectedly and tragically of a heart attack a few years ago. The family found him a plot right next to Sir Terry Wogan. As I said at the funeral, "Howard would have been terribly pleased with the idea of being placed next to the Irish broadcasting legend, but whether Sir Terry would actually relish spending eternity next to Howard, we shall never know. They were both great blokes and are both terribly missed."

Sir Terry had a really sharp sense of humour. He once looked at me and asked how old I was, and I dutifully told him. He shook his head, and said, "Christopher, the years have not been kind."

I loved what he did on the radio. I was a huge admirer of what he did on television, and he was great fun to be with. He and I both met a lot at Lord's Taverners functions. We were both past presidents, but also, considering that our combined ages were way over 100, for some reason whenever we got together, we behaved like naughty little boys.

We were both doing early morning breakfast shows, and because neither of us had a grain of discipline in our bodies, we would stay up as late as possible, misbehave as badly as we both knew how, and somehow get to work the next morning.

This came to a head one Taverners night, in front of various members of the Royal Family at The Savoy Hotel in London. After it was all over, Terry and I, along with our wives, found ourselves in a quiet corner of the Savoy bar. We both had to be on air at 6am the next morning, and Terry suddenly decided it was a good time for us to be drinking large port and brandies, a favourite tipple of us both.

We had several of them, told silly stories to each other and our yawning wives, laughed a lot, became sillier and sillier, and with our drivers waiting outside the hotel, and our wives saying, "Come on, you two. Drink up and let's go home," we threw caution to the wind and stayed up later and later and drank more and more.

Eventually, the bar staff started making noises that 'we really have to close', the wives continued to 'tut-tut', and we were forced to have just the one more and call it a night. A rather long night.

It was twenty past three in the morning. Somehow I got home. It was one of those dreadful nights, where as soon as I put my head on the pillow the alarm clock seemed to ring at once, and I crawled back into London to Capital Radio.

My driver was exhausted, I was exhausted, and I talked even more rubbish than usual for the next four hours of my life.

Lots of coffee helped. I think I did a lot of 'I'll let the music speak for me this morning' as well, and somehow got through until ten. The only thing that really kept me going was the wonderful feeling that somewhere across the other side of London, was a man considerably older than me, who must have felt much, much worse. I had a dreadful headache, and my mouth tasted like the bottom of a parrot's cage.

I went home. Jim, my trusty driver, went off to catch up on some twenty-four hours of missing sleep. Luckily I wasn't working later that day and I slept through till about teatime.

There weren't too many complaints about the morning's show, although funnily enough, I have virtually no recollection of any of it, and I forgot all about it and got on with my TV and radio commitments for the next couple of weeks.

Eventually I bumped into Sir Tel at yet another charity event, at yet another London hotel. We chatted and laughed and then I said to him:

"Oh, God. I've just remembered when we last caught up. What a night that was at The Savoy."

"Oh dear, yes, Chris," he said. "Oh dear, oh dear. I was in a dreadful state."

I said, "Well, we're only young once. What time did you wake up?"

"Oh," he said, "I don't know. I had a dreadful headache. I think it was about eleven o'clock."

"Eleven o'clock?" I said. "Well, somehow I was up at five. I wasn't quite late, but god knows what I talked about on the show," and then I blinked at him without any comprehension, and said, "So you must have missed your Radio 2 show altogether. What did the bosses say? I didn't hear anything about it. It usually ends up in the papers."

And with a wicked grin on his face, he said, "Oh no, didn't I tell you? I'd booked a week off."

The bastard, it was industrial sabotage. He'd stitched me up like a kipper.

THE INSURANCE MAN

After all the years of hurt with the English football team since 1966, and our on-off form particularly against Australia at cricket, at last in the year 2003 we won the World Cup, this time with our magnificent rugby team, who lifted the cup in a breath-taking final against the Australians in Sydney. They were all heroes, and as always, when we do something well, it lifts the spirit of the whole nation. So, when I was asked to present a World Cup winners celebration TV programme to a star-studded, all-celebrity audience, I jumped at the chance. I remember that when I said, "Please welcome the England rugby World Cup-winning squad," to the audience, I had never heard applause like it. The whole audience lost their normal composure, and a studio full of famous faces stood on their chairs and cheered and cheered as all thirty-one giant men came down the stairs through the audience. On they came, one enormous man after another: Martin Johnson, the captain, Lawrence Dallaglio, who is the size of an Alp, Mike Catt, Jason Leonard, Ben Kay, Richard Hill, Jonny Wilkinson et al, with their coach Clive Woodward. With no sign of a let-up from the cheering audience, they mounted the stage, all proudly sitting behind the World Cup.

It's a proper great big cup as well, not like the silly Ashes urn, and it was a glorious picture. Obviously, in the show that went out, we edited the applause down to maybe forty-five seconds, but in reality, in the studio, we timed it at over five minutes. It was wonderful, and of course the guys themselves and their families in the front of the audience were absolutely thrilled.

It was a great show, a wonderful celebration. We talked to the guys about what their memories were of that amazing afternoon. We talked to Sir Clive, we talked to the wives and the mums and the kids. We had all sorts of people coming on to pay tribute from all over the world, including Dame Edna, live from her home in Australia. Her praise was a little less than fulsome, very funny of course, as she always is, but with a distinctly Aussie we wuz robbed bias, but then what would you expect?

As the presenter I was loving it all. We had probably done about half an hour of the show when I noticed there was a funny little man in a suit, just quietly sitting, looking very ill at ease, out behind the screen at the back of the studio. Each time I came on or went off he was still there, and eventually, while a filmed item was going out, I said to him, "I don't want to be rude, but who on earth are you?"

"Oh," he said, "it's a bit silly really, but I'm from the insurance company."

"The insurance company? What exactly are you insuring?"

He said to me, in all seriousness, "I'm making sure nobody steals the World Cup."

Now, the World Cup was gleaming in all its golden glory right at the front on the stage, directly in front of the captain, and I said to this bloke, "The cup is out there in probably the safest place in the world. It's on stage in front of a live audience of about two hundred people. It's at the feet of the enormous Martin Johnson, and all around him are thirty of the biggest, baddest men on the planet. Nobody in their right mind is even going to contemplate stealing it. They'd last about a second before they were torn to shreds."

He said, "I think you're right. I do feel a bit redundant," and slunk off.

Needless to say, at the end of the programme, the World Cup was still there.

A PARKING MISDEMEANOUR

I'd had a very pleasant week off from filming, fishing down in France, and I was on my way up to Elstree Studios. Jane and I stopped off at our house in London, to sort a few things out, and pick up a few clothes. Because I'd come straight from my favourite French lake, I still had one of those great big roof boxes on the top of my car. They are great for extra camping gear, fishing rods, bait and so on, but above all, according to madam, for keeping the inside of the car from smelling too evil.

Jane wanted to get a couple of lamps from the electrical shop around the corner in Baker Street, and I said, "OK, I'll put the car in the garage and see you in the house."

To my annoyance, the car and the great big roof box wouldn't go into my garage. It was simply too high. This was a disaster because I couldn't remember how to take it off and I was planning to leave the car there for a week. I certainly didn't want to leave it anywhere outside on a meter, so I shot down to the nearest NCP, a few hundred yards down the road.

It was one of those where you don't pay on entry, there is just a bloke waiting at the box office down at the bottom. You give your keys to him and pay up on return. Well, that's what was supposed to happen anyway. This was one of those car parks that drop down below the street level and go down into a basement. So my vehicle and I, with the great big roof box on top, made our way carefully down the ramp. I didn't see anything about 'height of vehicle' or 'headroom' but it soon became obvious that my vehicle was simply too tall for the car park. In fact, much too tall. There were horrible clanging noises coming from the top of the box, and then a grating and a hissing noise, as I ripped some sort of a pipe out of the ceiling. I couldn't reverse back uphill, I was too far committed. It is almost impossible to describe the chaos that I caused in just a few seconds. I absolutely destroyed the roof of that small car park. I had torn out all sorts of wires, which came flying out of the ceiling, sparking. Then several great big fluorescent lights came crashing down on either side of me. There was a lot more sparking and flashing, and some sort of liquid came pumping out from above. I thought, for a few terrifying seconds, that it was petrol. Mercifully it was only water. Well, water but with maybe just a bit of oil. So, thankfully it didn't turn into one great ball of flame, but things were bad enough. I had absolutely trashed the car park.

I got to the bottom, completely shaken by what I had done, and I thought I had better lock it up, go and hand the keys in and try and make peace with the attendant. However, when I got to the little glass security box where he was supposed to sit, there was nobody there.

Now, to this day, I don't know whether he had gone to the pub, taken an hour off for lunch, was having an affair with one of Little Mix, or had been kidnapped by Hezbollah, but he wasn't there. And now I really didn't know what to do, but I thought the best thing was to get the hell out of it, working on the basic premise that I couldn't do any worse damage going up than I had done coming down. Wrong. Wrong. Wrong.

I actually managed to cause even more chaos on the way up, as more lights came flying out of the remains of the ceiling, great chunks of plaster fell off, and with an enormous clang the metal NCP sign, that hung proudly over the entrance to the car park, was ripped completely out of its sockets. As I drove away, I was shaking. I felt sick. I looked back in my rear-view mirror. I couldn't believe the damage that I had done in hardly any time at all. And there was absolutely nobody to even try to explain it to.

I rang my car dealers at home, and they explained to me, very patiently, how easy it was to remove the roof box. If only I'd made that call in the first place, but then life is never that simple. Well, my life isn't anyway.

I got back to my house, took the box off as instructed, parked up in my own garage and went upstairs to pour myself an enormous drink. I was actually in shock.

Jane came back smiling happily with two new lamps in her hands, and said, "Everything alright?"

"No," I said. "It's not. It's really, really not. You've only been away ten minutes, but you won't believe the chaos I have caused."

She listened aghast and eventually said, "I can't believe you drove away from the scene of the crime."

"But there was nobody there to tell," I bleated, pathetically.

I had visions of the bloke, the car park attendant, coming back from his brief lunch break, staring in absolute shock and horror at what had happened to his prized workplace, while he had only popped out for a sandwich, or whatever. It must have looked like there had been a nuclear attack.

I did nothing about it for twenty-four hours, because I really didn't quite know what to do, but of course, the situation resolved itself, because one of the few things I hadn't ripped out of the ceiling, apparently, was a very good CCTV camera.

Can you imagine when they watched the recording? "My God," they must have said, "it's Chris Tarrant! He appears to be having some kind of seizure." Seizure or not, I had a fairly terse, but actually very reasonable, letter arrive on my mat the next morning, along with a bill for £4,500 to be paid within seven days, or the matter would be put in the hands of the local constabulary. I was bang to rights. I promptly paid the four and a half grand; I think it was the most expensive bit of parking I've ever done.

MILLIONAIRE

W*ho Wants to Be a Millionaire?* was, of course, a monster all around the world. It was devised by David Briggs, my producer from the *Capital Breakfast* show. It was based on a game we did on the radio called 'Double or Quits', where you started with £1 and you went up to an infinite amount of money. Capital Radio, of course, panicked because they thought we were going to bankrupt this enormously rich company. Of course, that didn't happen, because basically once people got up to £64 or £128 they started to panic and would usually drop out.

Briggsy rang me out of the blue, a couple of years after he'd left Capital. He was trying to get a television sponsorship deal going. He had one or two programme ideas, but to be honest, he was struggling in the big bad world outside radio. He had an idea based on 'Double or Quits' and he wanted me to do a pilot.

I was busy doing Capital every morning and recording a new series of *Tarrant on TV*, which I'd taken over from the brilliant Clive James. It was a simple enough set-up: just the presenter with a pile of outrageous clips from all around the world and a television set.

Producers with a new host always want to change the set, or the music, or the titles, just to make their mark. So he said that instead of *Clive James on TV*, let's call it *Tarrant with a TV*.

"Brilliant," I said, "but everybody will shorten it to T W A T."

So *Tarrant on TV* it remained for the next ten years.

So anyway, I said to Briggsy, "I'll do a pilot, but I'm really too busy to do the actual show, if it takes off."

I can't believe it now, but I actually did nearly turn down *Who Wants to Be a Millionaire?*

He wanted me to do the pilot because we were both old mates, we'd worked together for a long time, and the only other person he really knew in television was Kenny Everett, who was, of course, completely potty. Having said that, Kenny presenting *Who Wants to Be a Millionaire?* would have been tremendous fun.

Anyway, as I did the pilot, I quietly thought to myself, "This is actually quite good. It's a really good format and I might even think about doing a series. It could last even for two or three years."

The original name for the show was *Cash Mountain*, which I always thought was pretty feeble, but then I didn't like *Who Wants to Be a Millionaire* either. I said that it would never catch on, which puts me on a par with the man at Decca who said there was no future for a band called the Beatles. I clearly knew nothing, because the show went on to become number one in 120 countries around the world.

I remember the morning after the first show. I was walking up from the studio to the Hilton Hotel in Wembley to do a few press interviews at lunchtime before the rehearsals in the afternoon, when a bloke with a lorry pulled down his window and shouted at me, "Phone a friend."

Now, over the years, I was very used to people shouting catchphrases at me in the street. Obviously for many years of *Tiswas*, it was usually all about custard or Sally James, and obviously then through the Capital Radio years, all sorts of things to do with my show on the radio.

But bear in mind, *Who Wants to Be a Millionaire?* had only gone out once anywhere in the world the night before, and within a matter of twelve hours, 'Do you want to phone a friend?' was on the nation's lips. Well, on one lorry driver's lips anyway. It did seem to me we were clearly onto something enormous. Which of course we were.

But – and I'm working this out, as I write – it's just over twenty years, four months, three weeks, and about twenty hours since I could last walk down the street anywhere in Britain without somebody shouting at me, "Hello, CT. Do you want to phone a friend?" Bearing in mind I haven't even done the show for five years, it still happens every single day. It's already happened once this morning when I went down to the petrol station just off the M4.

I honestly never mind it at all. Usually they suddenly get thoroughly embarrassed, go bright red, and think, "Oh Christ, he's probably heard that one or two times before." Yes, but make that one or two million times, and you're probably closer to the mark.

It's never been a problem, people are just saying they like the show, and phrases like 'phone a friend', 'we don't want to give you that', 'ask the audience', 'go 50:50', and so on, have become a part of world parlance.

I do love the ones who get it ever so slightly wrong. People sometimes shout things like, "Hello, Chris. Are you going to phone the audience?" "Phone the audience! How the hell would that work?"

But the catchphrases have been used in Parliament by people like Tony Blair, and Boris Johnson, and they were certainly used in the American senate by George W Bush.

I was talking to Bruce Forsyth once, who was always very kind about *Millionaire*, and asked him how did he handle all the cries in public of his catchphrases, because he must have created more than any man on earth: 'Good game, good game'; 'Cuddly toy! Cuddly toy!'; 'I'm in charge'; 'What do points make?'; 'Give us a twirl, Anthea'. The list goes on and on. He said he was fine with all of them, you just smile and become immune to them, except the one he said that drove him up the wall: 'Here kitty kitty'. Apparently they did a sketch on the *Generation Game* where somebody lost a cat and Bruce's cry of, "Here kitty kitty" followed him everywhere he went for the next two or three years.

Yes, that would become very wearing. So, when I say I don't

mind catchphrases, I don't … Well, mainly I don't, but a few years back on one of those rare, very hot days we do occasionally get in the summer, I was driving through Leicester, and I really desperately needed a beer. It was a baking hot day, I'd had a busy morning, and I wanted to get back down to London.

I don't usually go into pubs that I don't really know, because I do get a lot of very strange looks, and sometimes get dragged into even stranger conversations, but I thought, "I don't care, I just really want a beer." So I went into quite a busy pub, there were a few double-takes, but nobody actually spoke to me. The landlord hardly looked at me, and I said, "A pint of bitter, please." He stared at me in a gormless sort of way, started pouring out the pint. And you know that thing when you get the froth coming right up to the top and you are desperate for it? Well, we got to that point, with my tongue hanging out almost to my knees. He got right to the top, turned the beer glass over and said, "But we don't want to give you that." And poured it into the slop bucket. There was laughter right across the pub. I resisted the temptation to shake him firmly by the windpipe, was then given a fresh beer and a very nice lunch, all on the house. So I couldn't really complain.

Who Wants to Be a Millionaire? was an enormous show. Everywhere it went in the world, it went to number one, sometimes only for a few weeks, sometimes for years. It was just the format, which was so wonderfully simple. It just worked everywhere it went.

The most recent one I have heard of was Afghanistan, but it's almost certainly been banned by now. Anyway, when they were taking it, I discovered that the top prize of a million Kabuls, or whatever the currency is in that poor war-torn country, is actually something like £11,000. Now that doesn't sound a huge amount of money, but when you realise that the average annual wage in Afghanistan is about £200 per year, you do see that eleven grand is an enormous amount of money, probably one of the most cost-effective in the world.

The show has won literally hundreds of awards around the world and, as well as the awards, there were all the spin-offs. I remember when we did the CD-ROMS and all the video games. We sold thousands of them in this country, and I got mail saying things like, "Dear Chris, I've just won a million pounds on the Christmas CD version of *Who Wants to Be a Millionaire?*, but my cheque hasn't arrived yet. Is there a problem with the post?"

"No," I wanted to reply, "but there's clearly a problem with your ears. There seems to be solid bone between them."

I went into a pub in Cardiff once, when I was staying down there for a couple of nights, and they had one of those fruit machines that had the *Millionaire* game on. It was quite surreal. As I walked in, nobody looked up, but they had my face and my voice asking a question on the fruit machine. I tapped this bloke on the shoulder, and said, "That one's B, mate," and he turned around without looking up, and said, "Don't be so bloody stupid," and then suddenly said, "Oh, bloody hell, it's him." We laughed a lot and had a great evening.

We did nearly 700 shows, we gave away over 60 million pounds in prize money, just in the UK, and we had six, honest, million-pound winners. Well, five and a dodgy one. But more of him a little later …

Sometimes people go away with nothing. It only happened four times in the years I was doing the show, but it was always really sad. It shouldn't happen. They've got three lifelines. They should always get to at least £1,000.

However, there was one woman in America that went away with nothing on the first question, having used up all three of her lifelines. She was called Cathy, a 32-year-old housewife from Idaho. Regis, the American host, said to her, "OK, Cathy. Let's play *Who Wants to Be a Millionaire?* Question number one: 'Which of these is the largest, an elephant, a peanut, the moon, or an atom?'"

Surprisingly, Cathy decided to use her 50:50. 'Atom' and 'peanut' went, and 'elephant' and 'moon' remained.

Cathy said, "Wow, this has really thrown me, as it's taken away the two I was kind of inclined towards."

Nevertheless, she carried on. "I'd better 'ask the audience'."

"OK, honey," said Regis. "Let's ask the audience."

94% said 'moon'. Now this is a worry, because this means that 6% of the people in that audience thought an elephant is larger than the moon, but then this is the country that voted for George W Bush and Donald Trump.

So, she had only one lifeline left and she used her 'phone a friend'. She rang a friend called Betsy, who sounded clearly amazed that Cathy was on the show at all, but with only the two options left, Betsy screamed out, "For God's sake, honey, it's moon. Go Moon, baby."

They cut back to Cathy who, after a long pause, said, "You know that Betsy, she can be kind of dumb sometimes, and once in a while in your life, you have to follow your gut. OK, 'elephant', final answer." So, with Regis the host and the audience all banging their heads against the furniture, she made her way, still smiling and waving out of the studio, with absolutely nothing. But of course, America being America, the next day she was on every single chat show, radio and television across the USA, and probably made far more money than she would have done if she had even one single brain cell. "Tonight on Letterman, will you please welcome the stupidest woman in the world, etc, etc, wild applause and whoops …".

The list of people who came on *Who Wants to Be a Millionaire?* in the UK was extraordinary. Just about every TV personality in Britain: Stephen Fry, Jonathan Ross, Simon Cowell, Piers Morgan, Anne Widdecombe, Tim Rice, Bear Grylls, Vic Reeves, Bob Mortimer and his son, Eamonn Holmes and his wife, Dermot O'Leary and his dad, Frank Skinner, David Baddiel, Laurence Llewelyn-Bowen, the list goes on and on.

Terry Wogan came on the first time with Chris Evans. They were extraordinary. Mainly due to Terry's intelligence, they coasted to a million pounds in rehearsal, so we thought, "They're gonna be great." Come the show, and I don't know what happened, but it was a complete disaster, and they went away with 500 quid each.

Four months later, James Martin, the chef, came on, and for some incomprehensible reason he brought Chris Evans along with him. I said, "Why on earth have you brought him?" and James said, "Well, last time he went home with 500 quid," and Evans piped in, "So I couldn't possibly go home with less, could I?" But, do you know what happened? He actually did. James and Christopher left with 250 quid apiece.

Then there was Laurence Llewelyn-Bowen, who won 500 thousand, lost 500 thousand, then won 500 thousand all over again after consultation with VAR.

But one thing that really gratified me was the number of people that came on who would never normally go on a game show: Sir Alex Ferguson, Frederick Forsyth, Alastair Campbell, Greg Rusedski, Hugh Bonneville, Amir Khan, David Haye, Ronan Keating, George Michael, and Paul McCartney with his then wife Heather. The McCartneys were great, and after the show I remember saying, "They seemed a lovely couple, they are obviously really happy," which is one of the many reasons why I have never worked for Relate. There are a number of other reasons!

On the whole, though, I liked ordinary people doing extraordinary things. Judith Keppel was lovely, but decidedly odd. During rehearsals she came up to me, and said, "Do you stop the show at all?"

"Not really. We do stop for the amount of time it would take for commercial breaks, but otherwise it pretty well runs to time."

"Well," she said, "what happens if I faint?"

Puzzled, I asked, "Are you likely to faint? Do you have a fainting problem?"

"No, not at all, I'm just curious."

"Well, I suppose if you were lying on the floor at my feet, and I was asking questions that you couldn't answer because you were unconscious, yes we would probably stop, because it wouldn't be much of a show."

When you realise that, the next day, she went on to win a million pounds, it was one weird conversation.

I think my favourite was a guy called Dafyd Evans. He was very Welsh, his wife Blodwyn was in the audience, and the only thing we could find out about him was that he didn't live in the same house as her. They had two kids, so he must obviously have been at home a couple of times. His mum did their washing and Sunday lunch once a week, but otherwise they lived apart. I said to him on the show, after he'd got very happily to one thousand pounds, "So, Daff, why do you and your wife live in separate houses?"

"Well, to be honest," he said, "it's just a way of getting around the DHSS."

"Are you sure you're supposed to say that out loud on national television?"

He said, "Oh dear, I never thought of that."

NOTORIOUS

The contestant who is probably the best-known all around the world, from all those who have appeared on *Who Wants to Be a Millionaire?* is Major Charles Ingram. Sadly, he is remembered for all the very worst reasons. He appeared to have won a million pounds when he was on the show in September 2001, but some weeks later he was accused by the police, who brought the prosecution of cheating and fraud. He was subsequently arrested and in April 2003 he was found guilty of conspiring to cheat to win one million pounds.

Since the verdict, a documentary about the saga, called *Major Fraud*, was made and presented by no less than Martin Bashir, and was broadcast to 17 million in the UK and later on to huge audiences all around the world.

Charles was the third member of his family to appear on *Who Wants to Be a Millionaire?* The Ingrams seemed totally obsessed with the programme. Mainly, perhaps, as they saw it was a way of making lots and lots of money. Charles's wife, Diana, had already been on the show a year before his appearance, where she won £32,000. I remembered her as being quite fed up that it was only £32,000.

In the bar afterwards, I said to her, "£32,000 is a pretty good night's work."

"Yes," she said, "but I'm pretty annoyed with myself that I didn't beat my brother."

Her brother, Adrian Pollock, had also appeared on the show

earlier, having made an incredible number of phone calls to get on, and he too went away with £32,000.

So, when the Major appeared, I do remember myself and the production team feeling quite sorry for him. From what we had seen of him briefly in rehearsal, he seemed pretty amiable but unlikely to go very far.

He was asked this practice question: 'What country does Rupert Murdoch come from? England, USA, South Africa or Australia?'

He needed a 50:50 to answer this, which left just Australia and South Africa. He then had to phone a friend, who told him he was sure Murdoch was Australian, yet he went very stubbornly for South Africa. Murdoch is, of course, Australian. He is probably one of the most Australian people you are ever likely to meet, this side of Dame Edna.

We didn't fancy his chances at all. He seemed to have dreadful peer pressure from the rest of his family, to get at least £32,000, and frankly we didn't give him a cat in hell's chance of doing so.

However, he got in the hot seat after winning the last fastest fingers of the evening. When I asked him on the show how much he would like to win, he said the prophetic words, "I just want to hold my head up high." Which of course he did, at least for a while.

He seemed very hesitant and struggling from the word go, until he got to the question that would guarantee him leaving with at least £1,000. The question was:

The Normans, who invaded and conquered England in 1066, spoke which language?

A: German   B: Norwegian
C: French   D: Danish

Surely this is one of those questions that every schoolchild in England has known since they were about four years old. 1066 and all that. Charles finally answered it, but after a lot of hesitation. "I'm pretty sure it's French," he said. The whole country must have been screaming of course it's bloody French. He paused a lot on that question, but as the show went on, I realised that big, long pauses were very much his style.

On question number six, for £2,000, he got a *Coronation Street* question, and said, "Frankly, I've never watched *Coronation Street* in my life." So he used up a lifeline and asked the audience.

I didn't get any warning bells at this point, as I thought it was quite likely that a lot of serving army majors would not have time or the slightest interest in watching *Coronation Street*.

For £4,000 he got a question that certainly, if he had ever served in Northern Ireland, he would have known:

The River Foyle is found in which part of the United Kingdom?

A: **England**   B: **Scotland**

C: **Northern Ireland**   D: **Wales**

Charles said he thought it was Scotland. I knew this was the wrong answer, because I have fished the River Foyle in Northern Ireland many times, and I do remember thinking, "Poor sod, he is just going to go away with £1,000."

However, he phoned a friend who told him the answer was not Scotland, but Northern Ireland, and at that point the claxon sounded for the end of the show, and he was up to £4,000. But he only had one lifeline left when he came back for day two.

Now, to be honest, this is not at all the stuff of million-pound winners, nor did it ever cross our minds that he was likely to become one. Most of the big winners on the show in the UK haven't even paused for breath before they've got to about £125,000. So the idea of him plodding on from here with just the one lifeline left, seemed pretty hopeless.

Then a strange thing came to light at the end of the first day. Our main sound recordist said, "I don't know what was going on today, but there were really strange technical noises coming through the programme sound all evening. I've never heard anything quite like it before. We did manage to keep most of them from going out on air."

"Strange," I said, and thought no more of it.

Then Chris Burke, our studio manager, said he'd had trouble with one of the guys in the audience during rehearsal and during the programme. He kept walking about, going in and out of the studio during rehearsal, and whenever Chris went out to tell him he had to come back in, he seemed to be hastily putting away his mobile phone.

During the actual recording, he'd insisted on being seated in the VIP area which, interestingly enough, is the one spot where mobile phone interference could not be picked up by the TV sound engineers, and he had been spotted using his phone several times and admonished while he was there.

None of this meant much at the time, but much later we discovered he was Marcus Powell, Diana Ingram's other brother. He was interviewed by police after Ingram's arrest, but never actually charged. It was put forward, however, by the prosecution at the trial, that on day one they were trying to cheat by using messages sent out on the phone.

None of this was particularly significant at the time, although it now seems likely that they were trying some very technical way of getting the answers to Ingram on day one, but were forced to abandon it and go to a very much simpler method of beating the computer with the answers on day two.

The Major came back with £4,000, but with only one lifeline left. Interestingly, joining in the programme that day was a lecturer from Cardiff called Tecwen Whittock.

We all wanted the Major to do as well as he could, but we secretly hoped he'd just take £4,000 and go, as it was pretty unlikely he'd get to £32,000. It never occurred to any of us that he'd get much higher.

In fact, the odds against it were fantastic.

The first question he faced on the second night was:

Who was the second husband of Jacqueline Kennedy?

A: **Adnan Khashoggi** B: **Ronald Reagan**

C: **Aristotle Onassis** D: **Rupert Murdoch**

The Major now began what became his routine. Even though, after Jackie re-married, she was universally known as 'Jackie O', he admitted to being unsure and then went through each option verbally, out loud, with pauses between. This very significantly became a feature of the manner in which he answered every question that night.

He got to £16,000, then got a question about cheese, which after lots of umming and ahhing he again got to the right answer.

He then got the following question for £32,000. This, when we looked at the tape for hour after hour before the court case, was the first time we really noticed how manic his behaviour was.

Who had a hit UK album called *Born To Do It*, released in the year 2000?

A: **Coldplay** B: **Toploader**

C: **A1** D: **Craig David**

He could clearly now walk away with £16,000, with his head held high, or could go for it, get it disastrously wrong and go home with just £1,000.

I remember thinking, "It's a pop question, he won't have a clue," and of course he didn't.

He said, "I think it's probably A1 because I've heard my daughters playing them, but I've never heard of Craig David."

It was also equally obvious that he'd never heard of Coldplay or

Toploader either. The Major seemed inclined to go for A1, although eventually he decided to use his last lifeline, 50:50. I was hoping that A1 would disappear at this point, and then he could at least walk away with his pride intact, but infuriatingly A1 and Craig David were the two left. He kept saying "A1, A1, A1," right up to the point when I said, "Is that your final answer?" He replied, "Yes," but then equally quickly, he said, "No." He now paused and did something quite incomprehensible; he changed his mind completely, and said, "I think it's Craig David."

I said something along the lines of, "But you said that you'd never heard of him." And he replied, "I've worked out that 80% of my guesses are wrong, so I'm going with Craig David. Craig David, final answer."

The panel on the screen went to orange. There was no going back from that point. Craig David was, of course, the right answer, and Charles Ingram was now somehow guaranteed to leave with at least £32,000, the same as his wife and brother-in-law.

On the tape afterwards, it was interesting that there was no discernible coughing from Whittock at this point. But when Charles said, almost as a desperate throwaway, "I suppose it could be Craig David, whoever he is," you could quite clearly hear 'cough, cough' from Diana Ingram in the audience. And – surprise, surprise – suddenly her husband selected a completely different answer to the one he had been going along with.

By now the audience were in a frenzy, there was wild applause, and gasps of sheer disbelief, as this man, who appeared to know virtually nothing, seemed to be bumbling his way up to the big money.

He ummed and ahhed and paused his way up to £500,000, when he got this question:

> ## Baron Haussmann is best known for his planning of which city?
>
> **A** **Rome**   **B** **Paris**
>
> **C** **Berlin**   **D** **Athens**

Charles was confident straight away that it was Berlin. His logic was that Haussman is a Germanic sounding name. He rotated through the other three options and seemed to more or less dismiss them out of hand. He kept saying, "Berlin, Berlin, Berlin." But until he gave the other options, there was only silence from the area where Tecwin Whittock was sitting. Then he said that he supposed it could be Athens (nothing), Rome (nothing), Paris (cough, cough). Having deliberated for several minutes, that the answer should be C (Berlin), the Major suddenly made the most incomprehensible U-turn, and said, "No ... B, Paris. That's my final answer." He offered no explanation for his change of mind, nor did there seem to be any logical explanation to it. Paris was, of course, the right answer, and he'd just won about fifteen years' worth of the salary he'd earn tax free as a British Army Major. He had £500,000.

Now, over the fifteen years I fronted *Who Wants to Be a Millionaire?* there were probably no more than a dozen or so contestants who got to the £500,000 mark. Very few of them went on to win the million, several of them pulled out as this point, but there was a thing I said that always got a reaction.

"You have £500,000. If you go for the next question and get it right, you win a million pounds. But if you get it wrong, you lose £468,000. You do not have to play it."

Everybody I ever said that to suddenly had a look of real shock and panic. In their minds they had already banked £500,000, but the reality that they could still lose such an enormous amount of money suddenly hit home, and even if you're Gates or Branson the thought of losing half a million quid in the next couple of minutes was absolutely terrifying. And this only occurred to me months later while we waited for the trial: he never even blinked.

The Major was the only one who never paused for a second. "Yes, come on," he said. "Let's play." He knew he was going to go for it, and he knew he was going to get the right answer.

The question was:

A number one, followed by a hundred zeros is known by what name?

A	Googol	B	Megatron
C	Gigabit	D	Nanomole

Charles said, "I'm not sure." Inwardly I gave a big sigh of relief, thinking, "That's it, great, he's out of here." Nobody in their right mind would surely go for this unless they were absolutely certain. I joked with him, "Charles, you've not been sure since question number two."

"I know," he said, "but I think the doubt has now multiplied. I think it's a Nanomole, but it could be a Gigabit. I don't think it's a Megatron," and then uttered the famous words, "I've never heard of a Googol."

After his usual round-the-houses way of calling out each answer, he suddenly said, out of the blue, "I think it's a Googol. I think it's Googol. By process of elimination, I have to think it's Googol. I don't know what a Googol is, I don't think it's a Gigabyte or a Nanomole, and I'm pretty sure it's not a Megatron. I think it's a Googol."

There was a huge gasp from the audience, and in amazement I said to him, "But you thought it was a Nanomole, and you'd never heard of a Googol."

"Googol," he shouted. "Final answer." I genuinely didn't know if it was the right answer, until the screen went to orange and as I looked down, Googol was confirmed as the correct answer. I couldn't believe it, the mad Major was somehow a millionaire. When I told him he was right the studio erupted.

Diana came down from the audience and gave him a hug of delight, but clearly also surprise, and as they left the studio to hysterical applause, she said quite clearly, "No one is ever going to believe it. You are mad." These were meant to be private words between the couple, but of course both the Major and his wife were still wearing radio microphones.

It was an amazing night. It was probably one of the most extraordinary television programmes I have ever been a part of. Somehow, we had another million-pound winner. I went up into the box to say what an amazing show it was, but instead of the usual euphoric atmosphere, I found some very sombre faces and shaking of heads. Patricia, the director, said to me, "No, something is wrong. Something is definitely bloody wrong. Something was going on." I didn't believe it. Or maybe I didn't want to believe it.

I had to finish off the show, with one more contestant who bizarrely turned out to be Tecwen Whittock. He didn't do very well at all. In fact, he left with only £1,000.

I went back towards the Ingrams' dressing room, to congratulate them. But I was stopped in my tracks by Eve, a lovely girl in our research team, who was sobbing. "What's wrong, Eve?" I asked. "It's been the most amazing night." "No," she said, "the Major has just told me very forcibly to get out of his dressing room and eff off. I went to see them with a big bottle of champagne, but they were having this massive row."

Now, it doesn't matter who you are, and how unhappy you may be as a couple, if you have just won a million pounds, surely you would be in a celebratory mood. However, the screaming row was heard by Eve, the security guards, and Paul Vaughan my manager. He still berates himself for not putting one of those glasses to the wall to hear what was actually being said.

Theories on what they were rowing about came later, but one that the police and others put forward was that Diana Ingram had thought her husband had gone a couple of questions too far, and had blown the scam wide open, that perhaps they could have got away with it for many more years. However, this is pure conjecture, and it must be said there was no evidence of this.

I still went home on a high, but what happened in reality was that Paul Smith, the owner of the company, David Briggs, several others of the production team and the editors, sat through the tapes trying to find out what had happened. "He's doing something," Paul kept saying. "He's doing something." But they could spot nothing.

It was only when they were viewing it for a second time, at about a quarter to two in the morning, a young editor said, "Hang on, there. Hang on, there's a cough." The exhausted team said, "What are you talking about?" and he said, "There's a cough." They spooled back and there it was, from early in the second show, there it was, quite clearly a distinctive cough.

A clear pattern emerged. Ingram would call out each possible answer in his round-the-houses way, and to one of them there would be a cough, and he would then say, "Final answer." And that's what happened all the way up to and including 'Googol'.

At 4am the Fraud Squad were called in, and they agreed there was a case to answer, and the police brought a prosecution. Two years later we all went to court and all three of them were found guilty.

We were certainly very naive in those days. We didn't ever imagine anybody would come and try and cheat a million pounds in such great big close-ups on a game show, especially a serving British Army Major.

All we used to ask was, "Can you please all turn off your mobile phones." Since the Major's sensational appearance all show security has been completely updated and tightened. No mobile phones are allowed in the studio at all, and nobody is allowed to leave during the programme.

We have never got to the bottom of exactly what happened, but clearly if you do have a phone on and open in the studio the questions and answers can be heard from anywhere. You then only need a very basic search engine to find the right answer. The big difficulty then surely is getting the answers back to Tecwen in the studio to cough at all the right points. Quite what happened on the famous Craig David question, where it was the wife, Diana, who did the coughing we don't know. Something went wrong, but for all the later questions, certainly Baron Haussmann and Googol, it is very, very clear.

I have always said that I had no sense that anything amiss was happening on the night, and nor did David Briggs, my producer. But to be honest it was the most extraordinary programme with the audience yelling, cheering, gasping, and of course coughing, because people always cough in the heated confinement of a television studio.

There was an excellent drama made a few years later called *Quiz*, with Michael Sheen playing me, and the undoubted inference from the programme's makers that the Ingrams might just be innocent.

Watching Michael Sheen play me was really yet another bizarre experience. He is a superb actor, and not only got pretty close to my voice, but also from hours studying tapes, got all sorts of bits of my body language, which I didn't even realise I had. One thing is a sort of Fosbury flop, which I used to do to get in the chair each night, and also when I am standing with a contestant to go on, I do something very strange, waving one arm, like a sort of demented duck.

His performance was, as ever, quite brilliant.

The suggestion that the Ingrams were not guilty, however, was rather loaded by the way that Helen McCrory, superb as the Major's defence counsel, did a brilliant summing up, protesting the Major's innocence. However, the drama completely omitted to show any summing up by the prosecution. This would never happen in a court of law and certainly didn't happen at the Ingrams' trial. I do remember the prosecution summing up, as a brilliant drawing together of all the loose strands, all of the police evidence and then very clearly to the jury stating that all three were guilty. Which is, of course, what the jury found.

Although I saw nothing at the time, as I was too focussed on what on earth was happening before me to even think about somebody coughing in the background, I have now sat with the programme's makers and the fraud squad for so many hours viewing tapes, that I am convinced in my own mind that he is guilty as sin.

The suggestion at the end of *Quiz* that the Ingrams might be considering an appeal is to me absurd. It was twenty years ago, and to stand even the slightest chance of getting an appeal they would have to come up with some sort of new evidence. As far as I know, there is none.

Apropos of nothing … A footnote:

I was filming one wet winter's morning down in the Savernake Forest in Wiltshire, when a woman appeared out of nowhere wanting an autograph, which I happily signed. But then she added:

"Your mate's up the road today."

"Which mate's that?" I asked.

"You know … That cheating major."

"Well, he's not exactly my bestest mate," I said. "Not exactly top of my Christmas list. But anyway, what's he doing?"

"Oh, you'd have loved it. He's at a car boot sale with a sign up saying, 'Forced to sell all my worldly goods by ITV'."

"That's rubbish," I said. "It should say, 'Forced to sell all my worldly goods for being a cheat'."

"Anyway," she continued, "me and my best mate found one of those *Millionaire* board games at another stall and took it over to the major and asked him to sign it."

"Oh my god," I said. "How did he take it?"

Laughing manically, she said, "He told us both to piss off."

ROUND THE WORLD

The simplicity of *Millionaire*'s format, and the sheer human drama, made it a success not just in the UK but all around the world. The simple idea caught everyone's imagination on an unprecedented scale.

Before *Millionaire* it was very, very difficult, in fact almost impossible, to sell television programmes to other countries in the world, particularly America. Yet for the USA, the country that invented the game show, importing the biggest game show of all from the UK was a bitter pill to swallow, but swallow it they did, and of course it was a huge success across the Atlantic.

The show's been sold to over 120 countries as far apart, both culturally and geographically, as Japan, Kazakhstan, Russia, India, Colombia, the Philippines, Germany, South Africa, Venezuela, Israel, China, Kenya, the USA and Australia. It was the first western game show ever bought by a Japanese television channel, in this case Fuji. It has also gone to number one in the ratings in every country where it's been transmitted, sometimes only for a short time, but sometimes it has stayed there for month after month after month.

It has won the Queen's Award for Export Services to British Industry, and the style of it has spawned all sorts of other shows, like *The Weakest Link*, that in look, if nothing else, was very similar and almost certainly would never have got on air in the countries that took it had *Millionaire* not paved the way first. Anne Robinson, the black witch of game show hosts, and the malicious, unkind *The*

Weakest Link were the perfect antidote to cuddly, caring *Who Wants to Be a Millionaire?*

The ratings in the USA reached over 32 million viewers. The first celebrity show they ever did in the States gave the ABC network its biggest audience for almost twenty years.

There are so many great stories about contestants from around the world. One that I love is of a struggling American musician down to his last fifteen dollars in the world. He'd phoned in an almost last-ditch attempt to get himself solvent and when he learnt he had been called onto the show he hadn't even got a decent pair of trousers. So he told his local branch of GAP that he was going to be on *Who Wants to Be a Millionaire?* and they leant him a nicely ironed new pair. Quite how much notice the audience ever take of a contestant's trousers I'm not sure, but anyway, wear them he did, and he looked very nice. He left the show 250,000 dollars better off and was given a hero's welcome in GAP with wild applause and whooping as he returned the trousers on his way home.

Overseas versions of *Millionaire* are deliberately, virtually identical to the UK original. Celador's international team used to go to each country where they had sold the programme in order to advise them how best to produce it successfully, but after that they were on their own. Lots of countries wanted to veer away from the original format, but Paul Smith and Co were adamant: "We know this is how it works best. If you want to buy it you've got to take it as it is."

The Japanese almost certainly would want the contestants to have live snakes going up their trouser legs, and boiling hot chip fat poured over their heads, but Celador would have none of it.

The host still managed to berate the hapless contestants in screaming, abusive Japanese, and whereas those ridiculous pauses I used to do lasted for, say, seven or eight seconds, the Japanese host has been known to keep the pause going with the contestants pouring sweat and crossing themselves for almost a whole measured minute.

Because they had all been sent the UK tapes to make notes from when they first bought it, most of the foreign hosts tended to mimic exactly what I did in the UK. They point their fingers in the same way, they have the same poker face, they have the same intonation, no matter what the language. They all, of course, got a full set of master tapes of our version, which means, sadly, they had to sit through hours and hours of looking at me.

After a couple of years of the show airing first in the UK, and then increasingly around the world, we had a wonderful weekend in the south of France where all the hosts and production teams from around the world came for a mammoth conference. Well, a mammoth piss up actually. I did a spoof *Who Wants to Be a Millionaire?* with all the various countries' hosts taking part, except for the Hungarians, who for some reason got to the airport in Nice, but were never ever seen again.

There was real bonding between all of us. I got on like a house on fire with Eddie the host from Australia, where it's still on air, and probably one of the longest running of all, as well as American host Regis Philbin, who became a great friend.

My favourite though was a rather short and very young guy who was the host of the show in Georgia. He kept following me around all weekend, hanging onto my belt and calling me 'Daddy'. Don't ask, no, I'm not checking my blood group. And I refused a DNA test. Of course I'm not his father. He was a lovely young guy, but I couldn't shake him off. I had to check that he wasn't in the overhead locker on the flight home.

It's quite extraordinary watching the show, as I have done, in all sorts of foreign languages, because usually they keep the expressions like 'phone a friend' or 'we don't want to give you that' in the original English. I watched the Kazakhstan host when I was out in Almaty, the capital, jabbering away incomprehensively to the screen in Kazak, but then suddenly shouting, "Go 50:50" or "Ask the audience" in English, before carrying on with his high-speed Kazak ramblings. It was yet another strange out-of-body experience.

On the eve of the presidential elections in Russia in 2000, six candidates were invited to take part in a one-off charity edition of the show. Can you imagine having a collection of election candidates here in the UK? Having said that, Corbyn and Boris would make for brilliant TV viewing, as would Trump, Hillary Clinton and Joe Biden in the US. Four of the candidates actually did take up the offer, although surprisingly President Putin said, "Het." That's 'No', by the way.

Russia has no real history of TV game shows and there were big problems with the Russian studio audience. After a few nights it was clear that 'ask the audience' was proving disastrous, because the majority vote was invariably wrong. It emerged that the audience didn't see why they should help the contestant in the chair, and were deliberately giving the wrong answer, jealous that they hadn't made it into the hot seat. This created a massive job for the producers, re-educating each and every audience member before they came into the studio.

In Saudi Arabia, there were similar problems where many of the early contestants absolutely refused point-blank to use any lifelines because it is a mark of shame in many Arab countries to ask for help. All very laudable, but of course it meant that in many cases, virtue intact, they went home with sod all.

The Hong Kong television company that bought the programme wanted two hosts, one to ask the questions under the spotlight and one to participate with the audience. The UK producers pointed out that this would be very confusing and disruptive, and eventually they begrudgingly agreed to use just the one.

Each Chinese programme recording was filmed in Hong Kong, but broadcast from Beijing, so the tape had to be sent for government censorship before it was screened, and three days before the first show was set to be transmitted, the communist Chinese government decided to slash the top prize money by 50%, so it became something like *Who Wants to Be Half a Millionaire?* Still a lot of money, but somehow not the same.

In Malaysia, the host is an actor famous for playing the role of millionaires in TV dramas. For this and no other reason, he was chosen to play my role on *Who Wants to Be a Malaysian Millionaire?*

The Venezuelan host is also the president of the TV station, and in Chile the programme is presented by a man called Don Francisco, a famous South American TV star who lives in Miami and flies into Santiago by private jet for each programme. He wanted to turn it into a chat show, because, he said, "That's what my audience want from me." It was pointed out to him by the makers of the programme that, no matter who he was, if he wanted to present *Millionaire* he was obliged to host the game, and the game only. Begrudgingly, Chile TV still bought it, he still hosted it, and it was a huge success.

In Colombia, many contestants are very wary of appearing in the millionaire hot seat, understandably, in this very volatile, dangerous country. They are terrified that having won a huge amount of money in public, their chances of getting out of the studio alive are considerably reduced. Those who have been brave enough, or perhaps foolish enough, to go on the show, and have won big money, have been known to change their name. Some have even had plastic surgery after their appearance to off-set the very real danger that they could be murdered or kidnapped for their winnings.

The first series in the Middle East was bought by Egypt. Initially it was filmed at Elstree Studios, in between our own recordings, using our set, our camera crews, even our warm-up man, Ray Turner, whose knowledge of Arabic is non-existent. Contestants were flown into Boreham Wood from Cairo, and a local Arab audience was recruited for each programme and paid a hundred quid a go.

In Turkey, a million Turkish lira was worth less than a pound, so the show was re-named to *Who Wants to Be a Zin Zin Zillionaire?* Also in Turkey, some of those who had been invited onto the show visited their local priest beforehand to ask him how much money they would win. Human nature being what it is though, even if the priest told them they wouldn't win much, they ignored him and had a go anyway, just on the off-chance.

When the Israeli show had its first million-pound winner, the host danced around in the middle of the studio, stripping all his clothes off, as a mark of respect. Funnily enough, it was something I never did in front of Judith Keppel.

In Iceland, the population is only something like 250,000, so they had to reduce the number competing for the hot seat from ten to six. There was real fear that in only a few years they would literally run out of people to compete on the show. One of the country's favourite contestants was a priest from a little village. He promised his congregation that, if he won the top prize of a million Krona, he would build the village a new church. He did win the magic million, and I rather expected this to be the moment that he said, "I was never that religious anyway," and disappeared to Las Vegas. In fact, he was as good as his word, and he built the church.

A German lady declared, "If I get all fifteen questions right, all I want to do with the money is divorce my husband." She never actually did make it to question fifteen, but she went ahead and divorced him anyway.

In the first year of *Who Wants to Be a Millionaire?* in Bulgaria, the nearest television studio was over the border in Romania, and every week a convoy of buses would leave Sofia and head to Bucharest, the Romanian capital, to record a whole string of shows. There were eight programmes' worth of contestants, plus friends and family, and each bus was emblazoned with the show's logo and branding, and were dubbed the 'Millionaire Caravans'.

In Georgia, where my funny little friend came from ("You my daddy"), they had tremendous setbacks before they could ever get the show on air, but showed amazing tenacity. The country has constant power cuts, sometimes as frequently as every five minutes, so occasionally it could take a whole day to record one episode. The facilities in the studios are extremely basic. For example, the lift only carries five people at a time, so getting the contestants, the host and the audience to the set is a tedious process. However, it was well worth the effort, when it eventually aired, as it was the most successful show ever transmitted on Georgian television.

Also, of all the tens of thousands of contestants around the world who have appeared on various international versions, one of the most amazing winners is a guy from that very country of Georgia. Paraplegic and with a life-threatening lung condition, he had to have his temperature regulated twenty-four hours a day, and for six years had not left the safety of his own home. Having been called to appear on the show, he arrived at the studio by ambulance, and once he was there the temperature on the set had to be monitored constantly by the doctors. A specially developed machine was to be set up to enable him to do fastest finger first, which incredibly he won against the other contestants. In the hot seat, he won the Georgian equivalent of £125,000. The money completely changed his life for the better. He was able to buy his first ever computer, and having been unable to leave his house for years, he is now in contact with new friends all over the world via email and the internet. He became a real celebrity in Georgia and was even asked to open an art exhibition. When doctors advised him it was too dangerous for him to leave his temperature-controlled flat again, a crew was allowed to film him in his home, making the official opening speech.

And finally, the Indian show is made in Bollywood, the Indian equivalent of Hollywood. The host was a really impressive figure called Amitabh Bachchan, who was a legend in Bollywood films, known and loved all over Asia. In fact, many of the contestants were more interested in meeting him than in winning the prize money. When he came over to the UK, as most hosts did in the first few years, to observe the show first-hand and make notes, he had two bodyguards on either side of him, seemingly round the clock. He and I even went to the loo at one point during the rehearsals, and his bodyguards came with us. I took the urinal on the left, and they took the three on the right.

He was an incredibly decent guy, as tall as me, with a great big booming voice. He said to me one afternoon, "Chris, do you think I could have the great honour of sitting in the audience tonight?"

"Of course you can," I said, and the floor manager went off to sort it out.

However, on the night, he sat quietly in the audience with a bodyguard on either side. Nobody recognised him and nobody bothered him, until all of a sudden a couple from Southall who were sitting in the front turned around and screamed, "Oh my God, it is him, he is here amongst us," and started climbing over the seats to get his autograph. The bodyguards did what bodyguards do, we had to stop the show, and the studio was in chaos for several minutes. Eventually Amitabh and his bodyguards had to go and sit up in the directors' box and watch the show from there. The other 198 members of the audience had no idea what any of that was about.

When the first show finally transmitted in India, Hindu priests were brought into the studio, ringing little bells and sprinkling holy water to bless the set. Everybody, including some of the lads from Celador, who were out there to help the first show get made, were anointed with a little red dot on their foreheads.

The gap between rich and poor in India is enormous and getting bigger all the time. There are now more billionaires in India than there are in America. They play for a million rupees, which is about £100,000 in sterling. It doesn't sound a huge amount, but with a hundred grand you could probably buy half of Calcutta.

A lot of people living in India's slum districts have no electricity, let alone a television, so a great tradition has arisen whereby hundreds, sometimes thousands, of people watch the programme on a single massive screen on the beach. It is the most popular show in the history of Indian television. There are no taxis to be had when it's on air. Everybody stops and dives into the nearest house or beach to watch it on TV.

Bollywood and cricket are the other two huge events for mass viewing in India, and the audience for both were absolutely savaged when *Millionaire* first came on air.

I've caught up with Amitabh a couple of times since. He said the show has made him even more successful, and presumably even richer, but also now any chance of him having a private life is completely finished. He has several very nice sports cars, but he cannot go out anywhere in them after about four in the morning because people just take off the wing mirrors, windscreen wipers, even bumpers, to keep as souvenirs. The only other person this happens to in India is Sachin Tendulkar. They are probably the two best-known celebrities in a country that is obsessed with fame as a way out of abject poverty.

I interviewed Amitabh on his last visit to the UK. He loves it here as he can mainly go around unrecognised and undisturbed. He told me, with a hint of regret, that the ratings for the programme in India are no longer quite as huge as they were initially. But bear in mind, at this point, it had been running in India for over ten years. He said to me with genuine sadness in his voice, "It is a great shame, we always knew it would happen, but the audiences have begun to fall away. Last weekend we were down to only 230 million." Unbelievable, and this is in a country where only about a third of the 1.3 billion population have television sets.

TINY DANCER

Toby, my idiot son, the runt of the litter, all six-foot-five of him, rang me in hysterics one day, and said, "Dad, have you read Wikipedia this morning?"

I said, "Of course I haven't. It's a load of old rubbish."

"Oh no, it's not Dad. There's the most fantastic story there today about you."

"Oh yeah? What am I supposed to have done now?"

He said, "You haven't done anything for once, but apparently you've got Perthes disease, which means that your feet are very small, and that they haven't really grown much since childhood. You've got size two feet," he guffawed, "and when you go on *Who Wants to Be a Millionaire?* you have specially built-up shoes to enable you to get up into the chair. But also, this weekend, you are hosting a Perthes disease conference in Salford for similar sufferers from all over the world."

Now, this is complete and utter nonsense. I am six-foot-two, have size ten feet (which I think I've had since I was about 14), I do not need built-up shoes, and I never did address a conference on Perthes disease in Salford, or anywhere else.

I am not even sure that Perthes disease exists. Toby continued to howl with laughter. I must admit that I too found it very funny, but also you do wonder who on earth sits down for Wikipedia and goes, "I know what I'll do today, I'll just make something up about Tarrant." He was probably a former editor of *The Sun*.

But why choose me? And why, off the top of your head, would you just invent the fact that I've secretly been hiding size two feet all these years? It did cause huge merriment to all sorts of people for a few days. Then, I suppose, thinking enough was enough, it was taken off. No harm done.

I still do sometimes wonder though what sort of a strange creature would concoct such a bizarre idea, commit it to social media, and send it off around the world.

And people say I'm weird!

Making Phil laugh.

Not quite the blond one in the middle they're used to.

Looking bewildered.

Why do DJs have to be so loud.

I do make a truly hideous woman.

With Rick Parfitt working! On a yacht in Monaco.

George Michael took over my radio show.

Party in the Park live to 100,000 people.

Just chewing the fat with the future king.

They gave me a lovely spear to take home.

With Howard our newsman, live from the top of Sydney Harbour Bridge.

He told me
he was once
mayor of
Cincinnati.

Mmmm … Betty.

The funniest man
in the world.

"God."

That chair was my home for the next 15 years.

Vic 'n' Matt looking almost sensible.

Mr and Mrs Wossie …
He said he'd "never been so nervous."

Giving Fergie
the hairdryer.

George and
Ronan were
loving it.

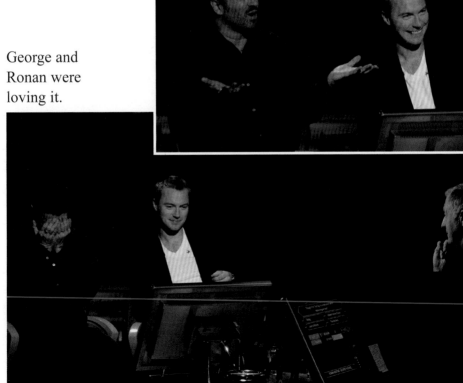

OMG! Those sideboards!

The obligatory cheesy grin.

Really, really, cheesy.

Even cheesier.

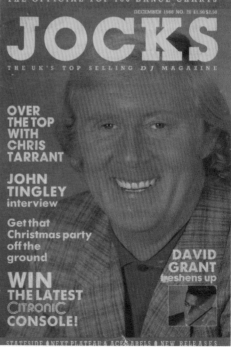

Rankin wanted to get
away from the cheesy
look … brilliant.

Either getting on or getting off.

Only an idiot would take his shoes and socks off in Siberia.

I'm six-foot-two.
These trains are huge.

Mike and I terrified on tiny ledge on north face of the Eiger.

Bathing in mu
well, I hope it

Looks beautiful, but was absolutely freezing.

This coat was a lifesaver in minus forty.

We only saw one other car all day.

Monsoon India … Breathtaking engineering.

A passing tramp with a carp.

I'm thrilled.
Fish very bored.

With my baby son …
He's six-foot-five now.

With dear Dad at the Royal Albert Hall.

At Buckingham Palace.

To get a doctorate you have to put all this on.

My OBE is in the hat.

He thought my head was a public convenience.

CONGO

I'd never worked for Channel 5, but when a very amiable and persuasive guy called Andrew O'Connell invited me over to chat about a possible new series of documentaries for them called *Extreme Railways*, I was very interested.

I'd been living in television and radio studios for the best part of fifteen years, and it would be great to get back to filming, which was how I started out. And although I'm not a train spotter as such, I love railways. I am fascinated by how they were built in the first place, often overcoming the most impossible mountainous or desert terrain and often ravaged by typhoid, dysentery, cholera, snakebite, sandstorms, solid ice avalanches, terrorists, even man-eating lions. Without the railways in many of the more remote parts of the world, most families would live and die having never travelled more, on average, than five miles from where they were born. Also, these incredible feats of engineering were usually developed by the British, 150 years ago, when we were still quite good at things. Most things actually, come to think of it. Whatever happened?

My enthusiasm was dampened a little when I was told that the first location they were planning to visit was the Congo. "Isn't it one of the most dangerous places in the world?" I had the temerity to ask in our first production meeting. "No, no, no. We're going to the Republic of Congo," I was told, "not the Democratic Republic of Congo. That's the really bad one."

I was not very reassured by this explanation of degrees of badness, and real, real badness, and I remember wondering why we couldn't go somewhere not bad at all, somewhere nice and safe. But then the series was to be called *Extreme Railways*, not *Nice and Safe Railways*!

"Actually, I was kidnapped there the last time," added Sam, our completely barking Irish cameraman, "by a load of big scary teenage kids with Kalashnikovs. It was really frightening. At a checkpoint, we made a run for it, expecting a bullet in the back all the time, but the kids who kidnapped us were too busy shouting at the police. Lucky, eh?"

"Yes," I said, "really lucky," thinking, "What the hell have I talked myself into?"

Roz, our director, who was in love with Roger Federer, and as far as I know, still is, was due to fly out the next day on a recce.

"OK," I said. "If you get back in one piece, we'll go and make the film in the Congo. If you don't get back in one piece, we'll go somewhere else like Monaco or Rome, or even Moreton-in-Marsh." They sounded so much more attractive. I remember thinking, "I'll never see the mad old bat again," but sadly, a week later, she re-appeared all in one piece, and I thought, "Oh sod it, Congo here I come."

After a really scary Air France flight through central Africa (Will somebody please tell me what the hell 'clear air turbulence' is? Whatever it is, it freaks me out), we landed bouncily, but happy to be on the ground at Pointe-Noire, one of the biggest ports in West Africa. Getting through passport control was chaos and getting through the yellow fever vaccination area was even more manic. It was very heavily policed. Luckily, all my jabs were up to date, but there was no messing with the Congolese. If you had no proof of current yellow fever inoculations, you were either pointed very roughly towards the next flight back to London. Or much, much scarier, you were taken by one of the three men standing at the foot of the escalator in white coats, holding up not particularly clean looking syringes, into a little tent and given a yellow fever jab on the spot. Mercifully, they accepted my paperwork, as nothing on earth would have induced me to risk one of their horribly blunt, and clearly second-hand-looking needles.

We got to the railway station in the morning for a 6am start. I had to produce my passport at the ticket office, which was a new one on me, although over the years, outside the UK, I've now come to accept it as pretty normal on the railways of the extreme world. Apparently, the train was due at 11am and was billed grandly as the Congo Ocean Railway Express. The COR Express was the pride of their fleet and we would soon be racing across the Congo to the capital city Brazzaville. Having got over my early misgivings, I was almost looking forward to the whole adventure. However, 11am came and went, then 11.30, 12 noon, and then 1pm, and although the station was packed with hopeful travellers, not one single train appeared.

Sometime in mid-afternoon one single locomotive came out of nowhere, but it was pointing in the wrong direction. There were no announcements and all day there had been absolutely nothing on the information board except clearly weeks-old information all written in chalk.

I didn't want to get on the wrong train, but I found a very important looking gentleman in a splendid hat along with gold epaulettes and a shiny uniform, who said, "Yes, indeed, sir. That is the right train. It's just turning round, then it will be off to Brazzaville faster than you can say Nelson Mandela."

I never saw that train or that man in those gold epaulettes and that splendid hat ever again in my life.

This was to become a pattern.

The hours dragged on, the only locomotive had disappeared, and slowly so did most of the crowd. There was no sign of the 11am to Brazzaville, and by 11pm we retired to the hotel bar.

The hotel was supposedly one of Pointe-Noire's finest. It had a huge five stars sign greeting us as we walked into the foyer. I don't think in any other country in the world it would have got an RAC two spanners. I had been told there was virtually no wildlife left alive in Congo. Well, there were plenty in my bed and they all had nasty little teeth.

The train had been scheduled for the Saturday morning, but by Sunday morning there was still no sign of the pride of the Congo Ocean fleet. I had to be back in London in about ten days' time to record another episode of *Who Wants to Be a Millionaire?* and the future of our brand new series seemed to be very much in doubt. Things surely couldn't get worse, but of course they did.

Two days in and we were suddenly given a Congo railway Mr Jobsworth, who had been told to chaperone us everywhere and help us with whatever we needed, which was of course pointless, as the only thing we needed was a train, and he didn't have one. We filmed the platform, we filmed the rails, we filmed a bridge, we filmed a signal box, we filmed an information board with absolutely nothing on it, and we filmed me pretending to be fast asleep on the platform, out of sheer boredom.

At this point, our supposedly helpful Mr Jobsworth blew a gasket, said how dare I suggest that their railway was anything other than punctual, and in a screaming tantrum insisted that we give him everything that we'd filmed so far to tear up. He screamed, "Give me all your film," even though nobody had actually used film for many years. After much shouting we let him have a reel of one of the crew's holiday snaps that he ripped triumphantly into shreds to teach us all a lesson.

The next few days were repetitive, to say the least, except that he'd stopped tearing up our holiday snaps, and more or less left us to our own devices to film anything we wanted, which was basically nothing. There was nothing left to film. We just wanted a train. And so it was on the Friday morning, exactly six days late, steaming proudly into the station, came last week's train to Brazzaville. We had a clue the evening before because people started to fill the station again. They were sleeping there overnight, waiting for the arrival of the train the next morning. How they knew this, we never, ever found out, because there was still absolutely nothing on the station blackboard. But the Congolese bush telegraph clearly worked perfectly, because by 7am the platforms were packed.

A huge cheer went up when it arrived and people spilled all over a very long passenger train. I'd never seen anything like it. People were jammed together, their faces forced against the windows in each carriage, although you couldn't see out of a single window on the train, because it was absolutely caked in thick clay. This made filming difficult, but not impossible, as we were allowed to open the doors anytime we liked.

Those who simply couldn't afford a ticket just sat on the roof of the carriages, and even on the couplings between the carriages. Two new mums were sitting on the couplings holding tiny babies that both looked like Jasper Carrott, only darker. At the time I found this absolutely terrifying, but seven or eight years later, having filmed *Extreme Railways* all over the world, it was not actually all that unusual.

At last we were happy and we looked like we might even get a film. The mood amongst the Congolese congregation on the train was joyous. There was even a Salvation Army band in one of the carriages. They talent-spotted me straightaway as a clearly musically gifted person, and Mother Superior gave me the great responsibility of lead tambourine.

As we headed deep into the Mayombe jungle, there was one particular point at which the train very obviously slowed down and all the locals around me started making the sign of the cross. Apparently, this area was very prone to landslides, falling rocks and trees, and four major accidents had happened at this spot in the railway's history. The worst was in 2012, when seventy-six people were killed and over 700 injured. Four passenger carriages had come off the rails and plunged down into a ravine. Gruesomely, a lot of the carriages were still down there, clearly visible at the bottom of the ravine, although covered with vines. Horrifically, the bodies of the accident victims were still inside. We were told it had been impossible, or just too dangerous, to get rescue crews down there.

Even more gruesome, and just a bit farther along the line, was the Bamba tunnel. At the start of its construction, hundreds of workers were digging and levelling the soil by pick and shovel to lay the lines through the long, dark and eerie tunnel. Then, one by one, they began to collapse and die on the spot.

No one could work out what was going on. It all happened so fast, but over 80% of the men died in a matter of minutes. For a long time there were rumours of voodoo and witchcraft, but eventually it was revealed that the earth they were turning over had probably not been disturbed for thousands of years and invisible, odourless methane gas poured out of the soil and into the lungs of the workers. Nearly all of the workforce died where they stood.

On our train to Brazzaville, sometime late that night, after we'd all had a couple of glasses of Congo's finest wine (which they are very proud of, and was not unlike dry cleaning fluid), all the lights went out on the train, and we became aware that it was slowing down. It then stopped altogether. People were shouting from other carriages, and it was quite alarming when the train was plunged into total darkness. So, after a six-day wait, we had now broken down in a long black tunnel in the Congo, in the middle of the night. This was the one time we could have done with some help from Mr Jobsworth of Congo Railways, but by torchlight we found him in a deep sleep, brought on, we discovered, by stealing our entire wine and beer ration. He was absolutely spark out in the corner of his cosy looking sleeper cabin, surrounded by *our* empties and snoring loudly. Sam and I both fought the urge to give him a damn good smack while he slept. In the end we didn't, but I still think we should have done.

The night was pitch-black, but we decided to make a walk

towards, hopefully, the nearest village. As we got out into the tunnel itself, we could barely see our hands in front of our faces, but there was warm sludgy water running down each side of the rock, and as we sloshed our way along, we realised it stank unmistakably of human excrement.

So, here we were in the middle of the night, in the notorious Congo, on a train that was six days late and had then broken down in the middle of nowhere, splashing about in total darkness, up to our knees in shit. Would the fun ever start?

We trudged out of the tunnel and along the main track with just the light of our torches to guide us. We had absolutely no idea where we were. I for one was genuinely scared. From what we could remember from the map earlier we seemed to collectively think there would be a village a couple of miles further down the line.

But who lived there? Would we be welcomed at this time of night? And if we were unwelcome, what would they actually do to us?

After about half an hour of trudging along we saw lights coming slowly towards us. It turned out to be a relief engine, come to hitch up onto our broken-down train and take us on towards Brazzaville. It seemed to us more than likely that this train would break down as well, and it was quite a long walk back, but at least we knew what we were going back to – a dead train in a tunnel smelling of shit, in total darkness, as opposed to going to a mystery village that might or might not exist and might or might not be friendly.

It was turning into the longest night of my life, but we got back into our carriage somehow, fumbling our way in the dark, to find a lot of completely new people in our seats. Suddenly all the lights came back on, everybody did a massive reshuffle, and we were all back in the same seats where we had started only a few hours ago, and still just the six days late. Most people didn't seem particularly fed up, so this was clearly no worse than what they were used to.

About an hour or so later, there were lights in the distance, and we pulled into the station at Dolisie. It was two in the morning and our train was just over eight hours late (well, six days and eight hours late, to be precise), and, funnily enough, there was no one waiting on the platform.

We were thirsty, we were starving, we were fed up, but we were very happy to be getting off without any more incidents.

There was nobody to help us. Our Jobsworth had disappeared in a drunken stupor, and we weren't even sure whether the hotel that we'd booked several weeks ago by phone from London would even still be open.

But as I've said before there does seem to be a wonderful bush telegraph in Congo, and not only was the hotel open, but they had obviously heard the news of our disastrous night. The restaurant was still very much open, with a big table just for us, and they had prepared an enormous feast with lashings of wine and whiskey.

Suddenly, the new programme seemed to be going terribly well.

The Congo film turned out really well after so many early setbacks and for the next eight years we filmed all around the world.

I don't want to turn this into a railway book, because I've already written one of those, but here are just a few headlines from some of the other *Extreme* journeys we made.

In making the programmes we travelled the equivalent of nine times round the earth. No wonder I always look knackered. The hottest place was in the south of Morocco where we filmed the temperature gauge in our car at 55 Celsius, and easily the coldest was Bovanenkovo in Siberia, where one night it was minus 40.

We went to Bolivia twice, because the first film was stolen by some little toerags at the end of a two-week, pretty exhausting shoot. We were checking in all our cameras and equipment at the airport in Sao Paulo, when we realised that someone had nicked the bag with all our rushes in. It has never happened to me before, in fifty years of filming, nor have I ever heard of it happening to anyone else. They are completely useless to anyone except the production team. We put up adverts offering a huge reward to anyone who found the bag with the tapes in. We hunted frantically all around the airport, searched every waste bin and all the bushes around the outside, but eventually we came home empty-handed. We were all sick to our guts. It was like a bereavement in the family.

They never turned up, and eventually, eighteen months later, we went back to Bolivia. What I found extraordinary was that when we rang all the various people that we'd interviewed before, and explained to them what had happened, and asked them tentatively if they would mind getting the same train out and doing the whole interview again, instead of screaming, "You incompetent bunch of idiots," they all said. "Yes, of course, we'd be delighted. It will be great to see you again." So back we went.

The heat was unbearable crossing the Atacama Desert. One of the trains got stuck and we all had to get out with shovels to dig it out of the thick clay. Another one, up and over the Andes, was fairly forgettable, except that it worked like a stop-go bus, and at certain points all the men pressed the bell, jumped out, and stood in a little line at the side of the track having a wee. But much more memorable, in a grisly kind of way, was the fact that a lot of the elderly women on the train did exactly the same thing. They all stood up, pointing forward in the same direction as the men, lifting up their skirts and petticoats and urinating, just like the blokes. The only time I'd ever seen a woman do that before was on *The Full Monty*.

When we got up to over 14,000 feet, we started to suffer from altitude sickness. It's weird stuff and affects everybody in different ways. Our fixer, who was Bolivian, was violently sick. I had a splitting headache, but only for a couple of hours, then when I came down in the morning, Sam, our normally very funny, extrovert Irish cameraman, was neither funny nor extrovert. He was lying on the floor in the hotel foyer breathing from a giant oxygen tank. He was unable to carry on filming.

Also in Bolivia, we stayed in the worst hotel we'd found anywhere in the world. We drove past it several times, because it was completely covered in tarpaulin and looked exactly like a building site, until we went around the back and they welcomed us in. They only had two small rooms for eight of us, and there were two enormous dogs the size of bears roaming about, so we spent the night all crammed together with a chest of drawers across the doorway.

In Japan, where every single train is on time to the second, we marvelled at their amazing bullet trains. I actually don't get that excited about locomotives. It's the railway systems I find fascinating and how they were built, often including how many died in constructing a particular railway, but the locomotives themselves don't really turn me on. I've probably seen too many. The bullet trains, however, were an exception. They must be the most beautiful locomotives on earth. We clocked ours travelling at over 207mph, and yet we could all speak at normal volume, and none of our coffee spilt even a tiny drop. The bullet trains even smell nice, with lavender being pumped around the air conditioning system. When did you ever get on a train in the UK and say, "Doesn't this one smell nice."

I also loved the fact that when the ticket collector came into the carriage, he bowed politely, and the guards did likewise when you got on and off the train. Sorry to be repetitive, but when did that ever happen to you between King's Cross and Birmingham?

We filmed in Alaska, where they had all sorts of problems on the line, including bears, falling giant fir trees and avalanches, yet they run over the Rocky Mountains every day of the year. If you told anybody in Alaska or Japan that in England trains get delayed by leaves on the line, they would undoubtedly say, "Are you having a laugh?"

We did have one very scary moment in Alaska. One of the ways they stop avalanches from coming crashing down onto the line was by going up in a helicopter, taking dynamite bombs and dropping them onto anywhere where the snow seemed to be impacting, before it could build up into an avalanche.

I'd never held dynamite before in my life (nor had Mike the

cameraman; in fact, nor has anybody else I've ever met) but just the two of us and the pilot went up and over the Rockies in a helicopter full of it. Then on cue, with dynamite in each hand, I threw it right out onto a sharp peak, where the snow was clearly piling up to form an avalanche. I was expecting a huge explosion to shake the helicopter. In reality there was a big bang, but the helicopter remained perfectly stable, and then as we turned to make our way across to a second point, to drop the second bomb, the pilot said the weather was suddenly closing in fast. We dropped the dynamite and turned to get quickly away, only to find that we were completely closed in by a thick blizzard. There was no radar, of course. All we knew was that we were hovering somewhere directly above the jagged peaks that we'd just climbed above in the chopper.

Our pilot very cautiously tried to find a way down, but our helicopter then started making a frightening alarm sound, and when I said to him, "What's that?" he said, "It means we are going down too fast." In my mind going down too fast sounds a lot like crashing, but somehow, we didn't. For the next few minutes he stopped even trying to descend, just kept us hovering there, even though he didn't know exactly where there was, and then suddenly the thick snow clouds cleared as fast as they had come and we could see the valley and the crew way down below us, and we gently made our way down to base.

"Everything alright?" asked the director.

"Oh, absolutely great," we said.

"Your lunch got cold ..."

"Gee, thanks ..."

In Australia we filmed The Ghan, which is a beautiful train that runs from Adelaide in the south to Darwin in the extreme North, a distance of something like 2,000 miles. We did some of it by train, some of it by four-wheel drive through the middle of the outback, which is one of the most remote places on earth. One day I drove for eleven hours, from eight in the morning till seven at night, and I only saw one other car all day.

We then hit some really bad weather in a light aircraft going into Alice Springs, which is memorable only because cameraman Mike was sick all down the back of my neck. We ended in a freight train doing the last twenty-four hours right through the night up to Darwin. We travelled on the footplate with two lovely Aussie drivers, in a train well over a mile long, that took something like thirty minutes to brake, and through the night we regularly hit cows, dingoes, kangaroos, and even camels, if they were foolish enough to go wandering onto the main line.

And in Georgia, in a place called Gory, where Joseph Stalin was born (probably one of the greatest mass murderers of his own people, ever known), we filmed in a Stalin Museum where people were queuing up for Stalin T-shirts, Stalin mugs, Stalin key rings, and stick-on Stalin moustaches, and even filmed the local supermarket which had a huge picture of Joseph Stalin over the doorway. He was a truly vicious, evil man, and I rather assumed that everybody else on earth, particularly Russians, thought the same. It seemed to me totally incongruous, about as likely as having a giant picture of Adolph Hitler to attract shoppers to my local Tesco.

And then to Ukraine, which by the way has the worst roads of anywhere I have ever been to, including Zimbabwe, Tanzania and Congo. Apart from its dreadful roads, Ukraine is also probably best known as the country that initially tried to hide a terrifying nuclear leak.

There is a clear pattern in this book of me agreeing to do things that are downright daft things to agree to. Filming in Chernobyl is a perfect example. It could be because I'm a very, very nice man, always obliging and helpful, or it could be because I'm very, very stupid. I'm pretty sure I know your answer, so I'll choose 'I'm a very nice man'. Chernobyl, as everybody surely knows, is a Russian nuclear plant that exploded back in 1986, killing hundreds at the time and killing thousands more by radiation during the years that followed. It was the worst nuclear accident in history. The Russians tried to keep it for a long time quiet, but when sheep started dying as far away as Sweden and Wales from radiation the secret had to come out. I will be quite honest and say that I was dreading going there and I refused point-blank on behalf of myself and the crew to climb onto a viewing platform right at the centre close to where the core blew. The big scary thing about radiation is that mainly you don't die on the spot, but you can develop tumours and cancers months, even several years, later; and of course it's invisible. I was told by an English guy, who was the boss of a security firm there, that in the original massive blast only 10% of the radiation actually escaped. The other 90% is still there sealed in a solid nuclear-resistant concrete dome. He told me proudly that it should last for two hundred years, but when I asked him what would happen to people after that he just grinned and said, "Well, we won't be here, will we?"

Whether there is still radiation on the site of this terrifying accident I have no idea, but a clue is that we all had to wear total anti-radiation suits from head to toe and were told by their head of security (presumably a new appointee because clearly the last one wasn't great) in no uncertain terms, "You must stay on the tarmac road at all costs. Do not, repeat, do not, stray onto the grass or go anywhere near the trees." We were more than happy to follow his barked instructions. We would keep off the grass, of course, we would get the film done, get our suits off, shower, and actually destroy our underclothes. We were taking no chances at all, except for Simon, a keen, young, assistant producer. I had just finished an interview with a lucky survivor, filmed of course with meticulous care, all of us standing on the tarmac, when I spotted Simon munching a big shiny apple. "That looks nice," I said. "Where did you get it?" "Oh," he said happily, "from that big tree over there."

I still see Simple Simon from time to time, always from a distance, and so far he's not flashing or even turning red and green, but it's early days …

And then our trip to Ukraine became more fun than I even dared dream. For no reason that I can actually remember, I was sent to interview a historian called Iryna Matsevko, but of course, with our producer, it couldn't just be in a nice, elegant bar, or a five-star hotel. Oh no, we had to do the interview down the town sewer.

This was actually in the town of Lvov, which suffered horrors in World War Two, under occupation by the Nazis. Then worse, as the Holocaust began all over Hitler's Europe, 160,000 Jews, which was about a third of the city's population, suffered brutal persecution and transportation to the death camps.

The story we were covering was about a remarkable Jewish shopkeeper called Ignacy Chiger and his family, who escaped murder at the hands of the SS by somehow hiding and surviving for fourteen months down the sewers.

The family survived thanks to a very brave Polish sewer worker, who found the family underground, and took pity on them, supplying them with food and anything else they required to keep them alive. The family emerged in 1944, when the city was re-taken by the Soviet Red Army. Ignacy described Leopold the sewer worker as their guardian angel. It was a remarkable triumph of the human spirit, although the kids must have been terrified.

I must say, I'd never been down a town sewer before and I wouldn't race to go down another one. I assumed there would be horrible stagnant water down there, but in fact when we got down to the bottom the filthy water was actually racing through in a fast-flowing river. It was disgusting, the smell was appalling, and it was also clearly very dangerous. You certainly did not want to fall in.

Iryna told me, "The family somehow survived on the few drops of fresh water that came down from a fountain above, but they were surrounded by disease and darkness for over a year."

Iryna, like me, having told the story, couldn't wait to get out of the stinking place, but throughout the interview she was very bright and very articulate. But suddenly, in the middle of giving a very detailed answer, she stopped for about ten seconds and then carried on. When we'd mercifully got back up to the surface, I asked her, "Why was it that you suddenly stopped in the middle of your interview?"

She said, "Because I suddenly saw something large, brown and evil moving behind your head."

Apparently it was a rat. Well, I certainly hope it was.

And then there was Zimbabwe. I had been there years before and it was a very different place. I was a young man, it was a beautiful country, and a new safari camp was due to open up alongside the shores of Lake Victoria, with fantastic lions, leopards and all sorts of wild game to be viewed, plus great fishing in the lake.

I was on an exploratory trip to help with the marketing of the camp, but once Robert Mugabe became President, the project, like so many others in that desperately struggling country, collapsed through lack of any funding, and it sadly never happened.

The country from then on went from bad to worse. White people, who ran most of the farms, in many cases, were beaten up and even murdered. Their lands were taken over by the Zimbabwean government and the economy just collapsed. The once beautiful country became a complete lawless shambles.

Whole areas of elegant housing were allowed to go to rack and ruin, and when we went there to film in 2018, the place was a nightmare. Absolutely nothing worked. The railway system was in a state of total chaos and everywhere we looked there seemed to be very scary gentlemen looking back at us holding big guns.

The country, after years of Mugabe misrule, was completely broke. I actually brought home a 100-billion-dollar Bank of Zimbabwe note. I've never seen a 100 billion dollar note before in my life, and when I checked it out, its real value was about two pence.

So, the idea of being a visiting white film crew and going to Harare, the capital, filled us all with a certain amount of trepidation, to say the least. Dread is probably a better word.

It didn't help that Zamo, a lovely young guy who became our guide and driver for the whole trip, was arrested and handcuffed when Neil, the director, went out on a recce a few weeks before. Thankfully, they let him out of jail after a few hours, but it wasn't a great omen.

As we made our way into the customs hall, with all our mountains of sound and camera equipment, it was clearly going to be no fun at all. Think overzealous bureaucracy in a sauna with loaded AK-47 rifles! The place stank. It was baking hot. It was airless, and although there were lots of men running around in flamboyant uniforms, with lots of big hats, braid epaulettes, and lots of medals, none of them seemed to have the slightest idea what they were doing or, when they finally got around to us, what they were looking at.

Zamo was busily explaining who we were, what we were up to, and showing them all sorts of pieces of very official looking paper, which clearly none of them understood. It was a scary place, there were huge wall-size pictures of Robert Mugabe everywhere. If you imagine coming into Heathrow and finding all the walls adorned with Boris, it would just be silly, but the pictures of Mugabe, inarguably, a very bad man, were somehow very intimidating. We were clearly going into a dangerous country.

Eventually, when we were given the OK to go through, it was a great shame that no cameras were allowed to be used inside the customs hall, as I desperately wanted to film the large 'Suggestions Box'. It was there unmistakably as you made your way through the exit. What it said, in totally ridiculous terms, was, 'If you have any evidence of Government corruption, please put your findings and your name and address in this box'. Unbelievable! I wonder if anyone was stupid enough to put in a single piece of paper: "I think Mr Mugabe is a rotter and he should be got rid of as soon as possible. C Tarrant, 92 Acacia Gardens, Bulawayo" … I don't think so.

Then, once we started our journey, there were the roadblocks, each one of them slightly more intimidating than the one before. Out of nowhere, a group of thugs with very serious looking machine guns and wearing hats with 'Police' written on them, appeared from the thick jungle that seemed to follow the full course of the only road to Bulawayo.

They would stop the car, come up to the window, muttering things like, "What are you doing in Zimbabwe?" and, "What is all this?" while poking at the camera bags with their guns. I became terrified that our script, which contained many unflattering references to Mr Mugabe, might be found. If they did find it the consequences could be really nasty.

In the end I agreed with Neil that we tore the relevant pages out and got rid of them. It was a weird sensation, but there did seem to be danger lurking just about everywhere we went.

Each roadblock seemed to only be lifted if we handed over a pile of dollars. It was outrageous, but it didn't seem the time to argue. In one place there was a big table in the middle of the road. Cars in either direction were being stopped, and the table was stacked with ever increasing piles of dollars. We had five roadblocks in less than forty miles, and at least one of the groups of 'police' were clearly nothing of the sort. They were just really young bad guys with guns, who just suddenly appeared in police hats as we rounded a bend. It didn't seem a good idea to ask to check for their credentials.

When we got to Bulawayo, the second largest city in Zimbabwe, it had clearly once too been a beautiful place: lovely houses with big sprawling gardens, lined with all sorts of wonderful trees, but the houses were mainly looted and empty and the gardens trashed. The centre of Bulawayo itself, by the station, had no glass at all in any of the windows and every single shop had huge iron bars across the doorway. Clearly crime was rife.

We were due to catch what was laughingly described as 'The Bulawayo Express', up to Victoria Falls. When we finally discovered the station noticeboard, there was a long list of trains to all sorts of exciting sounding destinations all over Africa, but every single one of them had 'cancelled' written beside it. Cancelled, cancelled, cancelled everywhere.

Then, eventually, we came across our train, the Bulawayo Express. It was the only one that wasn't actually cancelled. It just had the words 'may run' beside it. So we'd come all the way through this hellhole of a country to get on a train that 'may or may not run'. Amazingly, it did. Africa being Africa, it was, of course, several hours late. But suddenly in the early evening we found ourselves loading all our camera gear into two or three compartments, and the train actually left the station and seemed to be heading at least somewhere, possibly in the general direction of Victoria Falls.

We went into the bar, where there were a lot of locals, all men, who frowned at us and our cameras. I said to Mike the cameraman, "We'd probably better not do any filming in here." But then Zamo, who had been chatting to the locals, said, "No, it's OK. It's fine. They will allow it." So, we filmed a few of the locals drinking some terrifying looking hooch, that they drank out of cardboard cartons. They began to smile at us, and we smiled at them. I had a couple of local beers, I avoided whatever it was in the cartons, as their eyes seemed to be getting wider and wider and slightly manic.

I went back to my compartment to get some money. The bill would probably be a few thousand billion dollars, but discovered something I'd never seen before on any railway anywhere in the world: the door from the train, out onto the main line, kept flying open. We were actually going along at quite a steady lick, presumably because there were absolutely no other trains working on the whole railway system. We had Zimbabwe Railways to ourselves, but the chances of people falling out seemed to me distinctly possible. It was very frightening. I made my way, very carefully, past the swinging door, hanging on to the sides of the cabins for dear life. I also noticed that the offending door was handily placed between the bar and the gents, so as people became increasingly the worse for wear, from the contents of the cartons, whatever it was, and became less steady of foot, the chances of someone falling out seemed more than likely.

We eventually made our way to bed around midnight – and

locked our doors. Through the night I was sure I heard one or two loud bumps, and even an occasional scream, but when I woke up I was pretty sure that I'd been dreaming. However, in the morning, amazingly we arrived at our destination. As we were off-loading our equipment from the train to a beautiful hotel overlooking Victoria Falls, I said to a smiling guard, "It was a nice journey. Thank you. Everything alright?"

"Yes," he said. "The only problem was that three people fell out of the train during the night."

"Oh dear. How are they?"

"Probably dead," he said, and walked off whistling.

DON'T CRY FOR ME – ARGENTINA

O f all the countries we visited, Argentina was the one I was the most impressed by. I'd heard reports of a lot of crime and muggings, particularly in Buenos Aires, but I have to say when we got there, it was an absolutely beautiful city. They have planted trees everywhere and the blossoms when we were filming were just stunning. It's very much like Paris, except the streets are much wider. It is a lovely place and we felt safe everywhere we went.

It also has incredibly strong ties with Britain (although, obviously, these ties were broken for a while during the Falklands War), and there are still signs everywhere, saying, 'Give us back the Malvinas', which is what the Argentinians call The Falklands. However, I don't think there is any real expectation that we will be handing them over anytime soon.

This seems to be mainly because the Falkland inhabitants don't want to become Argentinians. They still very much prefer their ties with the UK. Everywhere in Buenos Aires there are red telephone and post boxes, a clue to a past British colonial presence, and of course it was the Brits who built the very successful railway system right across the country from Buenos Aires all the way down to Patagonia at the southern end of this huge country.

Football matches between England and Argentina have always been very bitterly fought. Alf Ramsey famously called them 'animals' back in the 60s and it's been like that ever since, with the famous David Beckham sending off, and so on.

Yet the locals we met couldn't have been kinder, couldn't have been more friendly.

We wanted to see a real Argentinian ranch, so we called on a family who'd had a ranch out there in the Pampas for a hundred or more years. Yorga and his wife Maria were real South American, hands-on farmers with a large number of gauchos to help them out with the running of the ranch.

They looked great in all their full cowboy costumes, and we thought we were in for a day of horse riding, lariat twirling, and six-gun shooting. Disappointingly, on the day we called with our cameras, it was a day when they all line up to castrate young bulls. It was done on a sort of conveyor belt system, the gauchos lined up with their scissors, the bulls came in, off their testicles were snipped, and back into the fields they went. The animals seemed to feel no pain at all, but as a background to our filming, I found it very off-putting. I couldn't help wincing every time I heard a sharp snipping sound. I was trying to do an interview with Yorga about the complexities of running such a big ranch, when out of the corner of my eye, I kept seeing gonads being passed from one gaucho to the next and put in a large bloody bucket.

When it came to lunch Maria had arranged a massive spread of beef, of course, which was great. Really thick burgers and great chunks of steak. Beef is very much the staple diet of Argentinians.

We all tucked into the steaks and the burgers, but one of our production team, Jake, was trying to be vegan. Now, Argentina is probably the worst place in the world to start giving up meat, but apparently he'd found a new girlfriend who was vegan and was very keen to impress her with his new diet. However, at lunchtime, confronted by all this meat, he seemed to have cracked under pressure and was the only one who seemed to feast on the delicacy that Maria had spread on one extra-large plate: freshly cooked bulls' testicles. To all of us they just looked revolting, but new vegan Jake bizarrely tucked in and munched his way through several of them.

When confronted by us, about how this could possibly be consistent with his new vegan principles, he insisted, "Oh yes, it's fine, because they're not on the animal, and the animal is still running free in the field over there." We weren't really convinced by his explanation. I don't think he quite got the hang of being a vegan, and several nights later he completely cracked in a famous Argentinian steak house and disappeared under a mountain of burgers and a T-bone steak. Predictably, the girlfriend is no more.

Big steaks and Malbec, the local red wine, are in every restaurant in Buenos Aires. On every menu there are whole pages of different cuts of steak and dozens of different types of Malbec. They are all good.

We travelled on down to Patagonia, which is a beautiful part of the country. Travelling on the Old Patagonian Express I met with a fascinating guy, a local historian called Abel Basti. It's a famous old railway line and I was talking to him about all the famous people over the years who have travelled on this legendary train.

"Oh yes," he said, "several US presidents, all sorts of film stars, many famous South American footballers, and, of course, Adolf Hitler."

"Adolf Hitler?" I said, completely thrown. "When did he travel on this line? Was it before the war?"

"No," he said, "in 1945. He did not die in the bunker, as was generally believed. He escaped from Berlin and was secretly smuggled into a submarine which landed off the coast fifty miles south of Buenos Aires. He had shaven off his trademark moustache and all of his hair and he arrived at this station where you and I are talking now in the dead of night. From here, he was spirited away by a local German landowner, who'd been here since the 1920s. He owned thousands of acres around here, and Hitler lived happily as his guest for many years."

When I asked how certain was he of his facts, he said, "I am totally certain. I have interviewed the guy who drove him around, and his chambermaid. After a while many people saw him drinking in the town. Don't forget people down here were a very long way from the war and really didn't care much. So many Nazis and SS figures came to live here in South America: Josef Mengele, Klaus Barbie, Martin Bormann and Adolf Eichmann. If they could get here, surely the most powerful Nazi of them all could make it. He lived here for many years and eventually moved to Paraguay where he died. I know the cemetery where he is buried, but I cannot yet get the Paraguayan government to agree to exhume his body. Although Argentinians don't seem to care either way, the Paraguayan government do not want it to be known that they harboured a monster. With modern DNA techniques, we could prove once and for all that Hitler died here in South America and not in a bunker in Berlin. The CIA were always certain he wasn't dead, and so was Stalin, who wanted him found and brought back to Moscow and paraded round the streets in chains."

It was an amazing, unexpected conversation, and when we put the cameras away I said to him, "Off the record, do you ever think you might be wrong?"

He looked at me, grinned, and said, "No, not all. I know I'm right."

HIRED GUN

In early 2000, I made a film about polar bears. I had been obsessed with them for years. I'd seen lots of grizzly bears, close up in Alaska and Northern Canada – one or two of them a bit too close – but the polar bear is the biggest of them all, and certainly the most dangerous.

I financed the film myself. It went out on ITV on Christmas Day, and I must say we were very pleased with the end result.

We flew to the extreme north of Norway to the island of Svalbard, which supposedly had a population of over 2,000 polar bears. But in spite of global warming, it was still then covered in thick ice most of the year. It has a breathtaking landscape of glaciers and heavy snow falls, with the sea around it just above freezing and packed with a constant procession of drifting icebergs.

Frustratingly, although we knew there were a number of polar bears around, after a couple of days of filming and only having seen one from a distance, we realised it was going to be much more difficult than we imagined. For such enormous animals they are surprisingly sensitive creatures. If they sense man or his machines anywhere near, they just disappear with their big white coats into the snow. Unless, of course, they decide to attack. In which case, unlike the grizzlies, which will often stop in mid-attack and back off, the polar bears are one animal that will hunt man down to attack and to eat.

We took a helicopter up for a whole day at the cost of $2,000 an hour, and even with my cameraman hanging out from the open door, we only spotted one, a long way below us, running along the shore. It was my first ever polar bear sighting, and it was a wonderful moment, but it was obvious that the noise of the helicopter was spooking the bears away.

We'd have to stalk them on foot, or take our small inflatable boat into the icy waters of the Arctic Ocean.

We went into the main town of Longyearbyen, and were told that if we were going to go walking anywhere out of the town limits, we'd need a guide and one of us would have to carry a gun. The police were surprisingly laid-back about telling me where to buy a weapon. There was a gun shop at the far end of town. He would let me have a licence for a gun big enough to kill a two-thousand-pound polar bear for the ridiculous price of nine pounds a day. It came with a box of very large bullets. It was only to be used in an absolute emergency and had to be returned after seven days.

I showed him no passport, no driving licence, no ID whatsoever, and I walked out of the shop, proudly carrying my gun. Remember that this is Norway where the prices of food and drink are exorbitant: five quid for a beer, sixty quid for a bottle of Scotch, but a mere nine pounds a day for a gun.

As we prepared for the next day's filming, word came through that two polar bears had been seen earlier in the morning, close to the small airport on the outside of town. It was a tiny little airbase, and when we got there we filmed some giant footprints, but there was no longer any sign of the bears.

But then, while I was standing there, a lot of large, square-shouldered gentlemen with earpieces appeared, doing a lot of shouting to each other in thick American voices. They seemed to be some sort of security team, and it was obviously something to do with a small light aircraft that could be seen coming in. I was about ten yards from the runway, standing quietly by a fence. The plane landed, and out got, of all people, Hillary Clinton. It was unmistakably her; she is very easy to recognise. She was immediately surrounded by security men, and slowly taken off out of the airport and towards a car. Apparently, there was some sort of big global warming conference going on and she was the star guest.

All this time, while the men in the suits were shouting instructions to each other into their walkie-talkies, I was just standing there quietly holding my £9 gun, that could blow a hole in a polar bear. At no point did anybody say, "Excuse me, sir, what the hell are you doing here?" or shout, "Let me see your hands!" or even spreadeagle me across the bonnet of one of their big black cars. It was a ridiculous moment and made a total nonsense of their much vaunted security.

Another day went by. Tragic news came in of two young girls who had foolishly camped up at the top of the glaciers outside the town the previous night, without a gun, and one of them had been attacked and killed by a polar bear. The other one escaped, but only by throwing herself down a ravine. She survived but with two shattered legs.

They seemed to be all around us, but still we hadn't got more than one decent sighting, and even that was only from the air. The next morning, Martin my producer and I were driving just outside the town, when we spotted a caribou all on its own. Now we had seen herds of caribou and reindeer over the previous few days, but like the polar bears they too are very nervous and almost impossible to get close up to on film. They seemed to be constantly looking over their shoulders, presumably terrified of the imminent arrival of hunters or a polar bear.

We stopped the car and got out, closing the doors very quietly. We made only hand signals to each other and silently moved ourselves downwind of him so there was no scent. Martin got his camera ready, and I started to creep towards the animal, keeping very low. It was a big male caribou, probably fifty yards away, grazing on some sort of coarse grass at the edge of a wood. We talked only in whispers. I got within thirty yards and Martin started grinning as he took more and more pictures of me getting ever closer to this beautiful, but very shy, animal. I couldn't believe it, I got to fifteen yards, ten, and then absolutely flattened myself against the ground as it looked up, for the first time. It clearly seemed to notice me, and I expected it to run, but after a few seconds it put his head down again and carried on grazing. I got within five yards, and then hardly daring to breathe, I got to within less than a couple of feet, within almost touching distance. Thrilled, we got the pictures of me and the Caribou together in great big close-up, and tip-toed away. Martin was ecstatic. We were absolutely thrilled. We had visions of my picture being on the front page of *National Geographic*. Surely nobody has ever got that close before to a wild feeding caribou.

Still no polar bear, but the caribou in itself was almost certainly a world first on film.

And that alone almost made the trip worthwhile.

The next morning, we went into town to get some supplies for the rest of the week, and as we looked up, I noticed a pile of happy children all taking turns to ride the very same 'wild' caribou that we stalked so carefully the day before. It was the town pet.

The days went by and me and my £9 gun were getting very frustrated. We saw one more bear late one evening, but it was a long way away on the far shoreline, right at the limit of our biggest zoom lens. Its white whiskers were covered in blood from a seal that he had clearly recently killed, but when we attempted to get closer, it left the seal and just disappeared into the snow.

Then, one afternoon, we took our little inflatable boat out just on the oars to keep noise to a minimum and tried to explore several of the ice islands, up around the north of Svalbard. We were very close to the Arctic Circle. We were freezing and feeling pretty fed up, when all of a sudden, a huge white head appeared round a big ice rock at the end of one island. We spoke in whispers. It had clearly seen us, but seemed intent on coming down to the shore in front of us. There were four of us crammed into our little inflatable. We were no more than about ten yards away from this massive creature as he made his way into the icy sea. It gave a few huge snorts in our direction, its icy breath on the air, as if to say, "I know you're here, just back off, stay there, stay quiet and you'll be fine."

It was one of the greatest moments of my life, as this huge creature swam across the channel in front of us, made its way to the shore of the next island about twenty yards away, shook itself like an enormous dog, and then disappeared out of sight. We had it all on film. We had the sounds of the bear's breathing and we had my whispered commentary. It was everything we had come for, and we were absolutely ecstatic. Even if we saw nothing else in the few days left, we'd made the film we'd come to make.

As we turned, all still grinning, to make our way back to our base camp, the paddle in our little rubber boat struck gravel on both sides. The bear was never more than twenty yards from the boat. We had assumed we were probably in thirty or more feet of water, but in reality, we'd drifted into something no more than two or three feet deep. At any moment he could have reared up on his hind legs and smashed us and the boat to pieces. If he had, I wouldn't have made the film, I wouldn't have written this chapter, and come to think of it, I wouldn't have written this book.

WHO WAS I?

I was wandering around Manchester a while back, and I popped into a newsagent to pick up the day's paper. The girl in the shop hardly looked up, as she handed me my paper and the change, but the exuberant guy beside her, who turned out to be her father, a very tall, silver-haired Asian gentleman, suddenly started wailing in the most extraordinarily loud voice: "Oh my God, it is him. He is here among us. Ohhh. Ohhh. I never thought I'd see the day."

I think I actually blushed, his daughter looked up and then became equally excited and he started pumping my hand: "It's such a pleasure to welcome you to our shop, sir. Thank you so much, you are doing us a great honour."

It was all a bit embarrassing to be honest, but he was obviously a very nice man, and then he called down his wife and kids from upstairs above the shop. They all came down and stared at me in awe. The very young ones clearly had no idea who I was, but the oldest son, who I guess was about ten, and the mum, both started doing the wailing thing the same as the dad. They were very nice, very excited, but I just wanted to take my paper, smile at everybody and then go. But, oh no, I wasn't going to get away as easily as that.

"Please, sir. Thank you, sir. Thank you so much for coming to our shop. Would you please do me the great honour of looking at my silverware and finest china items."

I looked at him blankly. I really had no idea what he was talking about, but the oldest daughter went racing up the stairs with mum and they came back down, very proudly holding some beautiful bone china plates. I think they were willow pattern and four big silver goblets.

"There you are, sir," he said.

"Yes, they are very nice," I mumbled. "Very nice."

"What do you think, in your professional opinion, sir, they are worth?"

By now I was completely flummoxed, I had no idea what to say.

"I think you really should get them professionally valued," I said to him, rather feebly, "but thank you so much for showing them to me. They are very beautiful, and you have looked after them magnificently. They are in very good condition."

"Oh, thank you, sir, thank you," he then said, and grabbed me in a kind of frenzied headlock and actually kissed the top of my head. Somehow, still shaking all their hands and looking thoroughly embarrassed and flustered, I beat a hasty retreat to my car, which was mercifully just around the corner.

He was a very nice man, they were a very nice family, and I'm very glad that I brought them so much pleasure. But who the hell did they think I was?

IN THE NUDDY

I don't know why I was filming in a nudist camp somewhere in deepest Sussex. It was probably something to do with money. Also I think it was an excuse for my producer to spend seventy-two pervy hours ogling all shapes and sizes of naked women, scampering about all around us. The reality though, we quickly discovered, was very different. Sexy it ain't.

I don't know what I expected, but nothing could have prepared me, when the five men and one woman of my crew all arrived to check in, the sight of a terrifying, grossly overweight, old battleaxe waiting to greet us at reception, with not a stitch on. We wanted to jump back into our cars and drive home, but there was no turning back.

The first evening over dinner we tried to pretend that it was the most natural thing in the world, to be surrounded by naked breasts, buttocks, willies and pubic hair. We all tried desperately hard not to keep looking down at everybody we were introduced to, but you could only maintain eyeball to eyeball contact for a limited amount of time. Sooner or later, and usually sooner, your eyes are forced down to their private parts, followed immediately by the guilty jerking of the head back upwards, accompanied by a bright reddening of the cheeks.

The regular nudists, of course, have seen it all before, so after quite a short time we became the ones feeling terribly conspicuous, by being fully clothed.

None of the nudists seemed at all fazed about our being fully clothed, but we began to feel thoroughly uncomfortable – downright silly, in fact, and of course it was the girl amongst us who just couldn't wait to get her kit off first.

We'd all worked with our PA for several years, and possibly had occasionally daydreamed, about seeing her naked, but when she came in dressed only in a clipboard and a stopwatch, all of us blokes went terribly red and started staring at the ceiling. She was, and still is, a very attractive woman, and she was magnificent with nothing on, but somehow the mystery was gone.

You soon realise that a hint of a stocking top or a scantily covered cleavage is one thing, total public nakedness is something else.

Nevertheless, shamed by our PA, we all slowly began to take our clothes off. It was a very strange feeling. I'd worked with most of the guys for several years, but I'd never seen any of their willies, and I sincerely hoped they'd never seen mine.

We all tried to carry on like it was the most natural thing in the world, but we felt downright stupid and incredibly self-conscious.

You find yourself doing absurd things, like looking for your car keys, that are normally in your trouser pocket, and suddenly realise you haven't even got any trousers, let alone pockets, and trying to cover your embarrassment by doing a strange slapping and stroking motion to the top of the thigh. It looks obscene, but it's better than the shame of admitting that you are hunting for keys in trousers that you aren't wearing. It was one of my very strangest filming assignments and I've done a lot of very strange filming assignments.

One source of great amusement was that the director, a man with a considerable paunch, but also I now know, a tiny little tinkle box, kept sitting on a huge cane chair, which left unmistakable cane chair marks on his buttocks. Whenever he stood up we all giggled uncontrollably behind his back, pointing at his backside.

Apparently three or four thousand people from every walk of life scamper about in the nuddy every weekend, in spite of the British weather, and often with not many really good places to go.

Our nudist resort, luckily, was a magnificent old country house with spectacular walled gardens and a lake full of carp. Mainly, though, nudists have to meet in places like chilly church halls and leisure centres, and it's the sheer pleasure of 'letting God's good air' getting to your naked body that's the attraction, apparently.

It was actually very invigorating, and every nudist had an all-over tan, with no silly little white bits.

There was a lot of sporting activity which we filmed and also joined in with, but we were downright cowardly about which ones we joined. Tennis and volleyball were great, as was soccer, although you felt very vulnerable when you went in for the tackle with your bits and pieces swinging free. And to a man and woman, we all said absolutely not to archery and darts.

AREK

No apologies. This next chapter is completely devoid of laughs, but I just wanted to write about the single, without exception, most amazing man I have ever met in my life.

As the *Extreme Railways* series progressed, filming in countries all over the world, it was inevitable, sooner or later, that we would feature the railways of the world wars. Of course, that meant we had to include the trains that Hitler used to make his unspeakable 'final solution to the Jewish problem' possible: the railways of the Holocaust.

We filmed various camps all over Europe, particularly in Poland. The Germans didn't of course have any death camps inside Germany, as they did not want their vile secret to come out.

The railways that ran to the death camps brought literally millions of people, mainly Jews, but also gypsies, homosexuals, musicians, artists, and any sort of political prisoner to their death, in camps like Treblinka, Dachau and, of course, the notorious Auschwitz.

I interviewed several very brave survivors from the camps, but one guy, Arek Hersh, was head and shoulders the most impressive. He had just celebrated his 90th birthday when I met him, and as I write this he is still hale and hearty and living with his English wife in Leeds. His early years from the age of just eleven, though, were almost unimaginably cruel. He saw things as a little boy that no one of any age should ever witness. He should have been traumatised for life and yet Arek was the only one of the Holocaust survivors who I met that was prepared to go back to Auschwitz. He even offered to go into one of the tiny, cramped railway carriages that transported so many thousands to their death.

Of course, I cannot blame any of the others for not wanting to go back to that monstrous place. The memories and nightmares must still be too raw to bear. The one thing Arek would not do was go into the gas chamber. He said, "I spent all those years trying to keep out of one, and I really won't do it now." And no one could possibly blame him.

By the age of eleven, Arek had already lost no less than eighty members, of what was once a very large Jewish family, to the Nazis. All of them had been taken away, and it emerged after the war that virtually all of them had been murdered. Though still just a small boy, with no members of his family around to look after him, he was forced by the Nazis to work on a railway line taking people from the ghetto to the camps. He said, "All the workers were very, very badly treated, so bad that many people actually jumped under the trains as they passed by, and I had to bury them. As a little boy I was scraping up the body parts. Some people were hanged by the Nazis, so I had to bury them as well. We had a cart to take the bodies away. We started with 2,500 men, by the time the railway line was finished there were just eleven people left, including me."

At the age of twelve, he moved into the Lodz Ghetto, and again he witnessed death every day.

"One day, the SS marched unannounced into the hospital and just threw all the patients in the hospital wings out from the second floor windows. Most of them died on impact with the streets, any survivors were killed. I have no idea why they just came here on a whim and emptied all the hospitals. Again, I saw bodies all the time. There were carts taking dead bodies away off the streets, sometimes little children just used to drop in front of me through malnutrition. I was immune to the sights I saw every day."

I went with Arek to the Lodz Ghetto cemetery, which had no less than 43,000 Jews buried there. On the gravestones the word 'Murder' was everywhere.

'Grandmother, Esther, murdered in 1942'.

'Mother, murdered in Auschwitz, 1944'.

'Sister, murdered in Treblinka'.

It was just not a word I'd ever seen on a gravestone anywhere else in the world, and the really shocking thing was that most of those selected for death were selected by the Jewish Council of Elders.

In reality, though, they had no choice. If they had not provided lists they would have been executed on the spot and immediately replaced.

In September 1942, young Arek heard rumours that he too might be chosen next. The SS told all the parents in the ghetto to hand over no less than 10,000 of their children. Of course, no parents could agree to this. A lot of the parents were killed on the spot. Many others hid their children, but then hundreds of the parents and sons and daughters, even babies, were killed when the SS found them hiding. Arek, alone with no parents, had become a master at tucking himself away and hid himself in the huge graveyard. He kept moving silently from one tombstone to another when German soldiers approached, because he had seen that any children caught were shot there and then.

Most of the people who were not shot on the spot at the Lodz Ghetto or the cemetery, were sent to Chelmno, supposedly to work. But on arrival, there was no work. It was the first experimental death camp. No one who arrived here survived. It was the place where the Nazis learned how to murder efficiently and in large numbers. Arek's quick wits saved him from being taken to Chelmno, but then he quietly slipped back into the ghetto and for a while even made some new young friends. However, the fear of death was everywhere and they dreaded being called to 'the transports'. None of the thousands of Jews who were 'transported' were ever seen again.

The Nazis set up an orphanage in the ghetto of almost 200 children, and for those few short months all seemed OK. Then they were told again that the Lodz Ghetto, the last one in Poland, was going to be cleared and over three weeks 68,000 inhabitants, including Arek, were marched to the station, and from here they were transported to what they were again told would be a work camp, with plenty of food and a much better life for their families. It was called Auschwitz.

Arek said, "I will never forget that journey, line after line of cattle trucks crammed with us desperate people inside. We had barbed wire on the window, not that we could possibly have escaped, the windows were so tiny. There were probably 100 people or more in each carriage. You couldn't sit down. There was literally one bucket as the lavatory for the whole carriage, with one tiny blanket to supposedly cover your modesty. Many people died during the journey. When we finally arrived, we'd had nothing to eat for days, but I heard men shouting and dogs barking, and I didn't like the sound of any of it at all. I was very scared. As we got out, all 182 from my orphanage were put into one line, along with women, children, babies, even old men. I didn't feel at all comfortable, I didn't like the look of the line I was in at all, and I thought, 'I've got to find a way out of this.' Then there was a commotion up front, a mother with a baby in her arms was screaming at the guards. They were trying to take the baby off her, and while all this was going on, I switched to the other line, which was mainly stronger looking, fitter men and some fit women. There were three high-ranking officers at the front. One of them I now know to be Dr Josef Mengele, the 'Angel of Death'. He asked me how old I was. I told him 17, even though I was quite small, even for 14. He asked me what I did. I thought up a lie on the spot and I told him I was a locksmith, because I thought they might be useful, and they sent me through the gates to prepare for work. The other 182 children, my friends from the ghetto, all stayed in the other line, and I'm certain they all went straight to the gas chamber, because they were never seen again."

He was alone once more, surviving in a world even more hostile than before. Starvation was the biggest problem.

"We cooked grass and ate it, to stay alive. I was staying in a men's barracks with 500 others. I'd had my head shaved, and given a pair of striped pyjamas and clogs. I got a tattoo on my arm, number B7608. And from now on I was no longer a name, they called me just by that number every day. We slept on wood, no mattress, no sheets, no pillow. There were about ten people crammed into each bunk, and people died during the night. Every morning they had a cart and collected the bodies and burnt them. Sometimes I found myself lying next to someone who had died beside me. It was horrific, but you become almost used to it. That's just how it went, every day. There are no excuses for how our captors behaved. They were just sick, vicious, cruel people."

Every day, more and more trains arrived bringing more Jews to their death.

The one thing we promised Arek we would not expose him to was detailed for filming the next day, and that was the gas chamber. Mike and I went in early in the morning, in total silence, and just kept shaking our heads and gasping at the horror of what we saw. The shower heads that secretly poured out gas, the little areas where they collected their soap, the little areas where they left their clothes and any valuables, because they were promised they would be coming back for them. There were the holes in the ceiling where the bulk of the poison gas was pumped in and you could still clearly make out the incinerators that burnt the thousands of bodies. You could imagine their sheer terror when they realised what was happening. The thing that made the most indelible impression on me was the deep scratching on the walls, maybe eight foot high up, where some prisoners, still gasping for breath, climbed frantically on top of others already dying or dead, desperate to find a way out. But of course, there was no way out. Nobody ever survived the gas chambers once the doors were shut.

On a good day, the Nazis worked out, people were taken off the train, gassed, cremated, and were just ash floating down the river Vistula within fifteen minutes of arrival. But still the Nazi High Command in Berlin wanted more and more to be exterminated each day. Quite often the incinerators broke down, as they couldn't keep up with the horrific workload demanded.

Arek said, "The chimneys were burning day and night, there were usually four chimneys burning, and when you saw the black smoke, you knew what it was."

After the invasions on D-Day, the Nazis' grip began to weaken and Hitler was losing the war on two fronts. By January 1945, the Red Army were advancing through southern Poland.

And on 27th January 1945, the Russians finally liberated Auschwitz, and even the most hardened Russian soldiers were absolutely horrified at what they found. Prisoners, some as thin as sticks, were helped to freedom, but Arek wasn't among them, because a few days earlier the SS had started evacuating the prisoners at gunpoint.

"We knew the Russians were close and we were praying for liberation, but the Nazis just took us out of the camp. It was minus 25 degrees with thick heavy snow, we were in pyjamas and clogs, and we marched and marched.

"They told us we were being taken to a different camp. There were thousands of us, and we were all very weak by then. Many fell as we tried to march. Anybody who couldn't walk was shot in the back of the head, and bodies were just thrown on the side of the road. We had no water, except snow, and we had absolutely nothing to eat. All I remember is hunger. We found grass through the snow, and I also ate my shoe. I managed to cut up the leather, and that somehow sustained me, just bits of leather. They gave us no food, most people died on the journey. I was one of very few who survived the march. Eventually we were put on a train in April 1945, for a month. Really and truly they were just sending us around in circles until we all died. There were 3,000 of us on the journey, it lasted four weeks and only 600 of us came out alive. I was just one of the very few survivors and I was still only 16 years old when we were liberated by the Russians on 8th May 1945.

"I can never forgive those people. They were just pure, pure evil. I had nightmares for thirty years."

Arek is the most incredible man. What he witnessed and what he went through is almost impossible to imagine. It is a miracle he survived, but six million others didn't. It was a chapter in human history that must never be repeated and must never be forgotten.

ENGLEESH ENGLEESH

I was scheduled to film in Jordan and Israel, two fascinating countries that I'd never actually been to, and I was really looking forward to it. But as I had a week spare before the start of filming, I treated myself to a few days off, on the beautiful island of Crete. This would be a nice week in the sunshine, and I was only about an hour's flight from where I needed to join up with the crew.

I'd never visited Crete before either. On the way down, I was reading in my *Lonely Planet* all about "this beautiful island with its lovely warm people, and everywhere is filled with their friendly laughter and the beautiful music of the bouzouki."

It sounded great. However, once I'd got myself checked in by a very unhelpful receptionist at my hotel, in Heraklion, I thought I'd take a walk around the city and try my first local beer.

I walked into the first bar that I came to, and the barman seemed to serve everybody but me. I'm big enough, but I just assumed he hadn't spotted me at the end of the bar. Eventually he came to me, asked me what I wanted, and begrudgingly poured me out a litre of the local ale. It lasted only seconds because I was a thirsty boy and I asked for another. This time I really was totally ignored, didn't get served at all and, a bit fed up, went looking for another bar where they might be a bit more welcoming.

In the next bar though it was no friendlier at all. The barman frowned when I gave him what was admittedly quite a large note. "Nothing smaller?" he grunted. I shook my head, and said, "I'm really sorry," and he turned to the till and almost threw my change at me, with a very dismissive gesture. I went back to my hotel and had an early night. I wanted to meet whoever writes *Lonely Planet* and have sharp words.

Over the next few days things went from bad to worse. I was frowned at, totally ignored, or occasionally jostled, by just about everybody I met. In one place the barman literally turned his back and refused point-blank to serve me, and in another one I was actually spat at.

"This is very strange," I thought. "I didn't realise they get ITV over here."

I really didn't quite know what I'd done to upset them, but upset they clearly were. I couldn't get my brain round it at all. I didn't have any tattoos, I wasn't wearing an easily misinterpreted slogan on my T-shirt, my flies were done up, but as the days went by my short holiday was becoming more and more of a nightmare.

It came to a head when I got on a bus to take me across the island. It was one of those great Greek buses, crammed with all sorts of people, and lots of animals, including a dog or two, several chickens, and at least one goat. The bouzouki was playing on the bus radio and everything was wonderful. We drove along the clifftops, looking down at the Mediterranean, and I felt good for the first time since I'd arrived. Then the ticket collector came wandering amiably down the bus. Amiable, that is, until he came to me.

He glowered at me, and said, in a very loud voice, "Allemand?" with a frown.

"Oh no," I said. "Not Allemand. I am English."

"Engleeesh," he shouted, grinning at me, shaking my hand and shouting to the whole bus, "Engleeesh, Engleeesh." They all started smiling at me and clapping.

The penny finally dropped. I was tall, big, raw-boned, with very long blonde hair at the time, and I suppose I did have a hint of 'the master race' about me.

It turned out that the Germans had invaded Crete in World War Two and there were a string of Nazi atrocities on the island where the SS had shot whole villages, men, women and children. Even though it was more than seventy-five years ago, there was still deep anger and resentment in many families who had lost loved ones brutally to the Gestapo.

From then on, the rest of my holiday changed completely. Everywhere I went, I made sure I said, "Hello, I am English and could I have a pint of bitter please?" "Engleeesh," they would say. "Engleeesh, of course, of course." In many cases they wouldn't even charge me for it. There was no more throwing my change or spitting at me.

It's easy for our generation to say we should all forget and forgive, but in many places the wounds from what happened in World War Two have still not healed. My own dad, who was a wonderful, gentle, kind man, yet spent the whole war from 1939 to 1945 fighting the Germans in France and then on into Germany, he too had no great love for the people who he had seen blow many of his friends to bits as they fought beside him. He didn't talk about the war much at all. Most of the ones who actually saw fighting never did, but he did once tell me a wonderful story. Ridiculously, in 1946, the company that he worked for and re-joined after the war, fixed up a 'goodwill' football match against their main German competitors, just one year after the end of hostilities. Dad always said, "What a ridiculous idea. It was the most savage game of football I have ever played in my life. There were vicious tackles, and some really heated exchanges on and off the pitch."

The Germans, of course, won 3–2. As they were walking off, an unsmiling German said to Dad, "Vee haf just beaten you at your national game."

"Yes," said Dad, "and we've just beaten you at yours."

So, having had what turned out eventually to be a very happy few days in Crete, once I had established my Engleeesh credentials with all and sundry, I flew on to join the crew in Jordan.

Jordan is the most beautiful country, steeped in history, and with some of the most stunning scenery on earth. I spent a blissful night in a Bedouin tent under a thousand stars in a place called Wadi Rum, which literally means the Valley of the Moon. We filmed right across the desert where Lawrence of Arabia made his name, and marvelled at the ancient tomb at Petra. But it was Israel I'd really come to see, and as we crossed over the Jordan we were all really excited. So much history to see.

We stopped overnight in the old port of Haifa, where Jews and Arabs talked amicably together about who made the best hummus, with no sign of tensions anywhere, and Tel Aviv the next day was just one fantastic place. It reminded me very much of Los Angeles. It had a very young vibrant population, and the beaches were crammed with kids playing volleyball, football, running and cycling. There was a real buzz about the place. They all seemed incredibly optimistic and super active, even though they were only forty miles from the Gaza Strip, which you can just about make out from the beach. Forty miles is probably just less than thirty seconds as the Exocet missile flies and, tragically, occasionally they do. But the residents all seemed to have a very fatalistic attitude to all of it. "We live for today," they said. "If a rocket comes, it will come." I loved Tel Aviv and I didn't really expect to.

But then I knew I was going to love Jerusalem, but didn't.

I was so looking forward to it, but it turned out to be a huge disappointment. The first thing I noticed was that there were guns everywhere. There is a very active national conscription system in Israel, every young man or woman has to join up for two years, and they all carry guns, proper guns, that would blow your head off. They carry them on the buses, they put them in their cars, they walk with them through the streets, they even carry them on their bicycles. I talked to one young recruit who had a very serious looking gun hanging off his shoulder. It was a Friday night and I said, "Where will you be going now? Are you going home for the weekend?"

"Oh, yes," he said, "I am going back to see my mum."

"And where will you put your gun and bullets?" I asked him, assuming he would say they'd be locked up in a big steel case, or something, like we do in the UK.

"Well, sometimes I leave it on the table," he said, "otherwise Mum puts it behind the fridge." It was a frightening conversation, and yet crime is very low. Terrorism is a constant threat, of course, but petty crime is rare. If you added all the kids with guns, with the weapons of the security services that are everywhere, for fear of a Hezbollah attack, or suicide bombers, there are far more guns on the streets of Jerusalem than you would ever see in any town, large or small, in America. The difference with America, though, is that in Israel the guns are hardly ever fired. If anybody does attempt to go against the Israeli security system, let's just say, it's sorted very, very quickly.

So, the guns were initially terrifying, but once you understood the system, they were almost reassuring.

There were still high, walled-off areas, topped with barbed wire, right in the middle of the city, an area where some Palestinians still live which was quite surprising and unsettling to see. But it was the main market area that was truly awful. What is supposed to be the holy place of the cross, the site where the crucifixion took place, was rammed with very loud tourists, mainly American, doing idiotic selfies, talking very loudly, chewing gum, and doing high-fives. There was not a hint of respect. It was nauseating. Far worse were the market stalls themselves. They were crammed from floor to ceiling with religious junk, utter tat, most of it sold at shamelessly high prices.

There were bottles of holy water available everywhere, there were bibles and hymn books (with signs like 'The Original'), there were prints of the Last Supper everywhere, and at every stall there were individual pictures of the disciples. In one shop, a guide told me he'd seen the disciples' pictures were actually signed. I admit I never did find that, but I could certainly believe it: "To Chris, best wishes, Judas Iscariot."

Every window had a huge array of little wooden crosses.

In sheer disbelief at the tackiness and exploitive nature of the whole place, I went through the motions of asking the stall holder, "How much is it for one of the wooden crosses?"

"Oh yes," he said to me, "they are very good, original wood from Mount Olive, and to you, sir, only 200 shekels," (about fifty quid) "but for 400 shekels" (about a hundred quid) "you can have one of the crosses with the little man on!"

I walked away without buying anything, shaking my head. Presumably the cross with the 'little man' on, referred to the figure of Jesus Christ being crucified. You can probably gather from this, I absolutely hated the place, although I must admit I didn't hate it enough to stop me buying a 'Guns and Moses' T-shirt on the way out.

BIG DADDY

We were in Florida, filming at a crocodile farm, one of those places that kids always seem to love. Personally, I can live without them because they are always smelly, the water is invariably disgusting, and the animals are one of the very few creatures I find revolting.

I love most wild animals, but I must admit I'm not at all keen on crocs, not since a huge one about fifteen feet long came up right beside our little wooden boat when we were fishing once in Lake Victoria. My guide started to panic and beat the water with his paddle, which just seemed to make the croc crosser, and he bit off the end of the wooden oar. He could have easily smashed the boat to pieces. I actually did think for a second about diving in and trying to swim for the shore while he was busy munching on the oar, but quickly thought better of it. He might have had brothers and sisters down there.

Anyway, luckily, that seemed to satisfy him for a while, and we got the hell out of there with the other paddle as fast as we could. Squeaky bum time.

I must say this particular crocodile farm, a few miles from Miami, was very well run. They had lots of big electrified fences all around it, and the guy who ran the place was an amazing man, known to everybody as 'Big Daddy'. He was a big old boy (what was left of him, anyway). He must have been at least six-foot-seven, had a big barrel chest, a cigar that never seemed to go out, and of course a big white Stetson. He had a big powerful right arm, but his left arm was chopped below the elbow, and it had been replaced by a hook. His injury, presumably at the hands, or rather the teeth, of one of his massive pets, didn't seem to deter him though. He was a great talker, and a real showman. He gave me a great interview, and all the time was putting whole, raw chickens onto his hook and into the mouths of the beasts that kept leaping up out of the water, from right under the feeding platform that he leant out on.

We really liked him, and we all agreed he was incredibly brave to confront the memories of what must have been a horrific attack. I thought it best not to ask him any details about what actually happened, but for Big Daddy to come back to face them day after day, putting his hand, even with his replacement hook, out over those terrifying jaws, called for a tremendous amount of courage, and mental strength.

At about three o'clock it was time to close the gates for the day. All the families had paid up and left and we'd got a nice bit of film with Big Daddy very much the one-armed star of it all. So we put the cameras away, said goodbye, and started to make our way back towards the crew cars. As we did so, Daddy got into his own car, unscrewed the hook, threw it into the trunk of his Mustang and, with a big grin at us, drove away with both of his two perfectly good hands on the steering wheel.

SWEET CHEEKS

I love Kenya. I've been there many times watching wildlife. The Masai Mara is one of the great wild animal reserves of the world. It was the first place I ever went to on safari. I've gone back many times since and even went there for a splendid week with Capital Radio. We actually covered lions trying to kill a herd of wildebeest live on the radio. Yes, I know, it doesn't sound much like a radio item, but actually it came over well. It was quite fantastic to be describing what was happening to an audience sitting in their cars in thick traffic back in London, but we were so excited, and the Africans with us became so excited, that it actually made a great bit of radio. Hundreds and hundreds of Londoners booked that particular safari camp for their next holiday.

We got on really well with the local Masai warriors. They came to do a demonstration for us one morning. Okay, dancing on radio isn't probably a great listen idea either, but then years before I had actually done radio card tricks, and that went down a storm. Yes, alright, maybe it says more about my audience.

At the end of the week, after five mornings of breakfast shows live from Kenya, the Masai leaders came to us very solemnly when we were on air, thanked us so much for being respectful towards them (which was easy, because they are a great people with a tremendous proud tradition), and very formally and publicly handed me a Masai spear. It was a huge thing that folded down into three equally scary looking pieces, and it had a deep slash in the steel halfway up the blade. When I asked the Masai leader what that cut in the spear was, he said, in all seriousness, "That is the mark from a lion that we killed with that spear on Tuesday." So, I thanked him profusely for the gift, and put it in my suitcase.

Being a bit slow on the uptake, it was only as I got into Heathrow that I realised that I was going through customs with a very dangerous object in my baggage. As I approached red channel or green channel, and I almost invariably go through green channel, I suddenly thought perhaps I had better go through the red channel and declare my spear. I needn't have worried. As we approached the entrance to both channels, a grinning customs officer said to me, "Good morning Chris, you'll be going through that one, won't you?" pointing to the red channel and laughing. Clearly, they were Capital Radio listeners, and there were two or three more of them grinning away at me when I got to the other end. "Anything you want to declare, Mr Tarrant?" they asked me, very pointedly, as I went past them.

"Well, I've got a spear in my case," I said.

"Yeah, we know that," they said, laughing. "We heard."

"But it's purely ceremonial," I said, "and is broken down into three pieces."

"Did you pay for it?" one bloke asked.

"No, of course I didn't. It was a present from the Masai."

"Is there any VAT due on it?" the other one asked.

"No, I don't think so. I don't think the Masai do VAT."

"Off you go then," he said, and to my amazement they let me through.

As I came out the other side all the crew were pointing at me and laughing, saying, "Did they take it off you?"

"No," I said, "it's still in my case, and when I get it home to Berkshire, I'm going to put it on the wall."

Where it still proudly hangs today.

When we filmed in Kenya for the *Extreme Railway* series, I was glad to be back. For a country I thought I knew well, I learned a huge amount about its history. The building of the railway across Kenya in the 1850s by engineers who were British, of course, is yet another amazing story of triumph over the odds. When the British engineers were trying to get funding from Parliament, they were almost laughed out of court. One loud-mouthed MP ridiculed the whole idea, calling it the 'Lunatic Line'. The name stuck.

Nevertheless, they eventually got just enough funding and when the British team arrived with mainly Indian workers at the Port of Mombasa, the plan was to go right across the country to the border with Uganda.

Kenya itself was thought to have been just a swampy wasteland, and the idea was to get through to Uganda, which was believed then to be an altogether richer country. However, the problems of building the railway were as extreme as almost anywhere in the world, but it slowly dawned on them, that Kenya itself was a very rich country indeed. Thanks to the railway, it is now one of the wealthiest and most productive countries in the whole of Africa. The problems for those first railworkers though were enormous. They were immediately confronted with sandstorms, snakebites, flesh-eating maggots, malaria, cholera, tetanus and dysentery. The large original workforce was reduced on an almost daily basis all the way through the project. They picked up more African workers on the way, but still they were losing men in big numbers.

One of the things that really struck me throughout the making of the *Extreme Railways* programmes was the sheer death toll (that has been almost forgotten) throughout the construction of the railways of the world, and none more so than in Kenya.

The worst of all though was yet to happen. When they got to the Tsavo River and set up camp, there was a new danger ahead of them, the most terrifying of all. They set up tents by the river, ready to construct the next stage of track across the Tsavo desert, but in the small hours of the morning terrible screams were heard coming from one of the tents. The next morning it was discovered that one of the workers had disappeared and the search party, following the tracks leading away from his tent, eventually made a grisly find. He had been eaten by what were clearly two man-eating lions. The size of the pad marks leading out of the camp were enormous and clearly showed two separate animals. The next night it happened again, and the next.

This went on for several weeks, and when I was being told this story, I assumed they would be talking about the loss of perhaps ten or a dozen workers, before the gruesome situation was resolved. But in fact the lions, while clearly ravenous and bloodthirsty, were also very clever at spotting danger, and avoided capture time and again, until eventually both of them were killed by marksmen. They were both shot to death a couple of weeks apart, but not before they had killed and eaten 140 of the beleaguered workforce. When I was told the figure of 140, I was understandably sceptical, but having checked several records since we returned to the UK, it seemed as if that figure was probably an underestimate. Terrifying.

We made our way on through Nairobi, which is a city that I've always loved and have stayed in The Norfolk Hotel, which is one of the great hotels of the world. It's where one of the rich local landowners famously rode into the bar on his horse, shouting, "Good evening, everybody," and fired his gun several times into the roof of the main bar. But, as always in Africa, our two-night stay in this beautiful old hotel was rather undermined by the knowledge that less than two miles down the road is one of the biggest and saddest slums in the whole of Africa.

Something like two million displaced Kenyans, men, women, lots of children, and many others, who make the trek from all over Africa just to get a roof over their heads, all live in the most appalling conditions of disease and near starvation.

This was made even more distasteful to us with the news that the Kenyan government were spending $3 billion on a new Chinese railway, scheduled to cross the whole country in quicker time than the current Lunatic Line. People were dying every day and the huge sum of $3 billion seemed just ridiculous and out of all proportion.

All in all though, it was a fascinating trip, until we got to the shores of Lake Victoria, and the boundary with Uganda. We made our way down to the lakeside, where we had to pass through a security barrier. We all handed over various official Kenyan government documents and copies of our passports and set up to do one last summarising piece to camera. The director and I talked through the sort of thing I might say. Then, as I started my end piece, and although I was looking squarely down the lens, I became aware of a hubbub going on somewhere just out of my eyeline. The soundman said, "Quiet, please," and I did my piece again, but the hubbub actually seemed to get louder.

Two camouflaged trucks full of soldiers had arrived, and a large, very angry woman, who seemed to be in charge, was doing a lot of shouting, mainly in an African language, which made it difficult for us to find out what the problem was. Eventually we pieced it all together, that this was a very sensitive place on the shores opposite Uganda, and we shouldn't be filming there. We showed them all our passes, which very clearly said, 'Mr C Tarrant and his crew are allowed in this place on this date'.

"No, no, no," she said. "We're not aware of this, nobody has told us."

It was a silly misunderstanding. Somebody hadn't passed a message on, and we thought we could clear it all up in a matter of minutes. Then, if necessary, we would move out of that area to almost any spot open to the public a bit further down the lakeshore and get this one final piece done. But she would have none of it.

"You've broken the law," she kept saying.

"No, we haven't," we said. "We've got permission to be here."

"We do not accept your permission," she kept saying.

Eventually, it was agreed that we would stop filming, go and sign a document at the police station, and be on our way. It was a ridiculous situation, but we thought we'd just go to the police station, which was down the road, sign something on the counter, and go and get this one final piece done. We still had to pack all the gear up and catch our flights, the crew back to London, me on to Cape Town to meet up with Jane for a week's whale watching and safari.

When we got to the police station, to our surprise, instead of being ushered to the counter to sign the documentation, we were firmly pushed past the counter and on around the back to a cramped area next to the cells. We were now five blokes beginning to get just a little worried. I got a lot more worried when a very large Kenyan gentleman in the opposite cell, surrounded by his large grinning mates, kept making obscene gestures about what he wanted to do to me, if I was unlucky enough to be in a cell with him at night-time, and kept calling me 'sweet cheeks'. Normally, the very thought of being called 'sweet cheeks' would have been very funny, but at the time it became more and more unnerving. I didn't want to have a shower with him, and I didn't want him anywhere near my 'sweet cheeks'.

Things were then compounded by the five of us having to hand over our passports. Nobody spoke to us in English, and we were getting very alarmed. This was a nonsense, we had done nothing wrong, and yet we'd all heard of cases where people just disappear for weeks and months in African prisons. It was getting scary. There was nobody we could talk to and we couldn't make the usual one call to our solicitor. In fact, we couldn't make a call at all. Nobody back at UK base had any idea that anything was amiss, and we were due to be on a flight out of the country at about six o'clock that evening.

We were all beginning to fear the worst, and my new boyfriend was positively rubbing his hands with glee through the bars opposite. It was very hot and smelly. 'Sweet cheeks' remained unimpressed and became slowly more and more frightened. I think five hours went by, we were sweating, we had no water, and I think it was one of the longest afternoons of my life. Then, all of a sudden, a man appeared saying, "I'm so sorry for the misunderstanding," and gave us our passports back and we were free. I've never been so glad to be handed my passport in my life.

We rushed out of the place before anybody changed their mind. I didn't even bother to say goodbye to my boyfriend, although he did start blowing kisses at my disappearing 'sweet cheeks'.

We piled back into our truck and made our way towards the airport, stopped for a very quick final piece to camera on the forecourt, and got on our planes.

The one abiding memory I have of this scary afternoon, was that one of the crew, who had been bursting for a wee throughout the ordeal, not wanting to risk the horrors of a Kenyan prison toilet, suddenly could hold it no longer and weed down the side of our transport right outside the police station. We all screamed abuse at him. If anybody had been looking out of the window, we would have been dragged back in and would probably still be there now. Luckily, he wasn't spotted. He apologised for the enormous stupidity of what he had just done, saying, "I'm really sorry, but I was bursting." In fairness, he had apologised, and out of respect I've never mentioned it again. Well, except for every single time I see him.

THE GREY LADY

For one absurdly lucrative twelve months we did a weekly Saturday morning show on Smooth FM with my old mates from my Capital days, Mike Osman and Sarah Jane, one of my favourite and silliest producers, and who took over as my producer when Annie could take no more getting up at the crack of dawn. Lightweight, she'd only done fifteen years. So I'd finished the show with Mike, and I was looking forward to a weekend back up in the Midlands, where, at that point, I still had a house. A beautiful old black and white house in the middle of nowhere, in deepest Warwickshire. Mike Osman, by the way, is one of the nicest, funniest men I've ever met. He is a fantastic impressionist, does a quite brilliant Donald Trump, complete with guest appearance of Kim Jong-un, aka Little Pocket Rocket Man, does a hysterical Boris Johnson, and an uncanny one of me. He even rings Jane up pretending to be me. He is also easily the clumsiest person I've ever met. He's not safe to walk the streets. We were once salmon fishing in northern Russia in the icy waters of the Kharlovka River, with all the waterproof gear, thick jumper and big waders on, and he fell in six times – and we're talking total immersion six times in a single day.

He then had to walk all the way back to the lodge, shivering and dripping with his boots feeling like lead, each time. We worked out that allowing time for changing, walking back again, and then taking time off obviously for lunch, dinner and sleeping, he'd set a record that will surely never be beaten. He fell in every quarter of an hour.

Anyway, I digress. I just wanted to share that with you. Stay with me.

Here we are back in Warwickshire. Jane, Ray my warm-up man, Tony my long-time writer, and a couple of old Midlands mates, went out to one of our favourite pubs for a long Sunday lunch. It's called The Kings Head at Aston Cantlow, a beautiful old inn with lots of beams, guest rooms, a nice bar, great food, and it's always been particularly famous for its roast duck suppers. So, we were having a nice couple of pints of Banks's Ale, the only possible drink when you are back in the Midlands, when people started trooping into the pub with pens and clipboards. It was obviously one of those treasure hunt things where you go driving around as a team from one venue, usually a pub, to the next, answering a series of clues at each stop, and then make your way back to HQ, which we learnt from them was a big pub in the middle of Stratford-upon-Avon, about ten miles away. They all had to get their answers in by five o'clock.

The questions about The Kings Head were pretty straightforward. One question was, "Which king's head is outside on the pub sign?" Well, that's famously the head of King Charles I, who was beheaded in 1609.

"What is the pub famous for?" That was an easy one: duck suppers.

Another one: "When did the pub receive an award for its cooking?" That was also pretty straightforward because there was a big plaque up on the wall.

One or two other equally simple questions, and then the one that we all couldn't get our heads around at all: "Which famous lady celebrated here was born in the middle of the fourteenth century?"

Now, because I was still recording *Who Wants to Be a Millionaire?* all the people that came in seemed to look upon me as some sort of fountain of knowledge, but to be honest, I hadn't a clue.

I said, "Look, I only do questions, not answers," but they wouldn't have it. One actually said I was being very unhelpful and went away thoroughly disappointed with Mr Tarrant's general knowledge. We could see this going on all afternoon and I thought, "Sod this. I only came in for a pint," when the landlord said to me, "That's an easy one. It's the 'Grey Lady'."

"Who the hell is the grey lady?" we asked.

"The grey lady," he said, "was supposedly born sometime in the fourteenth century, and was believed to have been murdered while still a young woman in her twenties. She is rumoured to stalk the rooms here sometimes in the small hours of the morning. I tend not to tell the guests this, as it might put them off staying here, but the few I do tell are quite intrigued, and in fact over the years there have been one or two sightings of the Grey Lady as she floats through solid walls from one room to the next." She was also, he was delighted to say, "completely harmless."

So when the next carload arrived, with their pencils and papers, they got the king's head, they got the duck supper, they got the cordon bleu award date, etc., and they came over to me and said, "Chris, who on earth is the lady born in the mid fourteenth century?"

"That's an easy one," I said, proudly. "The Grey Lady."

I told them the story, they happily wrote it on their answer sheets, and they went away terribly pleased with themselves and actually terribly pleased with me.

"That Chris Tarrant," they said as they were leaving, "he's a blinking marvel, he knows everything."

I didn't like to tell them that I only did questions, not answers, but as car after car arrived throughout the afternoon, we were happily telling them all about the Grey Lady. And I hate to admit it, but there was more than a hint of smugness about me.

It got to about four in the afternoon, the Banks's beer had been flowing nicely, and I thought the treasure trailers were pretty much finished, but there was one final motorist who came in, wandered around making notes. "King Charles," he murmured to himself, "cordon bleu award, yeah; duck suppers, yeah," and he hardly paused at all for any additional help.

He smiled at me, and I said, "Did you get the last one, the Grey Lady?"

"The Grey Lady?" he said. "What the hell are you talking about?"

I said, with great authority, "The Grey Lady, the famous Grey Lady, born and murdered in the fourteenth century, who still sometimes haunts the rooms upstairs in the small hours of the morning."

"Don't know what you are talking about, mate," he said to me, with a certain amount of disdain in his voice. "It's Stella."

"Stella?" I said. "Who the hell is Stella?"

"Stella," he repeated, and took me over and pointed at the pump behind the bar, and there it was, quite clearly for all to see:

'STELLA ARTOIS ESTABLISHED IN 1366', and he drove off shaking his head at my stupidity.

The landlord looked at me red-faced, and I looked at him in horror. I realised that about twenty different carloads had all got back to HQ in Stratford, and would have all got ticks on their papers, except for the famous lady who was born in the mid fourteenth century.

"Chris Tarrant told us it was the Grey Lady," they would have said.

"Well, Chris Tarrant's a pillock," the judges would have said, and I'm afraid to say they would be right.

"AND IN THE END
THE LOVE YOU TAKE"

At one point in the UK, after *Who Wants to Be a Millionaire?* had been on screen for a couple of years, in the TV Top 20 for that month *Millionaire* filled nineteen places. The only other programme that got anywhere near was *Eastenders*. It was just a phenomenon. We won TV award after award, year after year. I remember one year I woke up at 5am to go to Capital Radio and there was a big shiny award saying 'Best Dramatic Actor, John Thaw' by my bed, and somewhere across London John awoke, probably much later, with 'Best Game Show Host' beside his bed.

But one particular year, at the National Television Awards at the Albert Hall, we won 'Best Entertainment Show' for about the seventh year running. I went to receive the award from Sir Trevor McDonald, did the press interviews, and had just settled back to enjoy the rest of the show.

I knew my dad would be thrilled. I'd spoken to him earlier that morning and he'd wished me good luck for the night. "Mum and I will be watching." I was in a great mood chatting quietly to Briggsy. I had the award in one hand and was only half listening to Sir Trev, who was talking about some bloke who'd been a teacher and had then worked in children's television for a while, and I remember thinking, "That's someone with a similar career path to me," and then slowly the penny dropped. He was talking about me. I'd been given a lifetime achievement award for services to television. I really had no clue about it and as I made my way back up to the stage, I began to suddenly feel quite emotional. The whole audience was full of my peers, some of my heroes, and it was about to get worse. Trevor said something like, "There's one more person to give you a very special present," and in came the Phantom Flan Flinger, the man in the black mask holding a custard pie. I was a foot away from this person, staring at eyes that I knew really well, but couldn't place them. Who on earth was it? It couldn't be the original Flan Flinger because he was much fatter. It obviously wasn't Sally. It wasn't Lenny. It wasn't Frank Carson, because his mouth was closed. Who on earth …?

Then, on a cue from Trevor, he put down the custard pie and slowly removed the mask. It was my dad, my father, my best ever friend in the world. And all of them, Trevor, Dad, Mum, the producers, had kept it so secret. It was a wonderful idea, but it absolutely floored me. Tears were pouring down my cheeks and I gave him a huge hug. It was my daddy, my hero, the man I'd loved and respected all my life, the man who'd survived Dunkirk, the D-Day landings, fought his way up into Germany, won two Military Crosses, and somehow walked away from being blown up on a German landmine, now in his eighties, and still very fit, who was standing next to me on this world-famous stage. Once I'd recovered, as we both turned to face them, the whole theatre audience, even in the boxes at the very top, all stood up to cheer. Apparently, there were a lot of tears that night spilt by people in the hall and thousands more all over the country watching.

I was just so proud for us, me and him, my best mate, who'd stood by me through all of it, and for both of us now acknowledging the applause in the Royal Albert Hall. I have had one hell of a life, but of course this is my best ever memory. It really doesn't get better than that. It never, ever could.

ACKNOWLEDGEMENTS

To David and Ross at Great Northern Books, my tirelessly supportive publishers. To Jane for being my mate. To Tony Nicholson, Ray Turner, Sean OB and Mike Osman who have been so much a part of the many, many laughs along the way. To Nick Owen and Bob Warman from the earliest days at ATV. To Sally, John, Bob and Lenny for eight years of wonderful Saturday mornings that changed all our lives. To Paul Smith, David Briggs, Colman Hutchinson, Steve Springford at Celador and to Annie O'Neill, Sarah-Jane and Mike Osbourne for sharing so many cold, dark winter mornings together … Thank you all and so many more for giving me fifty fantastic years of fun …